THE DISASTER GYPSIES

THE DISASTER GYPSIES

Humanitarian Workers in the World's Deadliest Conflicts

John Norris

PRAEGER SECURITY INTERNATIONAL
Westport, Connecticut • London

Library of Congress Cataloging-in-Publication Data

Norris, John, 1964–
    The disaster gypsies : humanitarian workers in the world's deadliest
    conflicts / John Norris.
        p.   cm.
    Includes bibliographical references and index.
    ISBN 0–275–99365–5 (alk. paper)
    1. Disaster relief.   2. Humanitarianism.   I. Title.
    HV553.N67   2007
    363.34′9881—dc22   2006038817

British Library Cataloguing in Publication Data is available.

Library of Congress Catalog Card Number: 2006038817
ISBN-13: 978–0–275–99365–8
ISBN-10: 0–275–99365–5

First published in 2007

Praeger Security International, 88 Post Road West, Westport, CT 06881
An imprint of Greenwood Publishing Group, Inc.
www.praeger.com

Printed in the United States of America

The paper used in this book complies with the
Permanent Paper Standard issued by the National
Information Standards Organization (Z39.48–1984).

10 9 8 7 6 5 4 3 2 1

Dedicated to Brenda, my wife,
who fills me with love and wonder.

CONTENTS

ACKNOWLEDGMENTS

There are far too many people to thank than I could properly acknowledge in such a small space. I greatly appreciate all that Jill Buckley and Brian Atwood did to first allow me to slip away from my "day job" and begin doing field disaster work. Similarly, I owe a debt of gratitude to Nan Borton, Bill Garvelink, and the incredible disaster assistance response team leaders like Kate Farnsworth and Tim Knight with whom I had the honor to work. I also want to thank all the other members of the teams who did so much to both teach me the ropes and help keep life in perspective throughout all the mayhem.

In the same vein, I cannot say enough about those remarkable colleagues I worked with at the International Crisis Group. I owe special thanks to Gareth Evans who made Crisis Group a fantastic place to work and who is as talented as he is driven. Similarly, Jen Leonard, Bob Templer, John Prendergast, Colin Thomas-Jensen, Nick Grono, Jessica Bowers, Rob Malley, Mark Schneider, and so many others made my time there incredibly rewarding. All are wonderful friends, and seldom has a more exceptional and dedicated bunch been assembled in one place. Crisis Group is a testament to how much smart, well-informed people can achieve against very difficult odds.

I also want to express my gratitude to Strobe Talbott for all of his continued support and guidance. The phrase a "gentleman and a scholar" is frequently tossed around, but I cannot think of anyone who better fulfills its true meaning. I also consider myself incredibly lucky to have worked with Ian Martin at the United Nations. Although he enters this book only in its final pages, he is a remarkably effective diplomat made even more so because of his humanity. Hilary Claggett at Greenwood has always been a pleasure to work with, and made the publication process refreshingly painless, as has Saloni Jain. I would also like to thank my agents, Leona and Jerry Schecter, who did so much to get me published in the first place.

As always, I would like to thank my informal kitchen cabinet of friends who suffer through early drafts and odd ideas with impressive tolerance and good humor: Derek Chollet and Jason Forrester whose advice I treasure second only to their friendship; Greg Pollock who helped me edit early chapters into something approaching readable; Mike and Susan Petrosillo who have always been so supportive; John Raho, James and Mona Lares, Kevin and Meg Brennan, Matt and Jen Berzok, Mark and Meg Joyce, Greg and Julianna Caplan, Eric and Laura Weight and the lovely families of all of the above have been better friends than anyone could ask.

I also owe much to my family. They have offered support, insight, and great places to come home to throughout it all. I feel truly blessed to be part of such an easy, loving, and sprawling collective. They are with me always.

More than any other, I thank Brenda, my beautiful, talented wife and soul mate. Brenda is a terrific editor with an eye like a hawk, and she keeps me grounded in ways large and small. She is simply the best thing I have ever known. Brenda has made every difficult road infinitely worth traveling.

Lastly, I want to offer heartfelt thanks to the hundreds of people, many of them complete strangers, living in the countries I have written about who demonstrated so much kindness. These individuals lived among war, fear, and violence with a level of courage and grace that I could only hope to replicate if placed in the same position. Even as their own lives sometimes hung in the balance, they offered me time and wisdom. They helped me understand, as best I was able, what was happening and why. More than any aid worker, diplomat, or international official, these people are the true heroes of this book.

Author's Note

In a handful of instances in the text I have changed the names of individuals I interviewed. This was only done in two types of cases: first, where I thought the safety of those with whom I met with would be placed at risk by using their real names or even properly recording their names in my field notes, and, second, where the frank comments shared with me by officials would place their careers in jeopardy.

CHAPTER 1

Backing into Disaster

SNAPSHOT

Kathmandu, Nepal 2003. The student demonstrations erupted quickly after the royal government hiked kerosene prices. Nepal was already struggling to cope with a harsh Maoist insurgency that had claimed more than 8,000 lives, and a monarchy that often ruled with blunt force. With most people in the countryside living on less than $200 a year, life in Nepal was hard, no matter how you looked at it.

A persistent series of student protests and general strikes had brought business to a crawl. Shops and small factories drew their metal shutters down as Kathmandu's colorful and usually congested streets were virtually deserted. Throngs of college students and other demonstrators burned old car tires, chanted, and waved homemade banners in the narrow streets. The demonstrations over kerosene prices had taken on a sharper edge after the police shot and killed a prominent student activist.

I wandered into the protest by accident. The students controlled a stretch of roadway running through the middle of their urban campus. A few tires that had burned down to their steel belts smoldered acridly on the pavement. Broken bricks from an earlier bout of stone throwing littered the road. Students milled about. Two blocks in either direction, large phalanxes of policemen in riot gear looked bored and uneasy. The Nepalese police, never the most disciplined, wore helmets and shin guards as they smoked cigarettes. Several leaned against the long wooden sticks, *lathis*, they carried for crowd control.

I walked into the midst of the students. Despite Nepal's violence, neither the Maoists nor the government had targeted foreigners the way they were in Iraq or Afghanistan. Even when I had clandestine meetings with Maoist insurgents, they were unfailingly polite. Safety was not the first thing on my mind.

The students grew animated as a man on a motor scooter veered down the street. Bringing traffic to a stop was a pro forma goal of protests, and the students hurriedly launched a volley of stones and broken bricks in the general direction of the misguided commuter. They were not trying to kill him, nor did they seem particularly concerned if they did. The scooter quickly reversed direction, and the students reacted with glee.

Without the incitement of further traffic, the demonstration soon settled to a lull, and I contemplated walking back to my apartment. But the mood among the students changed abruptly, like a shift in wind before a hard rain. The police were becoming active, and the atmosphere of confrontation caused a ripple of adrenalin to pulse through the crowd. Many of the young men scrambled to pick up bricks and rocks as others looked nervously for escape routes. The police were preparing to charge. The students shouted in defiance.

With the police ready to surge forward, I eased a short distance away from the center of the crowd. I stood with my back against the closed steel shutters of a small kiosk. There were students in front of me with a wave of policemen to the left and right. Then, there was chaos. The police made a mad dash toward the protestors, and a shadow of fear and grim determination was plain on their faces. Students threw bricks and stones at the oncoming rush of blue uniforms before turning to flee toward the entrance of their dorm. Several police picked up stones and hurled them back at the protestors.

The police swirled in front of me, beating students sharply with long sticks. Debris rained down from the dormitory above. A cop repeatedly kicked a young man cowering on the ground who tried to protect his face. Too much resistance would ensure that others would join the beating. The police stormed into the dormitory, and the cacophony of shattering windows, breaking furniture, and angry shouts echoed wildly in the building's cement interior. Four kids, who could not have been more than ten or eleven, appeared on the third-floor ledge of the dormitory. They crouched low, scared and desperate. Several policemen near the dorm's side entrance threw broken bricks up at the boys, trying to drive them back into the building.

A number of students stumbled back out into the street, blood running down their faces. No arrests were made in the fracas. The entrance to Nepal's royal palace was only blocks away, and it was clear that the police would use any means to keep the students away from the king's gate.

With tumult all around, I stood oddly isolated. No one threw bricks at me. One policeman began to order me away, but seeing I was a foreigner, quickly turned his attention elsewhere. A student sidled up next to me, reasoning that he might find shelter in my translucent bubble of westernness. We talked—an island of conversation among the insanity.

"The police are like criminals," the student complained gasping to catch his breath. "Look at this: they are throwing bricks at children. They do not follow our own laws. Every time you deal with the police or they stop you on your motorbike, you know they just want rupees. The police only want bribes to make money."

We winced as we watched police pummel a student. "We are supposed to be a democracy. This is not democracy." The student was studying engineering. He hoped to move abroad. I asked him questions: What did he think about the war with the Maoists? What about King Gyanendra? What would happen if the king did not restore democracy? Was the violence getting worse? The questions were all part of my job. I was supposed to figure out what was happening on the ground in a country at war—even when it meant trying to make sense of the senseless. I was one of the disaster gypsies.

RESTLESS

I never planned to make conflict and disaster my profession. I grew up in a small rustbelt town in upstate New York, and no one in my upper-middle-class family expressed much interest in foreign affairs. My father was a civil engineer who ran a construction company. My mother was a homemaker who had her hands full with five of us.

Curiously, the first disaster came to me. I was in second grade. Heavy spring rains in Elmira caused the cancellation of the last day of classes. Not knowing better, it felt like an unexpected snow day. We rode our bikes through puddles that stretched half a block long, and our backyard became so saturated that we skimmed across the lawn on old pieces of plywood.

The rains kept coming as Hurricane Agnes worked its way north. There were no gale force winds or overturned cars, just more rain than I had ever seen. The Chemung River, which streamed through the center of downtown Elmira, was normally sleepy. During the summer, it looked shallow enough to walk across.

With the rain, the Chemung changed by the hour, and it soon became broad and improbably powerful. The current swept up entire trees, along with coffins from a low-lying cemetery. The tension in our house rose steadily with the water. After learning that we would soon need to boil the tap water, we filled every possible pot and pan with clean water. My parents moved the furniture up to the second floor, and we packed our bags. Despite reassuring words, the queasy feelings of things going wrong were impossible to ignore.

The river ripped away one of the large bridges that connected Elmira's two halves. It was almost incomprehensible. Dead cattle tumbled along in the filthy brown torrent. Elmira held its collective breath as the floodwaters worked their way steadily up the dikes that lined the streets of downtown.

For part of a rainy afternoon, the river brimmed at the top of the dike like water held in an overfull drinking glass only by its surface tension. And then the floodwaters cascaded over the cement walls along Main Street, hungrily seeking low ground. It was not long before water was on the *second* floor of buildings throughout downtown. The president of the United States came on television and called the flood the worst natural disaster in American history.

Our house on Euclid Avenue was about seven blocks from the river, but up a steady rise. The street looked like some strange American Venice with foul water lapping at every front door. Ultimately, we were incredibly fortunate, and the floodwaters stopped three doors down. A vast lake of damaged homes stretched out between our house and the river.

My mother volunteered at the local college campus to assist those made homeless by the flood. There were hundreds of people sleeping on cots, and the Red Cross served hot meals. It was the first of many times that I would see the blank look of people struggling to comprehend the magnitude of their loss. Bags of soggy donated clothes lined one wall. An army helicopter landed right on the college quad. I looked on in awe.

If you were to go to Elmira today and look at the Chemung River, you would not believe it capable of such destruction. No, I did not go into my line of work because of Hurricane Agnes. But those jarring memories of the flood did teach me one thing I did not forget: comfortable lives can fall apart with stunning speed.

More than anything, the travel bug propelled me toward my choice of profession. After four years of doing just enough to get by college with a degree in psychology, travel felt like a solution. I worked construction to save money, bought a good backpack, and hitchhiked across the States and Canada several times. It did not take long before I struck out for more exotic locales including Nepal, Pakistan, and Peru. Like a legion of other shoestring travelers, I crammed into overcrowded local buses with livestock and nauseous children. I ate rice and lentils, stayed in dingy little rooms, and shared stories and beers with fellow wanderers.

I usually traveled alone, or with friends that I met on the road, and the sense of adventure was intoxicating. The occasional discomforts were a small price to pay to see the Himalayas, Hindu Kush, and Andes. There was a feeling of genuine accomplishment in overcoming the anxiety of heading to places that were completely foreign. It was a big, fascinating world.

I became engrossed by the politics and cultures. The immense disparities between the developing world and America were shocking, as was the incredible turmoil of political life. The day I arrived in Peru, inflation was running over 1,000 percent and rebels tried to blow up the president at his inauguration. In Islamic Pakistan, "Death to America" graffiti was splashed on the mud and concrete walls of mountain villages, but all the men wanted to ask me about whiskey, sex, and American women. In Nicaragua, I watched thousands of fervent *Sandinistas* flood Managua's central square to commemorate a faded revolution in a city that had been left devastated by an earthquake and a civil war.

After working for a season aboard a small fishing boat in Pelican, Alaska, I decided to return to school for a graduate degree in public administration, largely focusing on international development. Not long after graduating, I landed a job at the U.S. Agency for International Development (AID), an offshoot of the State Department responsible for delivering American foreign aid.

Initially, I worked as a speechwriter for the head of AID. My job was to find ways to explain the importance of foreign aid programs to the American public—a laughably steep hill to climb. Foreign aid had such a bad reputation that one of my coworkers likened the experience to trying to "sell ground glass as baby food." But I enjoyed the work. While it was easy for the public to demonize foreign aid, immunizing and educating little kids in far-off lands was not such a bad thing to do.

As I settled into my job, I developed a familiar restlessness. Working in the State Department was not always as glamorous as it sounded. The government deserves its reputation for bureaucracy, and the State Department building was a dreary affair that seemed immune from daylight.

The work of our Office of Foreign Disaster Assistance was a noticeable exception. As the name suggested, the office dealt with humanitarian tragedies around the world, both natural and man-made. Whether it was volcanic eruptions in the Philippines or civil war in the Balkans, these were the people that figured out how to get food, clean water, clothes, and medical supplies to those in need. Because disaster relief, by its very nature, needed rapid delivery, the office did not suffer the same bureaucratic constraints that bogged down the rest of AID. In most cases, the office could deliver supplies or money halfway around the world within twenty-four hours. Its staff was younger and more irreverent than that of other offices. They reminded me of people that I might have met traveling. While some found it off-putting, I smiled when they served the ice for their office Christmas party in a body bag.

The office regularly deployed small squads of relief workers—Disaster Assistance Response Teams, or DARTs—to assess the situation on the ground and coordinate aid. DART teams did not deliver assistance directly to disaster victims. Instead, they channeled supplies and funding to groups like the Red Cross, CARE, and the International Rescue Committee. DART teams served as logistical miracle workers, expediting shipments of relief supplies like food, medicine, and plastic sheeting, while working as liaisons with everyone from the U.S. military to private charities. DART team situation reports were an exceptional source of information for Washington policymakers. DART workers often had the best feel for what was happening on the ground during times of anarchy.

When the Rwandan genocide exploded in 1994, I had only been working at AID for a brief time. Knowing that the Office of Foreign Disaster Assistance was overstretched, I offered my services. The first question the head of the office asked me was, "Do you know how to drive a stick?" I did, and it was not long before I was on the ground in Rwanda.

After my time in Rwanda, I quickly returned to do stints with other disaster teams. The contrast between the immediacy of relief work and the day-to-day grind of bureaucratic life in Washington was compelling. Over time, I came to lead a curiously divided life: working as a speechwriter in Washington for nine months out of the year while being detailed to disaster teams the rest of the time. As odd as it sounds, I liked going to disasters. I was hooked.

WORLD ON FIRE

I became involved in the disaster industry at a time when it was experiencing its own crisis. Hopes that the end of the cold war would begin an era of peace and stability foundered as conflicts in Bosnia, Somalia, Rwanda, Chechnya, Afghanistan, Colombia, and Tajikistan spun out of control. Fighting erupted in close to fifty nations by the mid-1990s. The violence drove more than 35 million people from their homes. The death toll from this spate of ugly conflicts quickly climbed over 4 million people. Up to three-quarters of the casualties in many of these conflicts were civilians.

The end of the cold war appeared to usher in an age of savagery, a Pandora's box full of obscene ethnic violence and territorial rivalries. Significantly, virtually all of these wars were taking place *within* countries rather than *between* countries. International institutions were poorly equipped to deal with civil wars under the best of conditions. The State Department and the UN's respect for the old rules of order led to terrible diplomatic indecision as innocent people were slaughtered. Lacking the lodestar of cold war politics, Washington, Moscow, and the world stared dumfounded as country after country imploded.

Less than six years after the Berlin Wall fell in 1989, relief operations cost more than $8 billion each year. U.S. contributions to emergency aid more than quadrupled. Prevention was largely an afterthought. The United States and its allies were unwilling to deploy a handful of armored personnel carriers and a contingent of peacekeepers to prevent the Rwandan genocide in 1994, but then proceeded to spend several billion dollars dealing with the fallout of the catastrophe. The pattern was no different in Bosnia or the other failed states that darkened the screens of CNN.

Aid workers were angry and frustrated. It was as if humanitarian relief was a substitute for resolving conflicts. Instead of decisive diplomacy or military action, millions of refugees had to make due with blankets and rations as their families were killed and their homes destroyed. A colleague described this approach as applying Band-Aids to gunshot wounds.

Equally appallingly, relief workers became targets. In Somalia during the early 1990s, CARE alone had more than forty employees killed, and militias held hostage more than a dozen aid workers for weeks. Hutu rebels killed six Italian relief workers in eastern Zaire in 1995 and left their decimated bodies as a stark warning to other aid groups. Insurgents butchered five women working for the Red Cross in Chechnya, four of them nurses, in their beds in December 1996. It was the worst premeditated attack on the Red Cross in its 133-year history, and the organization pulled out of Chechnya within days. The UN lost 140 relief workers in a stretch of five years, and hundreds more from private groups were also killed. The scores and scores of relief workers who have been explicitly targeted and killed in Iraq and Afghanistan since the United States invaded those countries are a sad continuation of this trajectory.

In a grisly new calculus, aid workers were now fair game. Many relief workers felt the United States went to incredible lengths to minimize the loss of military lives, but placed less of a premium on civilians. American soldiers wore full body armor and kept close to their bases in most of the places where I worked. Yet, the international community treated the deaths of individuals working for private aid groups as the cost of doing business in a dangerous world. Other than a headline in a hometown newspaper and the grief of families and friends, the requiem for a relief worker was callously brief. Until Iraq, which remains an unusual case, more relief workers and journalists were actually killed in these conflicts than Western soldiers serving as peacekeepers. It had literally become more dangerous to deliver food in a war zone than it was to be a soldier.

Relief groups did what they could. They added security training, upgraded their communication equipment, and treated more areas as off-limits. But short of hiring private armies, this only made a difference at the margins. It was much easier for a warlord to kill an aid worker than a heavily armed peacekeeper. Killing international aid workers became a means to an end, and warring parties saw it as an easy way to scare off continued Western intervention.

Although still distributing aid on a neutral basis, humanitarian relief workers had come to be seen as part of the West. More than ever before, the disaster business had become ensnared in a web of international politics and military force.

TRANSITIONS

By 1996 I had worked on DART teams in Rwanda, Haiti, and Bosnia, and received some formal training in field assessment. I had gained a much better understanding of the industry and its evolution. There was overdue recognition in Washington and elsewhere that the world needed new tools. The system was at a breaking point. More and more countries were in a nether world, somewhere between peace and war, with shaky ceasefires that threatened to disintegrate back into war. These countries had barely functioning governments, huge reconstruction needs, and multitudes of armed fighters still on the scene.

The United States was struggling to deal with such situations, in part because the conflicts often fell somewhere between the need for emergency humanitarian relief and long-term development programs. For example, a DART team could spend tens of millions to bring in water tanker trucks to save people from dehydration and death, but could not legally fund repairs to wells that would ensure these people had clean water for years to come. A DART team could deliver emergency medical assistance, but could not rebuild hospitals. Emergency funding could be used to feed refugees, but could not help create the jobs that would encourage them to return home.

By the same token, traditional development programs were long-term endeavors, with planning and budgets that required a horizon of years. Most development workers were not comfortable operating in hazardous environments, and they lacked the ability to move quickly and flexibly like a DART. In response, AID established an Office of Transition Initiatives in the mid-1990s to deal with countries trying to emerge from conflict. Like the DART teams, transition assistance was built around the idea of deploying small groups of people able to spend money quickly and effectively on the ground. However, in contrast to humanitarian assistance, which was supposed to maintain strict neutrality, transition programs were explicitly political. Transition programs demobilized former fighters by giving them jobs if they would turn in their weapons. Transition programs helped establish independent local newspapers and trained political parties in how to operate in a democracy.

Transition programs were new, sometimes controversial and usually understaffed. Having become friends with some of the people working in the office, I was soon able to do fieldwork in both Sri Lanka and Papua New Guinea in 1997 and 1998. In many ways, transition programs were an even more interesting challenge than DART teams because they required understanding the dynamics of a conflict rather than just its symptoms. Transition work required getting under the hood of the political, ethnic, and historical forces driving the violence.

Given the lead in designing a program in Sri Lanka—a country that had long suffered through a terrible civil war—I learned everything I could about the place. I was new, enthusiastic, and more naïve than I should have been. Although the program eventually fell apart when the war again intensified, I relished immersing myself in studying conflict. I also realized, despite the size of the U.S. government, there were not many people who got out from behind their desks and learned what was really taking place on the ground. Diplomats stayed within the cocoon of capital cities and cocktail parties.

After leaving AID, I worked for two years at the State Department and again war quickly became the central topic. Only a month into my new job, the United States and Yugoslav President Slobodan Milosevic lurched into war over Kosovo. NATO launched an intensive bombing campaign against Yugoslavia. Milosevic drove more than 800,000 Kosovar Albanian refugees into neighboring countries and NATO contemplated a ground invasion. I traveled with the Deputy Secretary of State as he tried to negotiate an end to the war, and I got a first-hand glimpse of high-stakes diplomacy. It was a striking change in perspective from working with relief operations on the ground.

On DART teams, I gained an appreciation for the difficulties of trying to deliver food and medicine to refugees in the middle of an ongoing war. Doing transition work, I explored what it would take to hold a fragile peace together. At the State Department, I gained a window into the geopolitics of war and peace. Without ever setting out to do so, my career had mimicked the natural arc of war and disasters from its most micro to its most macro levels.

In 2001, I left the government and began working at the International Crisis Group, an independent organization working to prevent deadly conflict. Crisis Group did not deliver humanitarian assistance or mediate conflicts, but used small teams of experts deployed on the ground in war-torn countries to develop in-depth reporting and offer practical policy recommendations to stop the fighting. In shaping this research, Crisis Group interacted with as many people involved in the conflicts as possible—warlords, diplomats, refugees, relief officials, politicians, businesspeople, military officers, journalists, and intelligence experts. During my time at Crisis Group, I worked in places like Zimbabwe, Afghanistan, the Gaza Strip, Nepal, Kosovo, and Liberia.

In 2006, I left Crisis Group to join a small United Nations team supporting the peace process in Nepal. I never could have imagined such twists of fate when I had started off trekking in Nepal years before. What began almost as an accident with my first assignment to a DART team in Rwanda in 1994 had become a vocation.

It is my hope that this book will provide a window into the hard realities and intrigues of working in countries that have fallen apart. Seeing both the very best and worst of human behavior first-hand is a mixed blessing. Those experiences have changed me in more ways than I can count. Millions of people in our world struggle to survive every single day. I would be remiss if I did not share some of their stories.

WHY DO WE DO SUCH THINGS?

For most of us, war is something that happens in distant places to people very different from ourselves. We see combat on the evening news, and give it only an appropriately sad shake of the head. For most of us, war feels fundamentally foreign. This is an illusion. The capacity for war is in people, not places.

On an intellectual level, it is easy to peel the onion and find the core causes of violence. They are rarely lofty or noble. The road to calamity is paved with the same greedy little slights and desires that are as familiar as everyday life. Violence comes through partisanship, and with stupid feuds that take on a life of their own. Fighting erupts over land and houses. Blood spills through the sheer stubbornness that makes mutual destruction more attractive than compromise. Countries do not wake up one day and decide that they should descend into war and ruin. Instead, conflict is the long slide of bad decisions—the conclusion of turn after turn down blind alleys of division and recrimination.

Hatred is a tool. When the economy stalls, you attack ethnic minorities and immigrants. If corruption in the presidential palace is exposed, you accuse political opponents of treason. If an election looks like it will be lost, you whip up hysteria over the language spoken in schools or about a piece of territory lost three hundred years ago.

I know it is difficult to perceive how such heated political arguments over ethnicity, religion, or land escalate into tens of thousands dead and hundreds of thousands of refugees. How could angry words translate into the senseless murder of women and children in their beds? The answer is in basic, painful math. It is not that hard to create a situation where one person is beaten, killed, or tortured because of their beliefs or identity. As soon as that one person is killed, there is a broader circle of family, friends, coworkers, and others who want revenge. One dead body can produce ten, twenty, or a hundred in return. Violent vendettas quickly turn into broader and more sprawling conflicts, with each side eager to gain the upper hand.

These are the rational explanations for war and violence, but the real reasons we do such things are ripe with uncomfortable implications. I re-member the bubbling anger that filled me after I first returned from Rwanda. I struggled to articulate what I had seen to friends and family. When people asked, "What was Rwanda like?" it was impossible to tidily encapsulate my messy emotions. Indeed, part of my anger was the way people asked the very question. There was always an implication that "those people" doing the killing were somehow different or that the atrocities were a product of ancient tribal hatreds.

I found it difficult to tell people that Rwanda had disturbed me most because it was not foreign at all. The understanding was repulsive: peo-ple everywhere would do similar things under similar circumstances. The slaughter was not tribal, ethnic, or African; it was *human*. That may sound simple or self-obvious, but everyone treats war as something that is outside of themselves—until they are in one.

People making conscious, and very personal, decisions start and wage wars. There is no mandate that any region, ethnic group, religion, or country needs to career toward carnage, nor is any group immune from such stupid-ity. There is no reason that better angels cannot prevail, but they will not do so if we stand with our hands in pocket. Even having seen terrible things, I believe in our capacity as a people to rise above them. It is our nature.

CHAPTER 2

The Seduction of Violence—Rwanda

In August and September of 1994, I served with a disaster relief team working in Rwanda. It was my first humanitarian experience and I was very much a novice. What I saw there was almost beyond belief. It was a wrenching introduction to the world of conflict.

LINES ON THE ROAD

There were two other passengers on the small United Nations World Food Program plane headed to Rwanda's capital, Kigali. We did not talk during the short flight from Uganda. I was anxious and wondering if I had made a mistake. As the aircraft banked sharply toward the Kigali airport, I looked down at the local soccer arena. The stadium served as a makeshift parking lot for a fleet of white UN armored personnel carriers. It was reassuring that peacekeepers held the city's high ground. It was also telling that they were not in the countryside.

I nervously scanned the streets below. Such terrible things had happened in Rwanda that I imagined the signs of chaos would be abundant. But Kigali was largely deserted. Traffic on the streets was sparse, and few people moved about. Over the course of a hundred days, more than three-quarters of a million Rwandans had been killed, but the damage to buildings was light. The massacres were dreadfully low-tech, and the killings were done mostly with machetes.

The plane pulled to a stop near the older of the airport's two control towers. Stepping off the aircraft, the signs of recent violence were more visible. Machine gun fire had raked the terminal, and the control tower's oversized windows were shattered. Several gutted vehicles cluttered the edge

Rwanda

DEM. REP.
OF THE
CONGO

UGANDA

TANZANIA

Ruhengeri

Byumba

Gisenyi

KIGALI

Lac
Kivu

Gitarama

Kibuye

Kibungo

Cyangugu

Butare

TANZANIA

BURUNDI

0   25   50 km
0   25   50 mi

Cartography by Bookcomp, Inc.

of the tarmac. The distinctive sunburst scars left by exploding mortar shells pocked the runway. Our pilot wasted no time in unloading several boxes of cargo, turning around, and taking off.

UN troops from different nations worked behind sandbag barricades, and the airport had been transformed into a military base. One of the UN officials on the flight offered me a ride into the city to drop me at the U.S. embassy. After some small talk with the soldiers, we loaded our bags and several boxes of medical supplies into the back of a UN vehicle parked next to the plane and left. We simply drove out of the airport and on to the road; there was no passport check, luggage carousel, or customs. Other than the military, Rwanda's government was not functioning.

Our's was virtually the only car to be seen. As our driver snaked his way along the curving roadway, he casually pointed out several spots on the street where someone had painted white lines around what looked like potholes. He inquired cheerfully, "See those circles? Those are land mines and unexploded ordnance—mortar shells, rounds from rocket-propelled grenades— that kind of thing." Almost as an afterthought he added, "You'll want to avoid those when you are driving." I felt a rush of panic: how could I not have known that white circles on the road meant explosives? What had I gotten into?

BACK STORY

Rwanda was divided between two primary ethnic groups, the Hutus and the Tutsis. The Tutsi population was always a minority, making up between 10 and 15 percent of the population. Despite this, the Tutsis ruled Rwanda and Burundi as feudal kingdoms for hundreds of years. The relationship between the two ethnic groups was not set in stone, and Hutus often emerged as senior administrators in some hill communities. Intermarriage was common, and Hutus and Tutsis shared the same language, religion, and most cultural traditions. The Tutsis enjoyed all the usual fruits of power: more cattle, better education, and land ownership.

The divide-and-rule approach of the colonial period only sharpened the divisions between the two communities. First under the Germans, then under the Belgians after World War I, Europeans cultivated the Tutsis as their ruling elite. The Europeans, relying heavily on pseudo-science of the period, thought the tall, skinny Tutsis looked more aristocratic than the shorter and stockier Hutus. The Belgians demanded that all Rwandans carry ethnic identity cards, one of the many policies that steadily widened the differences between Tutsis and Hutus into a gulf. Heavy-handed Tutsi policies also fueled an increasingly virulent strain of ethnic politics among Hutus who felt that they would only get political rights if they eliminated the Tutsis.

The situation eroded further as the sun set on colonialism. In 1959, the Hutus launched an uprising in Rwanda, and the violence continued into the early 1960s. When the Belgians pulled out of Rwanda in 1962, the Hutus shunted the Tutsis to the side under a rough democratic system. In the years surrounding independence, Hutus killed tens of thousands of Tutsis, and more than 250,000 Tutsis fled to neighboring countries. In 1973, Hutu General Juvenal Habyarimana overthrew his cousin and seized power in Rwanda. Habyarimana's wife, Agathe, was from a well-connected Rwandan Hutu family, and she was notorious for her virulent anti-Tutsi views.

Ethnic identity steadily became an overriding force in Rwandan society. At the time, Rwanda was Africa's most densely populated country. With plunging coffee prices, land becoming scarce, and growing international pressure for democratic reforms, the government brazenly tried to make the minority Tutsis scapegoats. The number of Tutsis who could attend college or get civil service jobs was strictly limited. The minority Tutsis became an easy scapegoat for a government that struggled to explain its many shortcomings. Ethnicity made the country resemble a small town where, just by the mention of a family name, Rwandans quickly determined occupation and social status. Fear and foreboding filled the hills.

In the early 1980s, Rwandan Tutsi refugees exiled in Uganda made common cause with local insurgents trying to topple the Ugandan government. By 1990, these exiled Tutsis, many of whom had grown up as orphans and never even seen Rwanda, invaded Rwanda as the Rwandan Patriotic Front. However, the French government, which played a key role in providing weapons and support to the Hutu-dominated government of President Juvenal Habyarimana, helped repulse the Tutsi attack. The aborted invasion triggered another round of reprisals against Tutsis in Rwanda, as hard-line Hutu elements within the government organized local militias— the *interhamwe*, or "those who fight together"—to direct attacks against Tutsi civilians. Bitter anti-Tutsi propaganda filled the media. Investigations of violence against those who opposed the government, whether they were Tutsi or Hutu, were rare. The government was quick to paint even its rival Hutu parties as "Tutsi collaborators."

For a brief period, it looked like it might be possible to avoid further bloodshed after the exiled Tutsis and President Habyarimana signed a peace agreement in Arusha, Tanzania, in August 1993. The accord allowed for power sharing between Rwanda's ethnic groups, repatriation of refugees, and established the framework for democracy. As part of the agreement, the UN deployed a lightly armed force of 3,000 under the command of a two-star Canadian General, Romeo Dallaire, to help keep order. Peacekeepers could only use force in cases of self-defense. A contingent of 600 Tutsi rebels entered barracks outside of Kigali as part of the deal. Hutu hardliners vehemently opposed the peace deal. The accord meant that large numbers of soldiers would be decommissioned, and many soldiers knew that peace would mean a loss of both salary and stature.

On April 6, 1994, things turned ugly. President Habyarimana and the president of Burundi were flying into Kigali, after reportedly finalizing the details of an agreement on a transitional government. As their plane approached the runway, a surface-to-air missile sliced through the air, probably fired by Habyarimana's own Presidential Guard—although some suspected Tutsi rebels. A portion of the planes' wreckage came to rest on the lawn of the presidential palace. Both presidents were dead. A wave of killings began with astonishing speed after the Habyarimana assassination. Hutu Colonel Theoneste Bagosora, a notorious hardliner, was effectively in charge of the government, and "Hutu power" radio stations exhorted the slaughter of Tutsi men, women, and children whom they referred to as "cockroaches." The extremist propaganda was brutally direct: cut down every Tutsi, or they will do the same to you. Every Tutsi was an enemy, and every defender of the Tutsis was a collaborator. For Hutu extremists in the government, the assassination provided the perfect pretext to liquidate all of their political opponents, Tutsi and Hutu alike.

The frenzy of violence and murder was so outlandish that it would have been easy to mistake it for a complete breakdown of order, particularly with Hutu military officers claiming that it was Tutsis, not Hutus, who had assassinated the president. But it quickly became clear that there was a method to the madness of the Hutu extremists. On the morning of April 7, Hutu extremists descended upon the home of the Prime Minister, Agathe Uwilingiyimana, who was also a Hutu. She tried to escape over a back wall, but the Hutus captured her, as well as the contingent of ten Belgian and five Ghanaian peacekeepers that had been guarding her. Although the Hutus released the Ghanaian peacekeepers, army officers killed all the Belgians in a gruesome fashion. The failure of the UN to mount a credible rescue mission to save its own soldiers projected an image of awful, accurate weakness.

The first targets for Hutu extremists were Hutu moderates, lending credence to the idea that the president's own party directed his assassination. Within hours of the plane being downed, Hutu hardliners wiped out scores of moderate Hutu politicians, journalists, and religious leaders, along with any effective Hutu opposition to the Hutu ruling party. The elimination of moderate Hutus was the essential first step of the genocide. The targeted slaughter of mainstream Hutu public figures and international peacekeepers was cynically effective, and it eliminated Rwanda's moderates. A contingent of French and Belgian forces swept in and evacuated international officials, including the U.S. embassy staff, AID workers, and other Americans in the country. A week later Belgium withdrew from the UN peacekeeping force. There was no one left to stand in the way.

With Hutu moderates eliminated and the international community having stepped to the sidelines, the slaughter of Tutsis commenced in earnest. Agathe Habyarimana, the assassinated president's widow, played a key role along with Colonel Bagosora in encouraging the death squads that were able to operate out of the presidential palace with impunity. Although the French government evacuated the president's widow to Paris a short time later, the killing had only begun. In almost every community across Rwanda, local radicals had carefully prepared lists of those they would kill, with soldiers and police facilitating this effort. The government manipulatively encouraged Tutsis to seek shelter in locations, like churches and schools, which had provided sanctuary during previous bouts of violence. This only made it easier for their attackers. One Rwandan compared this effort to "sweeping dried banana leaves in a pile to make them easier to burn." Guards became executioners. Hutus lobbed hand grenades into hospitals, turned machine guns on elementary schools, and set fire to crowded churches. The killings were mercilessly efficient, and the speed of the massacres outpaced even the holocaust.

It is crucial to understand the psychology of the killings. Those conducting the genocide were terribly shrewd. For several years, they had sent public signals that violence against Tutsis and Hutu political opponents was acceptable. By claiming that the Tutsis had assassinated the president, and stoking fears that the Tutsis had secret arms caches around the country, the authorities nurtured a kill-or-be-killed mentality. The government demonized high profile Tutsi and Hutu political leaders as conspirators and collaborators.

The authorities made slaughter and pillaging luridly profitable. Security officials and the *interhamwe* provided transportation, beer, food, and cash to those willing to commit violence. Searching for Tutsi was a good excuse for ransacking homes. One hundred dollars, a motor scooter and clothing from the victims—the rewards sound pitifully paltry for such horrible acts. But with some 80 percent of Rwandans living in poverty, greed was a powerful motivator. The government preyed on the easy aggrievement of the thousands of young Hutu men with no work and no prospects. Those who planned the genocide were well off, and they converted the poor into willing executioners by feeding them the right diet of incentive and invective. The militias gave one high school student they found to be a particularly good killer a boom box. In contrast, Hutus who looted without killing faced reprimand.

Rwanda was a land-starved country. Those who did the most killing got the most land. In a number of cases, this led to Hutus killing other Hutus over land disputes. Killing became a means to rise quickly in the military or local government. The government tolerated every excess. Men raped Tutsi women with impunity, and enslaved countless women solely for this purpose.

The government also took other steps to make the killing more palatable. Missions were broken down into discrete segments. While wiping out all of the Tutsis was too much for some to swallow, manning a roadblock, searching for fugitives, or guarding prisoners often was not. As one Hutu recounted to a reporter, "Many people contributed to killing one person.

Because we feared the blood of the victim, each man feared to kill alone. We would kill in groups. Even that old man hiding in the sorghum plantation—when we discovered him, Leonard, the militia leader, ordered everybody to hit the old man. Even after he was dead, everybody was supposed to take part in the killing. I used a club." Those who refused to participate in killings were mocked and, in some cases, killed. At every turn, the government reinforced the notion that killing was a collective responsibility.

The seductive power of violence was undeniable. When the president's plane went down, there were probably between 5,000 and 8,000 *interhamwe*, police, and soldiers committed to the killings. The ranks of those actively involved in the genocide quickly tripled or quadrupled. Many Hutus were too worried about their own survival to raise objections. It was a terrible race to fanaticism.

Alarmed by the presidential assassination and mass killings, Tutsi Rwandan Patriotic Front forces hastily launched another offensive into Rwanda, and the contingent of forces in Kigali broke out of their barracks in a desperate attempt to turn the tide.

Two days after the presidential assassination, Canadian General Dallaire, the head of the small UN peacekeeping contingent, cabled back to New York and warned of the dire consequences of a "very well planned, organized, deliberate and conducted campaign of terror" being directed by the Hutu presidential guard. Dallaire had earlier sent warning after warning back to UN headquarters in New York. Large shipments of small arms and huge quantities of machetes—enough for every third adult male in the country—had flooded into the country before the massacres began. UN headquarters had denied Dallaire's requests to seize arms caches.

In late April, as Hutu extremists and the *interhamwe* continued their rampage, Dallaire again pleaded for international assistance. The Canadian argued that he could stop the majority of the killings with 5,000 men and a handful of armored personnel carriers. Remarkably, just as General Dallaire was calling for reinforcements, the UN Security Council voted to slash the peacekeeping force by 90 percent, leaving less than 300 international troops in Rwanda. This small, virtually powerless, contingent could do little but stand witness to a bloodbath. In some cases, the *interhamwe* swept into compounds moments after UN forces withdrew, slaughtering Tutsis in plain view. Key UN members, particularly the United States, wanted no part of an African civil war that meant little to the public.

Rwanda's timing could not have been worse. The botched military operations to hunt warlords in Somalia—the events of the *Black Hawk Down*—had occurred only six months before. The debacle was still fresh in the mind of policymakers, as were the television images of the eighteen dead U.S. soldiers dragged through the streets. Consequently, neither the Pentagon nor President Clinton wanted anything to do with another African military adventure. In the spring of 1994, stopping genocide in Rwanda was less important to the Clinton White House and its struggling foreign policy team than sidestepping another potentially messy political problem.

Despite the huge numbers of Tutsi civilian fatalities, the Tutsi Rwandan Patriotic Front made significant military gains, in part because the Hutus were more intent on slaying innocent bystanders than engaging in combat. In mid-June, the French government deployed its own peacekeeping force, *Operation Turquoise*, claiming that they wanted to stabilize the humanitarian situation. But the French were still close allies with the Hutu government. Canadian General Dallaire later complained that the Hutu army "went mad with joy at the prospect of their imminent rescue by the French," believing, "that they now had carte blanche to finish their gruesome work." French troops mobilized in southwest Rwanda, the last region in the country that the Hutus still controlled, and declared the area a safe haven. Appallingly, the French continued to provide covert military assistance to the Rwandan government even as it carried out massacres. However, French aid was not enough to stop the rout of the Hutus.

By July 4, Tutsi forces had taken Kigali and, by mid-July, the Hutu government retreated across the border with Zaire. It was a remarkable turn of events. The Tutsis had suffered some 800,000 dead—more than half of Rwanda's entire Tutsi population—but Tutsi military forces had emerged from a generation-long exile and decisively won the war.

The Tutsi military victory in turn triggered a massive flood of Hutu refugees. One million Hutus fled west into Zaire in *five days*. The international community, whose deliberate dithering had allowed genocide to go unchecked, faced a humanitarian crisis it could not ignore. The demands for food, clean water, shelter, and sanitation overwhelmed AID and other foreign agencies. By late July, cholera exploded within the enormous camps in Zaire and disease began to take an unmerciful toll. Several thousand U.S. soldiers headed to the region to assist with the relief effort. In early August, I arrived in Rwanda with no official training, a weathered backpack, and a great deal of apprehension.

INTO THE FIRE

The UN vehicle dropped me off at the U.S. embassy, which our disaster team was using as a base of operations. The embassy had suffered only limited damage, the most obvious of which was a gaping hole in the second floor exterior wall from a stray artillery shell. The embassy was not looted—despite the evacuation of the entire American staff—mainly due to the efforts of one of the local guards. The guard admitted to me that he was something of an accidental hero. He had stayed at his post in part because he thought it was the right thing to do, but also because he did not know what else to do. He said he was terrified during the massacres, and added without an ounce of shame, "I wet my pants."

At the embassy, I met the other members of the DART. Kate Farnsworth was our team leader. Tall, skinny, fair-haired, and intense, Kate was one of the best in the business. Plainspoken and direct, she had grown up as a Foreign Service brat. Kate welcomed me, but I could tell she was quickly sizing me up to see if I would be an asset or liability to her overstretched operation. People sent from Washington were always suspect. I also met Kim Maynard. Kim had been a smokejumper with the Forest Service before joining the DART. This was less odd than it sounded, and the concept for DART teams was borrowed from the approach used by the Forest Service in fighting wildfires. A third team member, Buddy, was on the road traveling. The team was a skeleton crew, in large part because so many people were dealing with the huge refugee camps in Zaire.

There was no electricity, local telephone, or running water in Kigali. The embassy had a generator that ran during the day, and several pallets of bottled water stockpiled on the embassy loading dock, along with boxes of military rations. In the DART office, a small satellite dish, with its wires running out of the window, allowed the team to make international calls and access e-mail. The satellite phone was a clunky device about the size of a small suitcase, but it allowed for international calls from even the most remote locations. It was a crucial lifeline.

Other than the ambassador, a security officer, and a secretary, the embassy had ceased to operate. After passing through a series of locked bulletproof doors, I met Ambassador David Rawson not long after my arrival. As I listened to Kate give Rawson a quick briefing on events, the ambassador was distant. His detached, almost ghostly, demeanor was disconcerting, particularly in contrast to Kate and Kim's restless energy. I realized that the events of the previous four months had left Rawson with questions that would likely haunt him for the rest of his life.

Our team resided in the house of an evacuated AID employee. Although the woman had shipped out her most important valuables, half-packed boxes and furnishings left in haste cluttered the house. Our presence felt like an invasion of privacy. We slept on cots, and most of our dinners consisted of military "Meals Ready to Eat," or MREs, prepackaged foods wrapped in unattractive olive green or brown plastic. We bathed with buckets of water. The conditions were spartan but adequate.

Kate was up to jog at five thirty in the morning before going to work. I wondered where she got the stamina. The security presence in the streets of Kigali was lighter than I expected, and the Rwandan Patriotic Front soldiers at the checkpoints rarely interfered with foreigners. While the roads were clear of debris, shortly after the Tutsi army took the city, UN troops made large diesel bonfires to dispose of the thousands of corpses in the streets. Some soldiers took target practice on dogs that survived on the remains. Despite the cleanup, there were times when the smell from shallow graves in empty lots or by the side of the road was unmistakable.

Every day brought soul searching. In a Kigali orphanage, I puzzled over what could have driven someone to take a machete to the face of a six-year-old boy. He was shy, and wearing a stained red baseball cap two sizes too large. No mother was around to tell him to blow his nose or comfort him when he cried. It was hard not to stare at the angry red radial scars that lined his face. How had he survived? Making eye contact with him was hugely uncomfortable; it was as if I was afraid I would have to explain how this had happened. My smile was unconvincing. I felt emotionally naked when confronted by his wide-eyed sincerity. Kate casually scooped up the boy and held him on her hip as she engaged in a conversation with the head of the orphanage. It was an easy gesture, almost reflexive, and it spoke volumes about the way she went about her work. I felt ashamed that I had not responded the same way. It was hard. I did not even have my bearings, and my guard was up.

I fell into the rhythm of work over the next several days. Not far from the embassy, there was a large daily meeting chaired by the UN to coordinate relief efforts. I attended and took detailed notes. It was my first real introduction to the business of humanitarian assistance. There was a remarkable mélange of personalities and nationalities at the gatherings, with people from the UN, embassies, relief organizations, the military, and private contractors from every corner of the globe. All the relief workers knew each other. Rwanda was a huge family reunion for the industry. While it made sense, it took some getting used to. Aid workers were a tribe that traveled from disaster to disaster like moths to a flame. Understanding that there was a whole culture dedicated to dealing with war, famine, and disaster was equally comforting and disturbing. In the courtyard outside the UN meeting, long-lost friends embraced with gusto, and it felt like a glimpse into a secret society. "I haven't seen you since Mogadishu," was a common refrain, since many of them had worked in Somalia not long before. Knowing references to bad meals, broken-down vehicles, and other hardships—shared memories that they could laugh about in retrospect—followed the hugs.

It was an unavoidable camaraderie: in the places humanitarians worked, there were only a handful of dingy restaurants or bars. Curfews, roadblocks, and security restrictions made it almost mandatory for them to hang out together. Many lived in group houses just as we did. Humanitarian relief work was intense and demanding, and these people spent incredibly long hours in close quarters. Frayed nerves and exhaustion were a normal part of the job, but relief workers could still find time and energy after fourteen-hour days to drink too much wine and make dark jokes about the absurdity of it all. As I quickly learned, there was a lot of shared history. Relief workers competed for the same jobs. They all knew who had slept with one another or who had gone off the deep end during the last mission. They suffered the same hassles common to such disjointed lives: making infrequent visits to distant families; trying to find a decent place to live in the middle of a war zone; or even just keeping their belongings in storage for years on end.

The lines between professional and private were blurry. More women worked on the ground than you might expect, and it was easy for relief workers to fall into bed together after that last glass of wine at the end of desperate days. Emergency sex, as some have called it, was one way to keep sane. Many treated working and sleeping together as part of the business. People were reluctant to ask questions about lovers, or even marriages, left behind. Nobody really expected things to work out for the best in the middle of a disaster. The humanitarians did their best to be discrete, but with people sharing housing and driving white Land Rovers emblazoned with their organization's name on the side, things were easy to figure out. I did not ask unwelcome questions.

Huge maps detailing military encounters, population movements, security incidents, and refugee camp locations hung on the wall of the room where the daily coordination meetings was held. Planning a relief operation had the look and feel of a large, disorganized military campaign. The person leading the UN coordination effort was a Canadian named Charles Petrie, and he was impressive. Thin to the point of gaunt, he exuded a brisk efficiency that I did not always associate with the UN.

The scope of Rwanda's catastrophe made information a commodity, and the range of problems that relief workers were addressing was astonishing. A German-led group was trying to restore power in the capital, but finding parts for the antiquated generators was a problem, and the Germans were scrounging all over East Africa for what they needed. Another team was working on reestablishing running water, while ensuring that tanker trucks continued to distribute water to vulnerable sites like hospitals and orphanages. Others were airlifting in thousands of tons of food and other essential supplies such as plastic jerry cans that refugees used to carry water. There was back and forth about ports, ships, cargo planes, and the type of forklifts needed to off-load supplies. A planeload of cargo could quickly turn into a nightmare if the pallets were loaded improperly and every single item needed to be off-loaded by hand. Shipments of aid were also coming overland on large trucks from ports in East Africa, but many of these trucks were too large to navigate the hilly back roads that led directly to the camps. The amount of food, water, and shelter needed to keep millions of people alive—even for a single day—was mind-boggling.

Making matters even more difficult, relief workers had to deliver this mountain of supplies to a moving target. Entire villages and cities were picking up and leaving. Many of the large camps within Rwanda were receiving almost no humanitarian relief, as tens of thousands of people got lost in the shuffle. The swirling tide of humanity that swept across the country was unlike anything many of these hardened professionals had ever seen before. Rwanda's demographics were redrawn daily. Amid all this confusion, security was a constant concern, not just for Rwandans, but also for the people that were trying to assist them. Status as a relief worker did not protect against gunshots. The Tutsi's military progress had been stunningly fast, and there was a possibility that Hutu forces would regroup and counterattack. The situation in the southwest was particularly turbulent—with French soldiers deployed in the region, Hutu militias still active, and Tutsi military forces trying to consolidate their position.

After several days, Kim and I went to assess a cluster of camps in northwest Rwanda. We packed up a tan Toyota Land Cruiser with a box of MREs and a case of bottled water, and lashed several extra fuel cans to the roof. We carried a satellite phone in case of trouble. Even though I learned how to use the phone, I was skeptical that I could do so in a crunch. We left early in the morning, and Kigali was still misty as we headed out of town. Driving into the countryside, we passed a number of Rwandan Patriotic Front military checkpoints with no difficulty. The Tutsi soldiers were young, but professional. Their weapons were clean and well maintained—as were their uniforms. Someone was clearly in charge at each post. These were all good signs when you were an unarmed relief worker from home. Although the loss of life during the previous months had been immense, conquering Rwanda had been a lifelong dream for the Tutsi soldiers.

As we drove west, the low rolling hills were green and lush, but the entire countryside was vacant. Ripe fruit rotted on the vine because there was no one to pick it. Just months before, Rwanda had the most crowded country in Africa; its roads thickly congested with people, vehicles, and livestock. Yet, as we drove through the northwest, we had the streets to ourselves. There were no workers toiling in the fields, the markets were empty, schools, churches, and businesses abandoned. Those few people we saw lingered nervously near their homes, and melted away upon our approach. The numbers were stark. Rwanda's population had been just over 8 million to begin 1994. Eight hundred thousand people were killed in a hundred days. Well over 2 million people had fled the country as refugees. Countless more had fled their homes but stayed within Rwanda, living with relatives or gathering in large camps. More than 40 percent of Rwanda's population was either dead or displaced.

I got to know Kim during the drive. Kim had lived a vagabond existence before finding her way to disaster work, and she spoke fondly of hopping on empty freight cars as she explored the American west. She had enjoyed her time fighting forest fires as a smokejumper, and like most of the women I would meet in the field, she was tough as nails. Most recently, she had worked in Somalia when things had started to fall apart. Kim had been traveling in a military convoy when the U.S. army Humvee directly in front of her had been torn apart by a mine. Life in Mogadishu had been lawless and foreigners traveled from armed compound to armed compound.

Distributing the local payroll was a life and death affair involving armed guards and periodic shootouts. Her war stories from places like Angola and Afghanistan were curiously comforting. They made relief work feel like a logical extension of my own travels.

We arrived at the first camp we were inspecting. Because we were looking at the situation within Rwanda, we wanted to talk to "internally displaced" rather than refugees. The distinction between refugees and the internally displaced was something of a semantic curiosity. People who fled their homes and moved elsewhere within their own country were considered internally displaced. Only those people who had crossed an international border—like the Rwandan Hutus that fled to Zaire—officially received the title of refugee. While this might sound petty, the distinction carried tremendous practical implications in terms of international law and the behavior of aid agencies. For example, because of its mandate, the UN High Commissioner for Refugees was not normally able to assist the internally displaced. Internally displaced often faced horrible conditions, but because they had not crossed the magic line of a border, they were out of luck.

Rwanda was a good example of this phenomenon. Much of the international focus had been on the huge Hutu refugee camps just inside Zaire. Yet within Rwanda, there were scores and scores of smaller displaced camps, filled with people who had left their homes only to end up living on the side of a hill or in an open field. Rwanda's internally displaced would normally have been a headline-grabbing story, but with the mass killings and the gigantic refugee camps in Zaire, the displaced were an afterthought.

After the stillness of the countryside, the conditions within the camp were stunning. There were thousands of people. Some of them were living in a low-slung building that looked like it had been a school, while the majority of families sprawled out across a field that was stripped of its vegetation. Most were living out in the open, or in ramshackle temporary huts made of plastic, cardboard, or spare pieces of corrugated tin stolen from buildings. Our job was to do a basic assessment of the conditions within the camp. *Were there latrines? Was there a source of clean water? Did people have shelter? Were attacks taking place? Were aid agencies providing relief supplies and medical care? Were conditions getting better or worse?* We asked many questions. We jotted down comments in our small notebooks. Assessments were an imprecise science, and we were simply trying to develop a broad picture of what was happening on the ground. Humanitarian assistance delivered the greatest good to the greatest number, and in such a rapidly changing environment, our analysis had to be quick and dirty.

The displaced camp was an all-out assault on the senses. I did my best to keep composed when implausibly thin mothers clutching sickly newborns begged for medicine. I fought a rising sense of revulsion as I walked by an old man lying prone in the red clay with flies resting on his sunken cheeks. I pushed against the churning knot of nausea in my stomach as we toured the camp's filthy makeshift hospital ward and met children with crudely amputated limbs who stared listlessly off into the distance. I tried to act like a seasoned disaster hand, but it was a struggle.

I battled to stay calm when I realized that hundreds of people were surrounding us, all of them full of complaints and despair. People were angry, frustrated, and demanding help. The sour smells of body odor, sickness, human waste, and burning trash were stifling. It was intimidating, and I felt like I was standing in front of a tide I could not control. Imagine a sea of sick, malnourished, and agitated people all trying to speak to you at the same time. Most of the displaced were scared and convinced that they would soon be victims of reprisal killings. They did not know where to turn. This was just one camp, I told myself, surely not even the worst. If Kim could handle it so could I. My notes from the camp barely made sense.

The camp had received almost no aid, and only one or two relief organizations had visited the site. It was remarkable that Rwanda's disaster was so sweeping that the international community was not even able to keep track of all the camps—much less provide them with proper assistance. As we climbed back into the Land Cruiser, it was difficult to process what I had just seen. It felt like being in a car accident.

Locating such under-served camps was a key part of our effort, and we spent much of our day navigating rural dirt roads and asking directions from villagers. As I was driving along a thickly overgrown dirt track, I saw a small patrol of armed gunmen approaching. They did not have uniforms, and they could have been Hutus or Tutsis, militias or bandits. My initial reaction was to slow down; the men had guns. Without a second's hesitation, Kim insisted I rapidly accelerate away from the men. As we sped along, my heart raced, and I wondered if I would hear a burst of gunfire. With my adrenalin pulsing, the Land Cruiser muscled its way up a steep slope and into the clear.

Land mines were also a worry, and they killed about eight people a day at that time in Rwanda. Even larger numbers of people suffered devastating wounds, since mines usually maimed rather than killed. Armies knew that it was more difficult to deal with a wounded soldier than a dead one, and ripping the leg off a person was a sure means to slow down an opposing force. Soldiers were only a small portion of mine victims. Rwandan children often mistook land mines for toys or simply stumbled across them. In a conflict as chaotic as Rwanda's, military commanders had placed mines almost at random, with no real effort to keep track of their location. Land mines made the most mundane locations—small footpaths, fields, and empty lots—into deadly hazards. Always indiscriminate, the mines would ensure that senseless violence would continue long after the shooting stopped. The easiest way to avoid mines was simple: you kept to the pavement or walked along well-worn tracks. But Rwanda was rural. Lots of dirt roads and small footpaths did not get much traffic. Seeing a cow or goat in a field with its legs blown was a sure sign that the area was mined, and mines were a constant retrograde anxiety.

Kim and I took a short lunch break by a small lake. Pastures stretched out below. The landscape was a bucolic patchwork of terraced fields and small, tidy brick homes set against narrow streams and high lakes. The crops in the intensely cultivated fields were full and bountiful. With all the worries about gunmen, land mines, and dealing with the displaced, I was slow to realize Rwanda was beautiful. The country had once been called the Switzerland of Africa without a trace of irony. The scene was idyllic. It was only lunchtime and my head was overfull with all that we had seen. How was anybody supposed to deal with this?

AMONG THE BANANA LEAVES

As we worked in the northwest over the days that followed, we came across scenes beyond reason. In a hospital outside of one camp, a nurse explained how the Hutu doctor that had run the facility had methodically killed most of his Tutsi patients and staff. The nurse explained, "When the doctor heard that the Tutsis were coming, he started killing patients. Right there in the beds. He was very involved in politics, and he was very committed to Hutu power, but we thought it was just talk. We did not care so much about politics, and he was a doctor. He was a big man. He gave the same speeches over and over again. It was silly. We joked about it when he wasn't listening. He said we should be more patriotic. He was always saying, 'Tutsis are criminals; they want to kill us all. We must organize against them.'"

The killings began as the Tutsis advanced. The doctor looted the hospital's funds and killed the patients that remained. "I could not stop this," the nurse added in a preemptive defense. The nurse fled into the countryside, taking refuge with family members, and she had only just returned. She was hoping that the hospital would start functioning again. She needed the work. The nurse had heard that Hutu fighters forced some of her coworkers to retreat with them to "take care of the wounded." She did not expect to see them again.

The survivors we met spoke in matter-of-fact tones. The Rwandans, both Tutsi and Hutu, tended to be painstakingly soft-spoken, and it was difficult to imagine such personalities erupting in violence. One day stopping by the side of the road, I listened quietly as a young mother described having last seen her husband and two children six weeks earlier, "We heard stories that the Hutus had lists of names and were starting to kill people. It was no longer safe to stay in the house, and we went to hide in the fields. They had set fire to some houses near ours, and one man—we had known him all our lives—said, 'We will be back for you very soon.' It was as if we had never met before. Our children used to play together. At first, we thought they just wanted money, but you could see it was more. These men could do what they wanted. We had no time to take any of our things. There were checkpoints on all of the roads."

It was unclear from the woman's story exactly how exactly she separated from her husband and children. I did not ask. "I hid in the fields for days, and I could hear the men searching. They were drunk. They were singing and blowing whistles, celebrating when they found someone. I do not think I slept. I saw many bodies. Even then, some of the other families in the fields wanted to return to their houses. They thought it would be safe. This was so foolish. It made me angry. Even the police were involved. But some people would not listen."

Almost every Tutsi we spoke with offered an incredibly long list of dead relatives. A Rwandan working with one aid group calmly ticked off the names of seventeen of his murdered family members.

The massacres were so enormous that many of the aid workers could only understand them in fragments. One guy we worked with on the DART, Tom, was a logistician. He was an expert at arranging flights and cargo shipments. Tom could not get over the fact that the Hutus dumped more than ten thousand bodies in a single river, creating a grisly logjam that eventually made its way downstream to Lake Victoria. Tom not only wrestled with the extremity of the violence, but also in conceiving the organization required to transport ten thousand corpses in simple carts to the water's edge. To understand the amount of human labor that went into the massacres was to acknowledge how successful the hard-line government had been in drawing the public to its cause. At the height of the genocide, people stacked bodies in front of the houses of important Hutu leaders to demonstrate their fealty to the cause, much as cats proudly deposit eviscerated mice on the doorsteps of their owners.

For me, it was the shoes. I often spotted single shoes lying in the roadway or on the front lawns of houses. There was something about the footwear that was deeply disturbing. In a poor country, you did not just lose a single perfectly good shoe. A solitary shoe meant that a person fled for his life, or was pushed into a truck, or was torn apart from his loved ones. With each lone sandal, slipper, or shoe, I could almost feel the panicked last moments: sweaty, desperate with adrenaline, and sick with the realization that death would be ungainly and cruel.

The war was complex. While Rwanda had brought out the very worst in some people, it had also revealed remarkable strengths. There were Hutus that risked their own lives to save Tutsi friends and neighbors, sometimes literally hiding them under the bed or floorboards. Hutus helped Tutsis forge identity cards or claimed them as family members. Bizarrely, we even heard stories of Hutu soldiers who hid Tutsi friends in their closets—but then went out during the day and slaughtered other Tutsis for whom they had less compassion. In hospitals and camps, we saw Rwandan after Rwandan put their own mourning on hold to assist others. Those were the painful first steps to recovery: cleaning blood stains off the floor, sweeping broken glass, and taking an inventory of what remained.

There were too many displaced camps within Rwanda to keep them straight in my head. It was easy to spot the larger camps from miles away. Tens of thousands of people had stripped entire hillsides bare. They had uprooted or picked clean every single plant for food, fuel, or shelter. It was as if some terrible wave of locusts had descended. Vast low thickets of lean-tos made from cornstalks, banana leaves, and the distinctive blue plastic sheeting distributed by aid workers dominated the blighted landscapes. Quarter-mile-long lines of people stood with buckets and jerry cans hoping to fill them with water from oversized emergency water bladders. Medical tents were full of spindly infants being weighed on scales to determine the severity of their malnourishment. The children's heads were improbably large for their wasting bodies.

I would quickly learn that some aid organizations were better than others. To understand why, it is important to understand the philosophy underpinning the delivery of humanitarian aid. DART teams and their field-driven approach were a relatively recent innovation. The teams had people on the ground "pull down" resources by identifying the commodities and funding they needed to deal with the disaster. In the past, donors had simply "pushed" whatever resources they had toward a crisis and hoped they would be a good fit. Such an approach had led to aid operations that were little more than commodity drops, with American companies donating supplies as tax write-offs—whether they were needed or not. There were persistent tales of food rotting on docks and winter coats sent to the tropics.

Good will alone was not enough to manage a disaster. For example, when the American public watched the Rwanda refugee crisis unfold on television they came forward with tons and tons of kind-hearted, but often wildly inappropriate donations. A businessman generously offered two Chevrolet passenger vans for aid workers, not appreciating the cost of shipping the vans to Rwanda. One group donated brand new VCRs and Disney videotapes to help comfort refugee children, not realizing that most refugees were living without power, clean water, or shelter. Thankfully, the home entertainment packages never left the states. They did not tie up valuable space on emergency cargo flights stretched to the maximum. In short, it was important not only to help people, but also to help them in ways that made sense.

One American aid organization, AmeriCares, set off eye-rolling among the veteran humanitarians. After a visit to a large AmeriCares field hospital, I understood why. The hospital had been set up in the middle of a field, contained in huge, modern tents emblazoned with the AmeriCares logo.

Unlike many of the other aid groups, AmeriCares medical experts had little background working in the developing world. The doctors were plucked out of American hospitals, flown to Rwanda to work for brief stints and then returned home. When AmeriCares finished their respective missions, they would pack up their big white tents, fly out the doctors, and leave nothing behind. Other relief organizations went into the local communities and tried to identify previously existing health services. They found surviving local doctors and nurses and tried to get small clinics and hospitals up and running again. In contrast to AmeriCares, they provided training and basic low-tech supplies and equipment so the local health system could operate on its own. AmeriCares saved lives, but it did not offer lasting solutions.

With considerable help from Kim, I quickly learned the ropes. There was no other choice. Over beers, casual conversation, and during long car rides, I began to learn about the curious tribe of humanitarian relief workers. They had little in common with the Hollywood image of saintly good Samaritans saving the day. Yes, relief workers took incredible personal risks to help complete strangers in foreign countries. That was no small thing. Many of them were reasonably well compensated once things like hazard pay were included, but there were far easier ways to make money. It was obvious that the humanitarians took pride in the fact that their work made a difference. In a very unromantic way, this concept was central to their self-image.

Yet, relief workers were also rebellious. They disliked bureaucracy, took lots of chances, and could be full of themselves. Most were good at bending the rules, and this was very much part of their ability to get things done in a pinch. Relief workers did not look heroic. Most were unassuming. It did not take physical strength or lightning reflexes to engage in negotiations with a warlord blocking a convoy. Instead, it required the bravado to approach the situation as an equal. Relief workers had tough souls. In most cases, their toughness came across more as élan than machismo. They were willing to head to the hottest hotspot or to be the only person in a room without a gun. That was their business.

As people, they knew all too well that life was hard business, and the emotional landscape of humanitarian work was treacherous. It was corrosive to see thousands of innocent people die as part of your job. While despair was a reasonable reaction to so much tragedy, aid workers were not allowed the luxury of incapacitation. For relief workers it was a very fine line between being strong and growing utterly callous. Over every dinner conversation in Rwanda, I heard aid workers who were tired, raw, and angry at the international conspiracy of ineptitude that had allowed Rwanda's atrocities to go unchecked. I also saw the humanitarians who were more detached, who avoided unchecked emotions as if they were just another hazard to confront in war zones. The best balance seemed to be quiet resolve leavened with black humor.

It was unfair that the world asked people to work under such conditions. But it was also one of the great secrets of the industry: most people liked their jobs.

GOMA

Goma was located at the northern end of Lake Kivu in eastern Zaire, a very short distance from the border with Rwanda. Having watched scenes from the refugee camp on the news before I arrived, I was startled that the actual city of Goma was a dilapidated resort village. Zaire, having long suffered under the horribly corrupt leadership of President Mobutu Sese Seko, was lawless and run-down. The government could not provide security for its own citizens, much less the more than 1 million refugees that had poured out of Rwanda. We went into Zaire to meet with the DART team covering the Goma camp, and to transport some paperwork back to Kigali.

As we approached the Goma refugee camp, there were hundreds, maybe thousands, of women wearing brightly colored wraps walking on the shoulder of the road. The women, most of whom carried bundles of sticks on their heads, were scrounging further and further away from the camp for fuel wood. Some had walked miles for their sad collection of branches. As we got closer to the camp, it was no surprise the landscape was denuded. Groves of small spindly trees, like the stubble of a five o'clock shadow, were cropped to the ground.

A rush of movement caught my attention. Not far from the road, I could see three Hutus savagely beating a man who had fallen to the ground. Blow after blow rained down. We could do nothing. We were unarmed, and there were no peacekeepers in sight. I felt sick to my stomach, and uncomfortable that driving on was the only choice. I wondered if they would kill the man, and what had incited the beating. The women with the sticks walked faster. The scene left me with a sour taste that never went away.

The camp was perched in the shadow of an active volcano. The ground was craggy volcanic rock that was sharp enough to tear through sneakers. The ground was so hard that heavy machinery from Germany had been airlifted in to dig graves and latrines. The refugees had resorted to using small rock crags as toilets, but the frequent rains simply washed the human waste around the camp.

Getting refugees clean water was the single biggest factor in determining if they would live or die. Goma was no exception. Cholera—a highly communicable form of bacterial dysentery that triggered diarrhea and vomiting—was a fast track to death by dehydration if left untreated. Even though the camp was not far from Lake Kivu, providing drinking water was a huge problem because methane gas from the volcano fouled the lake. There were hundreds and hundreds of thousands of people living in close quarters with no toilets, no clean water, and not much in the way of shelter. The battle to provide water to the refugees in Goma had been epic, and tens of thousands had already died from cholera by the time we had arrived.

With a vast system of water pumps and filters in place, the situation was finally starting to improve. However, in a development that verged on the apocalyptic, a team of French vulcanologists flew in to inspect the volcano's cone amid fears it might erupt. Other than the methane gas, the active volcano, an airport designed to accommodate prop planes rather than cargo jets, the armed Hutu militias, cholera, the million people, the impenetrable rock and damp weather; it was an ideal place for a refugee camp. Imagine trying to establish water, sanitation, and shelter for a million people in a week under such conditions. It was madness.

It did not take long before we were in the middle of an overwhelming mass of humanity. With the windows of our Land Cruiser down, Kim warned me to keep my arms in the vehicle. In Somalia, people in the camps had been so aggressive that they had reached in vehicles to grab whatever they could.

The air was caustic with the smell of wood smoke and far too many people living packed together. The scene was a vast grim tableau of green and blue tarps providing temporary shelter. The camp was a study in the architecture of desperation, with lean-tos, huts, small igloo-shaped creations, and A-frames made from plastic sheeting, bamboo, cornstalks, wood, old raincoats, and straw. Mothers, often grasping children, waited in long lines for several gallons of water or meager rations of food. Thousands of people clustered around huge water bladders, thirty feet high, eager for their moment at a spigot. Hutu soldiers and militia men sat around drunk playing cards and killing time. The anger and bitterness was plain on their faces. None of their grand conspiracies for wiping out the Tutsis were supposed to end up with them sitting powerless in a refugee camp. Nothing was happening in Goma: there was no work; no plan; and not much hope. Everything was happening in Goma: young girls sold cigarettes and gum on overturned milk crates as harried relief workers tried to manage the chaos; a snarl of vans, cars, ambulances, and even school buses that had been looted from Rwanda were parked unevenly by the side of the road; doctors and nurses worked around the clock numbed by the sheer amount of patients passing through their hands. It was a swirl of color, sound, and activity. Many of the refugees had glazed expressions of shellshock.

Death was unceremonious. Bodies were stacked by the side of the road waiting to be loaded in dump trucks. People walking by did not give the corpses a second glance. This was the first time in my life I had seen dead bodies other than at a funeral. There was nothing enlightening about the experience. The bodies were tangled; their clothes dirty and disheveled. They looked like discarded, broken dolls unable to wipe away the grime or flies that clung to their faces. A heavy truck half-full of the dead moved slowly down the road, and the men in charge of its awful cargo wore bandanas over their mouths to dampen the stench. Making our drive all the more surreal, a cassette tape we had borrowed from the house in Kigali still absently played in the background. Neil Diamond's greatest hits accompanied a scene beyond imagining.

I was beginning to understand the depth of hatred and fear that drove the conflict. The enmity between the Hutus and the Tutsis was so great that, for the Hutus, eking out existence on a blasted piece of volcanic rock in Zaire made more sense than staying in Rwanda. A whole country of lush empty fields was only a short walk away. Yet, the Hutus believed that facing dysentery, disease, and deprivation was preferable to risking Tutsi retribution for the incredible slaughter of the preceding weeks. It was better to leave one's farm, land, and possessions than answer the hard questions about the killings. One Hutu I spoke with adamantly claimed that the mass exterminations were self-defense, shrugging, "If we did not do it to them first, they would do it to us."

Goma was bittersweet duty for relief workers. The very same Hutu army and militias that conducted massacres across Rwanda were using their fellow refugees in Goma as a protective cloak. Armed and uniformed men were present throughout the camp; most did not bother to conceal their weapons. It was accepted wisdom that soldiers never went hungry, because men with guns took what they wanted from women and children. This meant relief workers were delivering aid not only to innocent refugees but also directly to mass murderers. Would you want to deliver food to soldiers who killed entire families in cold blood? Would you prefer to let thousands of innocent people die because you did not want to feed those killers? A sense of unfairness suffused the entire relief operation: the international community had stood motionless during the killing of Tutsis, but swung into action to provide aid to the Hutu refugees.

Like it or not, by providing food, water, and medical supplies, the international community was providing tacit support for the men with guns, machetes, and lingering dreams of an ethnically pure Rwanda. One well-respected relief group, Doctors without Borders, complained that it had little choice but to "continue being reluctant accomplices of genocidal warmongers or withdraw from the camps, leaving the refugee population to the mercy of their jailors."

We were getting daily reports that armed gangs in the camp were intimidating Hutus who wanted to return to Rwanda. A number of Hutu families that had intended to return were hacked to death by Hutu soldiers in front of large crowds. The message was not lost. Hutu fighters also spread wild rumors that vengeful Tutsis had beheaded every Hutu who returned to Rwanda. In an effort to combat this propaganda, the UN took a test group of refugees across the border and then back to the camp so that they could report on the situation within Rwanda to their fellow refugees. Armed Hutus attacked many of these people as well. Those few people still willing to attempt to cross the border did so in secret, sneaking across small steep trails, vulnerable to two armies and countless armed bandits.

The Hutu military insulated itself from cross-border attacks by surrounding itself with civilians. If large numbers of innocent people in the camps returned to Rwanda, the Hutu army would be exposed, and no longer be able to receive food and other supplies from the international community. There was a growing belief among relief workers that something had to be done about the armed Hutus in the camps. If they were not disarmed, it would only be a matter of time before a new crisis unfolded.

But there was no stomach in Western capitals for putting a force on the ground to disarm the Hutus. The international community tended to lurch from disaster to disaster and was not very good at making the hard choices that might prevent such calamities. Wandering through Goma it was impossible not to feel outraged at the world's stubborn refusal to do the right thing. By failing to deal with the problem of armed Hutus in the camps, it was almost certain that most refugees would not return, and Zaire would remain a chaotic mess. Those responsible for perpetrating genocide would escape justice.

How could France, the United States, and the United Kingdom—countries that bragged about intelligence gathering so sophisticated that they could read the name on a mailbox from space—not have turned up evidence of the plot to commit genocide in Rwanda? Fifty armored personnel carriers and a few thousand UN troops parked in front of hospitals, schools, and churches could have saved tens of thousands of lives. Sadly, ten dead Belgian peacekeepers and memories of the Somalia fiasco were enough to scare the most powerful nation on earth away.

During the height of the killing, a memo even circulated in the State Department that cautioned against using the word "genocide" to describe the situation in Rwanda because it might raise public expectations that the U.S. government would actually do something about it. At one point in Kigali, I spoke with a U.S. congressional staffer over a beer. He commented, "Well, the American public just doesn't have much taste for intervening in this kind of thing." True, most Americans gave little thought to Africa, but was America so jaded that the notion of doctors murdering patients in their beds and teachers slaughtering children in kindergarten was of no consequence? The failure to act in Rwanda was not due to a flaw in the American character, it happened because American leaders stayed silent. Nobody stood up and articulated what was happening with clarity and passion. *Schindler's List* was one of the most popular movies of 1994, yet the American government was afraid to utter the word genocide for fear that it would have to stop it.

Kim and I dropped by the DART office in Goma, and the team was exhausted but in reasonable spirits. We were staying at a guesthouse not far from the camp, and it was well after dark when we finally headed for our lodging. We hoped the hotel had not given our rooms away. During our drive, the cone of the volcano illuminated the night sky an iridescent shade of orange. The scene was magnificent and otherworldly.

The guesthouse was nicer than I had expected, and it had been part of a lakeside resort. International relief workers and journalists had rented every room in the hotel. It was more business than they had seen in years. In thinking about Goma, I had never imagined a nice hotel just down the road from the world's worst refugee camp. Tables in the dining room were set with white linen tablecloths. The relief workers and journalists were drinking heavily. A few tables away, Ed Bradley and his crew from *60 Minutes* were finishing off a large dinner. Bradley, of whom I had always had a good impression, was smoking a cigar. When the check for the meal arrived, Bradley heatedly berated his Zairean waiter. Everyone else in the room was dead silent. Bradley called management over to review the bill, and Bradley continued to gripe about the price of his meal. Bradley may or may not have had good reason to believe the hotel was abusing his expense account, but several miles away more than a million people were sleeping in misery on volcanic rock.

Relief workers regularly used the term "disaster tourist" to refer to luminaries who jetted into war zones for brief visits. Disaster tourists came in many forms, whether it was politicians, actors, religious leaders, or rock stars. Disaster tourists held babies and press conferences with equal fervor, basking in the reflected glory of suffering on a grand scale. They then promptly returned to their comfortable homes. An hour in a refugee camp provided a disaster tourist with months of media coverage and cocktail party banter. Relief workers held disaster tourists in special disregard because they required a great deal of care and feeding at a time when there were a million other things worth doing. But television cameras meant attention and more donations, so aid workers gritted their teeth. Bradley behaved like the worst kind of disaster tourist, and it left me unsettled. Wasn't he supposed to be a good guy? Was my foray to Rwanda simply a way to feel better about myself? Was it all just macabre fascination? It made me wonder: was I some sort of disaster tourist?

A LONG DAY

By mid-August, the French government announced its intention to withdraw from the Turquoise Zone and hand over peacekeeping duties in southwest Rwanda to the UN. In reality, the French were simply acknowledging reality: they could no longer prevent the Tutsis from taking over the region. Fearing that Tutsis would take advantage of the French withdrawal to exact revenge, Hutus in southwestern Rwanda flocked toward the border with Zaire on the south end of Lake Kivu, with more than 25,000 people arriving in the border town of Cyangugu in a single day. At the UN coordination meeting in Kigali, dramatic aerial photos showed refugees jamming the bridges into Zaire. Making matters worse, Zaire repeatedly opened and closed the border, fearing it would be permanently stuck with another huge influx of refugees. Much time and energy was dedicated to contingency planning for what looked like the next wave of disaster. On

August 21, the French pulled out, leaving Rwanda's Tutsis in control of the entire country.

Kim and I traveled to southwest Rwanda to conduct assessments on displaced camps. The region was still in turmoil. With the French having pulled out only days before, neither UN peacekeepers nor the Tutsi military had established their positions, and there were steady reports of violence by small bands of armed Hutus. Our agenda for the day was to look at a series of nine camps, large and small. It was a lot of territory to cover, but the situation on the ground was changing rapidly and everyone wanted to know what was happening.

Our day began as we woke up in the Land Cruiser, which we had parked several hundred yards off a dirt road. It had been after dark when we stopped the night before, anxious about encountering checkpoints. Car camping in Rwanda was nerve racking, and my head was full of ominous imaginings as I had drifted off to sleep. Hutu militia still roamed the southwest, and relief workers were attractive targets because they drove good vehicles and carried cash. I stirred with every cracking twig and animal noise. It was difficult to feel safe in the middle of nowhere. The light of day did much to improve our spirits.

The first camps we visited were along the main road. It was startling how quickly my perspective had changed. The camps felt small in comparison to Goma and others that we had seen. Most held a few thousand families. Weeks before such camp conditions would have shocked me. Several sites looked more like squatter settlements than traditional displaced camps, with people occupying abandoned schools, clinics, and warehouses. It took a minute to remember that even though this was not Goma, there were still more than twenty people crowded into even the smallest of rooms.

After our first few stops, we had a several-hour drive to reach one of the larger displaced camps in the southwest. Our route took us along the edge of a security zone, and we had been careful to check our route with UN officers before leaving Kigali. However, security information quickly grew dated. For a lengthy stretch, we drove along the perimeter of an enormous tea plantation. The tea plants formed a beautiful vivid green carpet in the abandoned area. Years of hard work were wasted.

It looked like a cyclone had hit the tea processing facility in the heart of the fields, with scrap metal, broken glass, lumber, and paper strewn across a clearing. Every moving part was stripped from the remaining machinery. The destruction was pointless—more vandalism than looting. Patsy Cline played on our tape deck, and the borrowed music gave the plantation a dreamlike quality. As we slowly drove out of the gate, a middle-aged man lurched out of a shack, stumbling toward our vehicle. Mumbling incoherently, he carried a frilly parasol and wore an ill-fitting pink dress. He was drunk or crazy, and maybe both. We did not slow down. In parts of Africa, guerilla fighters sometimes wore outlandish costumes to make their spirits less culpable for the acts of violence they committed.

A few field-workers in a house told us that a wealthy Hutu who had left the country owned the plantation. Most of the workers had fled or been killed. The people in the house were eager to get back to work. They were still tending the fields even though there were no bosses to pay them. The sense of commitment to the tea plants was awkwardly and sadly sweet. It was impossible to explain that things would never return to the way they were. We drove on.

We passed through several sleepy checkpoints. For two hours we did not see a single other vehicle on the winding dirt and gravel road. It was almost a relief when we arrived at another checkpoint not far from the displaced camp that we were trying to reach. There was still no traffic. About twenty men milled about at a makeshift guard station. Roughly half of them were armed. Only a few of the men wore uniforms. They were Tutsis.

Looking surprised to see us, the men gave us a brusque reception. The soldiers demanded to know our identity and destination. Their angry questions felt odd given that the displaced camp was only about three miles from the checkpoint. The men grew even testier when they learned we were headed for the camp. They were upset that the Hutus in the camps were getting relief supplies. *Why are you helping to feed murderers? Those people deserve to die for what they have done. Some of these men are no better than animals. Why haven't you done more for the Tutsis? Tutsis are the real victims in this war. Our people are getting nothing. Where was America when Hutus killed our people?* Our chief interrogator was a short thin man in mirrored sunglasses wearing a maroon beret. He was angry. *This area is off limits. You are too close to the frontier.* He refused to let us pass and demanded that we get out of the Land Cruiser.

My instinct was to comply. The men had guns; we did not. Kim refused to get out of the Toyota with a vehemence that took both the Rwandans and me by surprise. "There is no reason for us to get out of the car," said Kim, her voice flat and hard.

Kim reasoned that once out of the Land Cruiser, we would lose what little leverage we had. The soldiers would search the car. They might confiscate our supplies, take our money, or worse. The situation could rapidly turn ugly, and we were both acutely aware that Kim was a lone woman among a group of armed men. We tried to negotiate with the man in the mirrored shades, stressing our status as humanitarian workers, and pointing out that we assisted Tutsis as well as Hutus. We emphasized that the Land Cruiser had diplomatic plates and should be immune from search. We also argued that the Tutsi military commanders in Kigali, some of whom had trained in America, would be very upset if they learned these soldiers harassed us at a time when the U.S. was doing so much to assist the new government.

The day was getting warm. We kept the engine running. I had quietly shifted the Land Cruiser into reverse and kept my foot on the clutch, waiting. We had a clear path behind us, and could gain speed quickly, but the men with guns were right next to the Land Cruiser. They could easily interpret sudden flight as a hostile act.

The soldiers came up to our windows and cajoled us to get out of the vehicle. "You can wait here all day; you will not pass," insisted one. The roadblock consisted only of a slender tree limb stretched across the road, but for our purposes, it might as well have been the Berlin Wall. The men gathered in angry conferences further away from the Land Cruiser, discussing our fate. A man wearing a yellow T-shirt increasingly took the lead in discussions. It was not clear if he was a soldier or not. It was also not obvious who was the ranking officer. We sat in the car and negotiated. Although the man in the yellow T-shirt was more moderate than some of his colleagues, five minutes soon stretched past an hour. The soldiers were baffled and irritated that an unarmed woman refused to take their orders. For the time being, there continued to be something in Kim's unflinching manner that thwarted the men from simply dragging us out of our seats.

It was impossible to tell if the soldiers would allow us to go back the way we came. The guerillas peered in the windows and tinkered with their weapons, sometimes laughing loudly at jokes at our expense. Kim and I spoke to each other in low tones trying to figure out the dynamics of the group. My knee was sore from holding in the clutch. The man in the yellow T-shirt and the soldier in the mirrored sunglasses approached the car. The soldier launched into another scolding, but his heart was not in it. The man in the yellow-T had convinced him to let us pass. With a dismissive gesture, the man in the mirrored shades ordered a subordinate to drag the tree limb out of the road. We drove through the roadblock with tight-lipped smiles. The displaced camp was ten minutes away, but the episode at the roadblock had made me appreciate our vulnerability.

The displaced camp stretched across two steep knolls. A large church, a school, and several other low-slung brick buildings sat on the crown of the larger hill. A mass of tents and people surrounded the buildings and covered the slopes below. As we drove through the dense crowds, there were many more people with weapons than we had seen at other displaced camps. After the experience at the checkpoint, it was hard not to be nervous.

Most of the relief workers were stationed on top of the hill, and despite being damaged, every building was being used by either aid agencies or the displaced. A handful of UN armored personnel carriers parked behind rows of barbed wire. The Red Cross was preparing for a large food distribution, and several trucks were fully loaded and backed into position. Bringing a huge mass of hungry people together with the promise of food was always dangerous work. There were thousands and thousands of people lined up in anticipation, and some of the old women in line clutched black umbrellas to ward off the sun. Even though the handout was well organized, there was always the potential for the situation to dissolve into pandemonium with even a minor provocation. Amid the steady din and jostling for position, security guards slapped at the unruly with sticks.

Ensuring that food actually got to those who needed it was difficult. Food meant life or death in the camps. It also served as a de facto form of currency. Even in the best cases the displaced resold and bartered food, and Rwanda was far from the best of cases. People employed every means imaginable to get what they could. To cut down on cheating, relief workers registered families before they could receive food. Beneficiaries got their hands stamped with indelible ink when given rations. In extreme cases, aid workers carried out "wet" feeding programs, where people received cooked food to ensure that others did not steal or resell the rations.

The young woman overseeing the food distribution wiped sweat from her face with a soiled bandana, and walked quickly as we asked her questions. She had been brought in specifically to organize the food deliveries, because earlier efforts had been badly mismanaged. We ran through our checklist of potential problems, and she indicated that water and sanitation were her biggest headaches. She sighed loudly when she contemplated life in the camp during the rainy season. The winding roads would be hazardous for the heavy trucks that brought in food and other supplies, and the hillside encampments would become a muddy mess. Standing in the baking sun, I could only have admiration for anyone holding back the mayhem while distributing tons of food to tens of thousands of hungry people. It felt like her will alone was keeping the situation from falling apart.

Kim and I made our rounds. We visited the makeshift infirmary and the feeding center where infants clung to life with eye-droppers full of nourishment. We inspected the water spigots and held a meeting with the Hutu camp representative who we had been warned was a pathological liar. We also stopped by the UN military compound where the officers were openly unsure who actually controlled the countryside.

Kim wandered off for several minutes, and I stood at the crest of the hill looking down on the camp. Hazy gray-white smoke wafted up from cook pots and burning garbage. As far as the eye could see, families were doing what families do—talking, arguing, washing clothes, playing, and yelling—in homes that consisted of only a small sheet of plastic and some cornstalks. I was standing in Rwanda's living room.

The church at the top of the hill had been a modest structure. Its brick walls vaulted upward, and its broad front doors were gone. A young boy stood on the front stoop. His clothes were tattered and grubby, but he smiled. We kidded around in small ways that did not require language. He had done nothing to cause the war, but he would live with it his entire life.

The church was empty. I walked inside and gazed up at the clear blue sky through the jagged timbers of what remained of the roof. The church had been full of people when it was attacked. I could see the dead body of a man still sprawled across a broken truss above. He must have tried to climb his way out. The young boy trailed behind me, curious as to why I was curious about the church. While every other building for miles around was crammed full of people, none took refuge in the church.

The solitude was eerie, but oddly welcome. Moments of peace were hard to find in the camps. The young boy wandered off, leaving me alone with my thoughts. What level of malevolence did it take to kill all the men, women, and children huddled in a church hoping only for sanctuary? The sky above was impossibly blue. I leaned against a wall and looked out across the thousands of displaced, their voices muted by the distance and the breeze. Some of the killers were still there. On the heavily terraced hillside, the dull desperate business of staying alive was the only task at hand. There were no answers for my question and no whispers of remorse. I walked on.

We finished our work at the camp and departed. Hoping to visit all the camps by the end of the day, some of which were smaller and more remote, we did not want to linger. Our route took us over increasingly narrow and steep roads near Rwanda's southern border with Burundi. The hard-packed clay roads were jarring and slick even with a good four-wheel drive. The smaller camps were receiving only token amounts of assistance, and there was concern that they would become inaccessible with the rains.

Although exhausted, we managed to make it to all of the camps on our list. By the last camp, my notebook was crammed with messy details scribbled during the drive. Because it was near the end of the day, we also needed to figure out where we were going to spend the night. We planned to drive south to Burundi the next day to pick up an extra vehicle. Given the continued fighting in southwest Rwanda, the safest route would mean an extensive detour, driving three hours north back to Butare and then three hours south to reach the main border crossing. Neither one of us was excited by the prospects of so much backtracking when we were already virtually on top of the Burundi border.

We noticed a small border crossing marked on our map. We asked several people if it was still open, but got conflicting responses. The afternoon shadows were starting to get long. We had to make a decision. We decided to find the small border post. We reasoned that if it was closed, we would simply drive to a nearby UN military compound and sleep in the car. We were not leaving ourselves much margin for error.

Navigation proved more challenging than anticipated. There were no signs or markers, and as we worked our way toward the border, the roads tapered into dirt tracks. It was a rural area with little traffic. The locals spoke only Kinyarwandan, a language of which Kim and I spoke only several handfuls of words, and we did not have a translator with us.

We asked directions the best we could, and traversed an intersecting series of dirt roads. Nothing bore any resemblance to our maps. As the last of the daylight drained from Rwanda's deep valleys, apprehension welled inside me. We were no longer on anything resembling a road, and we drove rapidly along the skinny, narrow ruts that cut through the fields. We came across several groups of deeply inebriated men with machetes that glared as we accelerated past. The track took us under canopies of thick brush adding a sense of claustrophobia to our predicament.

Several times, the trail dead-ended on the doorsteps of small huts, forcing us to slide to an abrupt halt. We had to face the unpleasant but obvious truth: we were lost, and we were lost in a place were people would kill us for our vehicle alone. We could find neither the way we came nor the border crossing. Having already spent part of the day at an armed checkpoint, we were driving in the dark in an area filled with Hutu militia. No one knew where we were. If we disappeared, help would be very slow in coming.

We crisscrossed back and forth through the fields, our exasperation and adrenalin steadily rising in equal measure. At every turn, I worried our headlights would splay across a checkpoint or an ambush. Stopping and setting up the satellite telephone in the dark to report that we were lost was not promising. We were violating almost every principle of good security procedure: it was dark; the area was not secure; we had no radio contact; and we were completely alone. Worse still, there was no obvious path out. One of the fuel cans we had tied to the roof rack worked itself loose and spilled gas down the rear window. Things were coming apart.

We ground to a stop. I scrambled up on the roof of the Land Cruiser to retie the gas can. Anxiety and fear gripped me as I worked clumsily with a flashlight clenched between my teeth. I could hear people yelling and running toward our vehicle. Fuel covered my hands, and I lashed things down quickly. As I jumped down from the roof, and the clamor of unfriendly voices closed in, the sky above was thick with stars. The Land Cruiser threw off a spray of dirt as we sped off.

Kim and I spoke in short terse sentences as we debated our course of action. We were caught in a maze, and although still certain that the border was nearby, we were disoriented. Discouragingly, when we encountered a small family and asked directions, they reacted like Burundi was a million miles away. The situation became more dangerous every time we crisscrossed the same ground, with the likelihood increasing that someone would be waiting for us.

We turned on to a dirt track that we had not taken before, and came across a dirt road. Through the darkness, we saw a house and a group of old men sitting around a fire. While still reluctant to interact with a large group, and knowing full well we could be putting ourselves at risk, we stopped to talk to them.

We had given up trying to reach Burundi, and hoped only to reach the UN military compound or even a more recognizable road. We asked directions back to town. After a halting back and forth, one of the old men tilted his head quizzically and asked, "Rwanda?" The old men looked at each other in confusion, as did Kim and I. After more questions, it became apparent what had happened: we had crossed into Burundi without realizing it. There had been no border guards, no sign, no building, and barely even a road. To the further bafflement and amusement of the old men, when we realized we were in Burundi, we stopped asking directions to Rwanda and started inquiring how to get to Bujumbura, the capital of Burundi. They pointed us down the road.

It was still a long drive to Bujumbura, and Burundi's countryside was also dangerous. But the fact that we were no longer in Rwanda sapped a good deal of the tension. It was late when we arrived in Bujumbura. Our colleague asked about the drive down, surprised that we were arriving so long after dark. We both shook our heads and mentioned that it had been a "long drive" without adding any detail. Kim and I never shared the story with Kate or others on the team. We had been stupid and lucky.

THE SHAPE OF THINGS TO COME

Driving back to Kigali the next day, the main Burundi-Rwanda border crossing was congested with Tutsi families returning to Rwanda. Most were long-term Tutsi refugees that had been in Burundi for years, some for more than three decades. Given the long exile, it was no surprise that most of the families did not look like refugees. They were well dressed and traveled with cars and considerable belongings. Many Tutsis had achieved relative affluence during their long years in Burundi, although society had never fully accepted them. Tutsis from Burundi, Tanzania, and Uganda were flocking back into Rwanda to reclaim their property.

We were getting reports that Rwanda's new Tutsi government was clearing Hutus out of the southeast and seizing their homes and properties. The government insisted that it was discouraging such behavior, but most Hutus were defenseless. In fairness, the government had intervened in a number of Hutu eviction cases, and the level of revenge killings was lower than most had feared. Watching the stream of Tutsi refugees waiting to get into Rwanda, I was convinced that Tutsi leaders thought they could run Rwanda without the Hutu refugees ever returning.

Back in Kigali, investigations into the genocide were off to an atrocious start. While the UN had brought in a Commission of Experts to identify war criminals and help bring them to trial, the commission had only four staff members on the ground, one borrowed vehicle, and a single laptop computer: Four people, one vehicle, and a laptop to investigate 800,000 deaths. The lone competent staffer quit in abject frustration. It was difficult not to be pissed off.

It did not take long once back in Kigali for Kim and I to get in trouble. After one of the coordination meetings, a reporter from the *New York*

Times, Ray Bonner, approached us. Bonner had heard us making the case for disarming the Hutus in the refugee camps and giving more support to war crimes investigators. He was eager for an interview. We spoke with him at length and argued passionately that development in Rwanda would be largely impossible until there was accountability for the genocide. Kim pointed out that less than $1 million had been allocated for the war crimes investigation—about what it cost to fly in a single C-130 flight of relief supplies. Bonner was quietly delighted to get such quotes from U.S. government employees, and his subsequent story filled a good part of a page in the *Times*. He had used our quotes on the record. The reaction from Washington was quick, and we were told in no uncertain terms that we were not to talk to the press. I did not regret talking to Bonner, but it was also clear why veteran relief workers strived to keep themselves out of the story.

Near the end of my time in Rwanda, I drove to the Gisenyi border crossing between Rwanda and Zaire, near Goma. I was waiting for several people to enter Rwanda so I could give them a ride to Kigali. Because they were late and I had time to kill, I struck up a conversation with a Rwandan border guard.

"Where are you from?" I asked.

"Butare," he replied, which was one of the larger cities in southern Rwanda.

"When was the last time you were there?" I inquired.

"Oh," he said, with a fleeting look of embarrassment on his face, "I have never actually been to Butare. That is where my parents are from, so that is my home."

The soldier's parents had fled to Uganda from Rwanda in 1959 during an earlier round of ethnic purges and violence. He had lived his entire life as a refugee. The only chance for him to return to the city he considered home came when he helped invade Rwanda.

It was hard not to be sympathetic. The guy would finally be able to return to the modest house and small piece of farmland that his parents abandoned thirty-five years before. But it was impossible to ignore the bigger picture. The return of the Tutsis had brought a new and larger exodus of Hutu refugees. Just miles from where we stood, countless young Hutu boys were now experiencing life without a country to call their own. Darting between temporary huts and cookfires, a whole generation of Hutu boys played with toy guns and dreamed of leading a triumphal army back into Rwanda.

The people I was waiting for appeared. Thanking the border guard, I tossed my bags in the back of the Land Cruiser before promptly setting off. I wanted to make sure we got to Kigali with plenty of daylight.

Bosnia

Cartography by Bookcomp, Inc.

CHAPTER 3

Ocean Blue—The Former Yugoslavia

After a short stint on a disaster team in Haiti, I worked with the DART team operating in Bosnia and Croatia in the fall of 1995 and spring of 1996. The crisis in the former Yugoslavia was the world's largest humanitarian emergency at the time, and it was a hard lesson in how hatred and violence could consume even a modern, European nation.

SPLINTERING

By 1995, Bosnia's slow-rolling catastrophe in the heart of Europe embodied all that was wrong with the world. Unlike Rwanda, there was no pretending that what was happening was either out of sight or out of mind. The evening news was filled with appalling images of snipers shooting women in the streets of Sarajevo and hoping to lure out fresh targets in the process. Sarajevo's former Olympic stadium was a makeshift graveyard. Commentators coined a new euphemism, "ethnic cleansing," to describe the systematic elimination of ethnic groups in the Balkans through forced relocation and murder. By September 1995, more than 100,000 were dead and more than 2 million people driven from their homes.

Yugoslavia's demise was a story of rivalries manufactured among people who were not that different. The Balkans were largely populated with southern Slavs, and over the course of history these people—who essentially looked the same and spoke the same language—were overrun by different empires. Consequently, the different corners of the Balkans took on the complexion of their primary conquerors: Serbs became Orthodox Christians, Croats converted to Catholicism, and much of the populations of what are today Bosnia and Kosovo converted to Islam.

With Europe's borders redrawn at the conclusion of World War I, Yugoslavia was established. For much of the 20th century, a single man, Josip Broz Tito, held Yugoslavia's complex stew of orthodox Christians, Catholics, and Muslims together with his iron will. Tito became a national hero during World War II by leading communist resistance fighters against Croatian fascists backed by Hitler. Under Hitler, the Croatian fascists operated some of Europe's deadliest concentration camps, slaughtering more than 300,000 Serbs. After World War II, President Tito gained almost legendary status as one of the few communist leaders to stand up to Joseph Stalin and avoid Soviet occupation. He adroitly played east against west during the cold war.

However, Tito viewed Yugoslavia's ethnic rivalries as a persistent threat and suppressed them with brutal police state tactics in each of the country's six republics—Serbia, Croatia, Bosnia, Slovenia, Macedonia, and Montenegro. When Tito died in May 1980, the complicated political structure that he left behind quickly became unworkable, and by the late 1980s, some of the republics were openly advocating democracy. Two powerful nationalist politicians emerged during this period: Slobodan Milosevic in Serbia and Franjo Tudjman in Croatia. Both men recklessly played long-forbidden ethnic cards as they rapaciously dusted off nationalist symbols that quickly brought back the bloodiest memories of World War II.

Slobodan Milosevic, the leader of the Serbian communist party, was particularly confrontational. Sensing increasing pressure in the republics for independence, Milosevic pushed Serb hard-liners across Yugoslavia to seize territory and he dreamed of creating a "Greater Serbia" culled from across the different republics. Militias formed, and the Yugoslav military, long a powerful symbol of national unity, was steadily transformed into a predominantly Serbian force. Retired Croatian general Franjo Tudjman was equally nationalistic, and he hoped to create a "Greater Croatia" consisting of the Republic of Croatia and large parts of neighboring Bosnia. Conflict became inevitable, and the international community was dangerously distracted with the fall of the Soviet Union and Iraq's invasion of Kuwait in August 1990. Europe and the United States wanted nothing to do with the messy politics of the Balkans, and as U.S. Secretary of State, James Baker, infamously said of Yugoslavia, "We don't have a dog in this fight."

By June 1991, the republics of Slovenia and Croatia both unilaterally seceded, and fighting erupted in Slovenia, which emerged as a sovereign country after a brief series of clashes with the Yugoslav military. With almost no Serb population, Slobodan Milosevic had little interest in Slovenia. But Slovenia's breakaway gave Milosevic the pretext to unleash his plans for "Greater Serbia." Combat soon ensued in Croatia, and by the beginning of 1992, Serb insurgents had captured about a third of Croatia, forcing tens of thousands of ethnic Croats from their homes. The UN inserted a token force along a shaky ceasefire line, but there was no peace to keep.

Bosnia was next to feel the wrath. Located dead center between Serbia and Croatia, Bosnia was the most multiethnic republic in Yugoslavia with an intermingled population of Muslims, Serbs, and Croats. Bosnia took great pride in its tradition of coexistence, and intermarriage between ethnic groups was common. Fearing that Bosnia would be reduced to a second-class status in a Serb-dominated Yugoslavia, the republic declared independence in February 1992, but because Bosnia was home to many ethnic Serbs and Croats, and possessed little in the way of a military, it would soon fall prey to Serb and Croat forces.

In April 1992, the siege of Sarajevo began, and many of the residents of the city were dumbfounded as Serb mortar shells rained in from the surrounding mountains. Well-armed Serb militias savagely attacked civilian populations in largely Muslim towns in northern and eastern Bosnia. Serbs executed community leaders in cold blood, raped women, and drained entire cities of their Muslim populations. If Bosnia's ethnic map were not conducive to tidy division, Milosevic and his allies would change the map through ethnic cleansing.

As the situation on the ground eroded, Europe and the United States flew in large shipments of food aid, but refused to mount an effective military response. As one resident of Sarajevo grumbled, "They simply want to make sure that we are well fed when we are shot." By the end of 1992, Bosnian Serbs, who made up only 30 percent of Bosnia's population, controlled close to 70 percent of its territory. Sarajevo suffered through a miserable winter under siege, starved of food, water, and fuel. With continuous sniper fire, even the scramble to fill a bucket of water at an outdoor spigot was a life or death struggle. Intense fighting broke out between Bosnian Muslims and Croats, and word leaked out that Yugoslav President Slobodan Milosevic and Croatian President Franjo Tudjman had made plans—literally drawn on the back of a napkin—to divide Bosnia in two.

In the spring of 1993, the UN declared six Muslim enclaves in Bosnia to be "safe havens," but the UN peacekeeping force in Bosnia had too few men and too many political constraints. Tragedy finally helped propel the United States into a more forceful role. A Serb shell landed in the middle of a crowded marketplace in Sarajevo in February 1994, killing 69 and leaving more than 200 wounded. Media footage of the carnage sharply escalated pressure on Washington to respond militarily. American officials pressured the Croats and Bosnian Muslims to stop fighting each other and make common cause against the Bosnian Serbs. After a brief ceasefire collapsed in 1995, the Serbs seized UN troops in an effort to prevent renewed NATO bombing. Humiliatingly, the Serbs chained UN soldiers to bridges and other important strategic targets, using them as human shields. Criticism of President Clinton's foreign policy rightfully reached a crescendo.

In another devastating blow, Bosnian Serb forces overwhelmed the UN safe haven at Srebrenica in July 1995 after steadily strangling the city. After the enclave's fall, Serb forces—with UN assistance—separated Muslim women and children from the men. The Serbs then took the men into the surrounding hills, killed them, and dumped the bodies in mass graves. Almost 8,000 men and boys were slaughtered at Srebrenica. The UN's vow to make Srebrenica a safe haven had proven bitterly hollow. Only a year after the Rwandan genocide, the United States and Europe sat on their hands in the face of the largest European massacre since the holocaust.

NATO air strikes and an increasing flow of arms to the Croats and Bosnian Muslims dramatically changed the battlefield calculus. In early August 1995, Croatia unleashed Operation Storm, pushing Serb forces out of almost all of the territory they occupied in Croatia. Bosnian Muslims and Croats also stepped up the pace of offensives in Bosnia, and the Serbs began to lose ground for the first time in the war. After a grenade attack killed more than thirty people in a Sarajevo marketplace in late August, NATO finally unleashed more widespread air strikes, launching over 500 sorties by the beginning of September as I arrived in Croatia. With NATO serving as their air force, the Croats and Bosnian Muslims were making rapid gains. The fate of Bosnia hung in balance.

INTO THE POCKET

Tim Knight headed the DART team. Initially headquartered in the Croatian capital of Zagreb, the team had been in place for several years—a lifetime in the world of disaster operations. I kidded Tim that he could run for mayor if he stuck around much longer. He was friendly and dapper, and ran the team with a laid-back corporate efficiency. Like the other DART team members I worked with, Tim went out of the way to make me feel welcome, and his views on the war were illuminating. Although Tim thought the international community's handling of Yugoslavia bordered on farce, his demeanor was dispassionate. He carried himself as a professional. Those on DART teams cleaned up the mess of war, but were rarely given a voice in major foreign policy decisions. Such mandatory stoicism was not always easy to maintain in the face of such florid political failures.

After only a few days in Zagreb working with the DART team, I realized that I fostered a great misperception about war. I had always pictured war as total chaos: guns firing, mortar shells slamming to the earth, and people barely able to move ten feet without getting shot. That was the war we knew from movies, and there were times and places where war was like that. But after Rwanda and Haiti, and then being in the Balkans, a different picture emerged. War was intermittent. Even in countries in the middle of full-scale conflict, combat did not take place all the time. Life could be deceptively, almost absurdly, ordinary just miles from the front.

Serbs and Croats who tried to kill each other during the day met in the dark of the night to sell each other gasoline, weapons, and cigarettes. A village that was the scene of total horror one day looked calm and commonplace the next. Ten people could go through a checkpoint with no problem, while soldiers killed the eleventh for no good reason at all. Even in cities where there had been vicious house-to-house fighting, sidewalk cafes quickly reopened after the shooting stopped. Television reinforced the stereotype of war as total bedlam, because networks broadcasted only the ugliest scenes. There was never footage of bored looking villagers selling scrawny vegetables on a blanket by the side of the road. There were no stories about surprisingly well-dressed children heading for schools that still functioned amid the mayhem. There was no coverage of the luxury hotel that catered to war correspondents and remained open by bribing government officials.

Zagreb was a good example. Croatia was involved in major fighting, but the capital, other than a few rocket attacks, had been spared. The city looked prosperous, and the young people I talked to were obsessed with computers, music, and cell phones. They were eager to shake off the country's image of clunky, square-shoed socialism like teenagers embarrassed by their parents at the school dance. As I walked back from the office one afternoon, the light cast the city in heather tones. I did not pass a single damaged building, and modern commercial goods filled the stores. Streetcars emblazoned with ads for Nike and Benetton rumbled by the old city square.

Despite the veneer, war was close at hand. Old men clustered around a magazine kiosk, animatedly debating a map on the front page of the newspaper that detailed territorial gains in Bosnia. The local staff in our office lived in fear that someone would discover the ethnicity of their aunt, or their grandfather, or stepbrother. The wrong family ties could mean the loss of a job, an apartment, or even a life. Friendships that had lasted decades could end in a second amid accusations and betrayals. Questions that had once been casual, such as "where are you from," had taken on disturbing intent. The concept of identity was treacherous.

Just an hour-and-a-half drive from Zagreb, every house, barn, and shed for miles was shattered. The roads that ran through the once quiet farm country were modern and good, although many of the larger concrete bridges on the highways had been blown up. These towns in the Krajina region of Croatia, which bordered Bosnia, had been caught in a deadly surge of back and forth offensives between Serbs and Croats. It was the first time that I had seen the impact of heavy artillery on a battlefield. Scorched and broken red brick roof tiles littered almost every yard. Yet even with tanks, mortars, hand grenades, and machine guns, it was difficult to imagine what battle could have decimated every single house without fail. Indeed, many of the buildings were not totally razed, as you would expect from damage inflicted by unceasing heavy artillery, but were gutted by fire and pocked with countless rounds from small weapons.

The destruction was purposeful and systematic—designed to drive out the people who lived in the houses and ensure they would never return. In fact, Croatia passed a law that mandated that any person who had fled the country had to return and claim their house within ninety days or forfeit ownership. To reenter Croatia you needed proof of citizenship, and the new government issued identity cards only to those already in the country.

In the Krajina, I toured an orthodox church that had been abandoned as the ethnic Serbs were driven out of the area. Splintered glass littered the pulpit and most of the furniture was overturned. Fake plastic flowers sat next to a cross that no one had bothered to loot. Municipal officials had brought me to the church in an effort to demonstrate that the Croats were tolerant. To bolster their argument, they pointed to a nearby Catholic church the Serbs had burned down. Despite the tour, the bitterly nationalistic attitude of many Croats was impossible to ignore. A Croat unhesitatingly dismissed my concerns about the tens of thousands of Serb civilians driven from their homes at a point of a gun. He scoffed, "The Serbs have only been in the Krajina for 350 years; they do not belong."

A colleague showed me a picture she had taken shortly after the Croatian military had driven the Serbs out of the Krajina. The picture was grainy and taken from a slow-rolling car at dusk, but it was clear enough. It showed several Croatian military officers sitting in lawn chairs, drinking beer, and watching the houses they had set on fire burn.

I set off with a colleague, Joe, to do a field assessment of several refugee and displaced camps. Like me, Joe usually worked in Washington, but deployed frequently to the field. He was married with children, sported a thick mustache, and had an understated sense of humor. We headed for a small enclave of territory in far northwestern Bosnia known as the Bihac pocket. Because of the intense fighting still taking place on the ground, not to mention the NATO air strikes, our safest route was a long circuitous one through the Krajina region of Croatia. At the border crossing between Croatia and Bosnia, we waited in a long line of trucks carrying relief supplies into Bosnia. As Joe relieved himself by the side of the road, he came dangerously close to stepping in a minefield.

We spent the night in a small guesthouse just inside Bosnia. I could hear the steady plink of small arms fire in the distance. I lay awake for a long time, getting edgy as the shots grew closer. My bed, like all of the ones in the guesthouse, was pushed away from the walls and the blanket covered windows to cut down on the odds of being hit by a stray bullet. I had all of my belongings packed in case we needed to leave in a moment's notice. My dreams were full of violence.

Our first stop in the morning was the Miholjsko refugee camp, back inside the Croatian border. Because the Croatian authorities had stopped the Bosnian refugees in the middle of the road as they migrated north, the camp was literally built around a traffic jam, and the refugees were pinned down along a two-mile corridor. Cars, tractors, and horse carts choked the road, and pedestrians and livestock milled between the long-stopped vehicles.

People lived out of their cars, camped out in the muddy field that adjoined the road, and occupied small wooden farm sheds. A number of refugees had tried to take shelter higher on the adjoining hillside, but the Croatian military had made clear that it would fire on anyone who strayed too far out of camp. Croatian security services had killed several people who had gone into the forest seeking firewood. Old women washed clothes in a dirty trickle of a stream and middle-aged men unhappily smoked cigarettes outside of small plastic-sheeting tents. Mud was everywhere.

Most of the refugees had come from the largely Muslim Bosnian city of Velika Kladusa. Before the war, the majority of people in Velika Kladusa had worked for a large agribusiness enterprise run by a wealthy Muslim entrepreneur and politician by the name of Fikret Abdic. When the war erupted, Abdic was eager to both get the region under his control and stay out of the conflict. So, while the rest of Bosnia's Muslim population was locked in a death struggle with the Serbs, Abdic carved out side agreements with the Serbs to protect his corrupt business empire. In return for his political commitments, the Serbs gave Abdic and his militia arms and free reign in northwest Bosnia. Abdic even rallied his troops to battle against their fellow Muslims in the Bosnian army, setting off a complex chain of events that shed light on the political difficulties inherent in relief work.

As Serbs conquered territory throughout Bosnia and Croatia early in the war, Abdic seized control of much of the Bihac region. But the tides repeatedly turned. First, the Bosnian army routed the Abdic militia and forced it to retreat into Croatia. Then Abdic's men mounted a counteroffensive and retook Bihac. The Bosnian army then again got the upper hand, and the Abdic militia and their families fled into Croatia for the second time, taking whatever they could carry. This exodus came to a rapid halt when blocked by the Croatian military, leaving a traffic jam on a country road with no moving forward and no moving back.

While relief workers were doing their best to take care of the Abdic refugees, it was not easy, and the refugees were a political problem as much as a humanitarian one. The last thing the fiercely nationalistic Croatian government wanted on its hands was a refugee camp made up of Muslims that had been fighting in allegiance with the Bosnian Serbs. The Croatians wanted to rid itself of the Abdic refugees, and refused to relocate them elsewhere in the country. Most other European countries already had their fill of Bosnian refugees, and had little desire to accommodate a Muslim militia force allied with Bosnian Serb war criminals. The Abdic refugees refused to return to Bosnia and into the arms of a waiting Bosnian army. The traffic stayed stuck.

The camp inhabitants were not typical refugees. There were many healthy young men with short haircuts—militia fighters stuck in the camp with their families. Just as in Goma, the militia fighters threatened families that were contemplating a return to Velika Kladusa because they needed a human shield of refugees. The militia men were still armed, and there were a number of weapon caches in the camp. An Italian relief worker explained to us how only several days earlier a refugee who received bottled water had offered a hand grenade as a token of gratitude because, "We have plenty of them."

There were a few Mercedes, looking out of place, mixed in with the tractors and other cars stuck on the road, although the richest of the refugees had been able to bribe their way past the Croatian guards. Some of the bored looking kids played handheld video games. One of the refugees disdainfully complained, "We are engineers and doctors living in this mud and filth. We are not Rwandans. This is not Africa. We are professional people." Although I did not debate him, his comment made me surprisingly angry, and not just because of its racist overtones. If Bosnia was so superior to Rwanda, what was the country doing in the middle of such a ghastly war? Was it really an accomplishment to be better educated and have nice cars but still be killing each other?

The Croatians had done everything they could to ensure that the conditions in the camp were wretched. In the camp's makeshift hospital, the patients, many missing legs because of mines, slept on thin mattresses scattered on a cold floor. The camp was low-lying and swampy with bad sanitation. Human waste flowed directly into the same streams where women washed clothes. Croatia had prohibited relief workers from bringing in heavy equipment to improve drainage in the muddy fields where the refugees slept, fearing that if conditions were too good the refugees would not leave. Guards stole relief supplies coming into the camp. Croatia had also denied the refugees official status to ensure they got less help. Although everyone pretended that humanitarian relief was apolitical, it was rarely the case.

The UN kept trying to push responsibility for the camp on to private aid groups, most of whom remained reluctant to accept an impossible mandate. Everyone said they wanted to help the refugees, but nobody wanted to make waves. There was always another form that needed filling out, or approval that needed to come from headquarters. The nights got colder and soon frost would creep across the muddy fields.

Traveling back into Bosnia, we visited the town of Vrnograc, a key transit point. As Muslim and Croat refugees from Bosnia fled north into Croatia, they often passed Serb refugees fleeing from Croatia to Bosnia. There were even reports that the refugees were swapping property deeds as they met on the road, coming to sad terms with the fact that they could not return home.

After talking to several local officials, we headed to a house that had been converted into a shelter for thirty people displaced from central Bosnia. Hurrying in from a steady, cold rain, it was like stepping into another world. As we entered, we were almost forced back down the narrow pine plank stairs by a surge of angry and pleading people. The house's ceiling was oppressively low, and all the windows were broken out of their wood frames. Blankets that served as uncomfortable beds were scattered across the floor. There were piles of trash in the corners of the main room, which was thick with the smoky pall of cheap Turkish cigarettes. The refugees had picked clean the discarded food tins littered about the space. The Bosnians were dirty and underfed.

A thin woman with a lazy eye roughly pushed her young daughter toward me, stretching her hair back to show me lice. The woman's other children cried plaintively and fought with each other. The stench of body odor and rotting food made the overpowering cigarette smoke almost welcome. Another woman pulled her pants away from her hip in a telling demonstration of malnourishment. She was two months pregnant. A man repeatedly waved a rock-hard chunk of bread at us as if all of Bosnia's ills resided in that single stale loaf. Everyone knotted around us, with three or four people speaking over one another, leaving our translator, Danica, to interpret the emotions as much as the words. *People from the UN come every day, but they do not help us. We are not getting enough food. We do not want to be here. Anyplace would be better than this. The cousin of the man who owns this house came by and said that we all have to leave or there will be violence. If things do not get better soon, we may kill ourselves.*

It was overwhelming. I wanted fresh air and five minutes of silence. I wanted it to stop, and I felt petty, gross, and small for wanting it to stop. I could walk away. I knew there was a chocolate bar and bottled water in the car. I would sleep in a bed that night. I would not be surrounded by feverish infants and rancid food. I did not watch a land mine shred my mother's right leg or see my family home reduced to rubble in a cascade of mortar fire. I did not have to beg foreigners to feed my children knowing that I once owned a farm that fed a hundred families. I did not have to sit in a small room, fumbling for words to comfort my sister after she was raped by the police.

The people in the house were pawns in a sick, violent game of musical chairs. The one thing they all had in common was that they were not Serbs, and that is precisely why the Serbs had driven them out of the city of Banja Luka. Those expelled from Banja Luka had first fled to Croatia. The Croatians welcomed the refugees who were ethnic Croats, and quickly resettled them in the houses left behind by Serbs. However, the Bosnian Muslims and other refugees were given a cold shoulder, and a deal was struck with the UN to bus the refugees back into Bosnia and settle them in Vrnograc. Officials packed 200 refugees into buses before dropping them at the school in Vrnograc at three in the morning, confused and disoriented. The refugees had little information about what was happening. During the days that followed, they were relocated around the city in houses that had belonged to Bosnian Serbs or members of the departed Abdic militia. There were so many refugees and displaced that even the UN was willing to look past the dubious legality of resettling refugees in other people's houses.

The Mayor of Vrnograc indicated that the thirty people we interviewed in the house were a core of individuals unhappy with the relocation, and he suggested that many of them were still in shock. The mayor thought they would adjust, but as we sat in his modest office, conflicting sentiments tore at the mayor. He felt badly that the people were living in cramped and difficult conditions, but he was also adamant that the city was doing all it could. The mayor had been forced from his own home during the war, and Vrnograc had repeatedly been on the frontlines of fighting, with considerable suffering all around.

Joe and I visited the local school, which continued to serve as a transit center for those being resettled. We spoke with some of the other people from Banja Luka who now lived in Vrnograc. Most were grateful. Standing on the steps of the school, the day's steady drizzle dripped through holes in the grenade-damaged roof. A nineteen-year-old woman, Jasmina, described her experience. It was her first time in Vrnograc, and she did not complain that the house to which she had been relocated was damaged. "Of course I am happy here," she told us through our translator. "In Banja Luka, I could not go out on the streets. I could not say my last name. I was afraid all the time. The Serbs would have killed me if they knew my name."

"Here it is better," said Jasmina running her fingers through her auburn hair, "We have a house, and I can go outside. Things are hard, yes, but I have life again." Jasmina wore jeans and a faded jean jacket. Shifting her weight from one foot to the other with restless emphasis, she could have been a teenager anywhere. "It is funny," she added, "Now I have freedom, but it is almost difficult. I am beginning to remember what it is like. The habits are very hard to break. I have to remind myself that I can go outside, or tell people my name. Life is better."

Pausing for a moment, she asked earnestly, "Do you know Moosejaw?"

The conversational detour puzzled Joe and me. Jasmina wanted to know what Moosejaw, Canada, was like. "Flat," we responded. Jasmina and her fiancé had planned to seek asylum in Canada, but they had been separated. He was a Bosnian Serb, she a Bosnian Muslim. According to the last information she had, he was in Belgrade trying to make his way to Canada. However, authorities took Jasmina's passport and her fiancé had no idea where she was located. Jasmina had questions about visas and plane tickets. We answered to the best of our ability, while being careful not to raise undue expectations that we could do anything about immigration issues. Jasmina could stay in Vrnograc or try to get to Canada. Getting out of Banja Luka had lifted Jasmina's burden of daily terrors. She was allowing herself the luxury of thinking about the future and weighing plans for something beyond sheer survival.

As Joe, Danica, and I headed back to the car, the woman with the lazy eye and the daughter with head lice rushed toward us. She wanted to go back to Banja Luka and her family home. Her oversized yellow sweater was soaked from the rain. A Bosnian soldier standing nearby vehemently cursed at the woman. Banja Luka was still an enemy stronghold as far as he was concerned, "If you want to back to Banja Luka," he spat, "you can wait ten days until we take it back." The exchange was soggy, desperate, and mean-spirited.

As we got into the car, Danica hastily lit a cigarette. Danica was a young woman and she had been in the Bihac pocket for the entire war. She inhaled the smoke as if it provided sustenance. Gazing off into the distance, Danica spoke softly, almost as if we were not there. "I worry about myself. Before the war it would have been very different, but now ..." She paused, thinking about how best to frame the words for outsiders. "Take that woman back there. If she does not want help, we cannot give her help. I think maybe she has gone crazy. She is confused, like all the refugees. It is a mental problem. She was saying that she has enough money to bribe the soldiers so she can go back to Banja Luka. It is insane. If she went to Banja Luka now they would kill her. That is it, they would just kill her." Danica paused. "It sounds very cold hearted, yes? The war has made me a colder person than I was before. We all suffer."

As we began to drive, Danica went on, "I am not hating these people." It was not clear if she was referring to the Bosnian Serbs, Abdic's militia, or the Croats. Maybe it did not matter. "I try to be objective, but it is difficult. My father, my uncle, they were killed very early on in the war. I try, I really try, to be reasonable and see the other sides of how this fighting happened." The car was a warm cocoon after the frigid rain. After being exposed to so much raw emotion during the day, Danica's words felt achingly intimate. "The saddest thing, the greatest thing being lost," Danica said, "is that we all did live together. I do not want to be separated because of Croat, or Muslim, or Serb. I grew up with all these people."

Danica's voice took on an edge, "It is not right that everything should be divided this way. This is not a war of the people; it is a war of the people who are our leaders. There is so much that needs to be done here. All of this is such a waste of time and money." She did not mention the cost to her own family, and she did not need to. Danica smiled a wry smile, "It is funny. Well, funny in a way that it can be here. Bosnia funny. You know the way it is. When they were shelling in the towns around Bihac, and every day there was so much shelling, people were running away from their houses." She waved her hands in the air, replicating the manic moments when artillery was falling, with a burst of exuberance that could only come from looking back at disasters survived. "But these people would run to the next town and the shelling was even worse there. It is funny to try to run away and then, 'boom,' shells are falling all around you. Sometimes we just do not know what to do."

"I think more than the electricity or the gas," said Danica, "I miss being able to get away. I would love to take a week of holiday." She grew animated at the thought, "It would not matter where." The border with Croatia was only a few miles away, but it had become impossible for Danica, like so many others, to leave Bosnia as anything other than a refugee. Turning in her seat, Danica faced us, her voice plaintive, "Last week, one of the women I work with started crying. She was crying so much. I asked her why. This woman explained that her family had taken its holiday every year on the Dalmatian coast—you know how close we are to the ocean; it is only two or three hours by car. It is very beautiful. Because of the war, they have not gone to the coast for several years now. So one day, this woman's daughter asked her if the ocean was blue. Can you imagine? Her daughter did not even remember the color of the ocean. It was too much. What has happened to us?"

THE LUCKY VEST

The military situation unfolded with a speed that caught everyone by surprise. By the third week of September 1995, the Serbs were retreating across a wide front in western Bosnia as the Bosnian and Croatian armies recaptured more and more land. NATO planes continued to pound Bosnian Serb targets, as U.S. negotiators at a military base in Dayton, Ohio, tried to hammer out a peace deal among the warring parties.

More than 50,000 Bosnian Serb refugees fled into Banja Luka as Muslim and Croat offensives continued. The assaults came very near to Banja Luka itself, one of the most important Serb strongholds in Bosnia. If Banja Luka fell, an even larger flood of Bosnian Serbs would pour out of central Bosnia.

Negotiators at the Dayton peace talks heralded it as a great victory upon reaching a formula to divide Bosnia: Muslims and Croats would control 51 percent of territory; Serbs 49 percent. But in a bizarre twist, American and European diplomats were concerned that the Bosnian government was doing too well on the battlefield and was reacquiring too much land that it had lost earlier in the war, potentially invalidating the 51-49 split.

The continued negotiations and the NATO air presence largely ended the siege of Sarajevo. Brian Atwood, the head of AID, announced that he would be traveling to the city to get a first-hand feel for the devastation. Tim Knight, the head of the DART team, asked me to accompany him during the visit. We would fly into Sarajevo, literally for a day, and then return to Zagreb.

Tim told me that I would need to wear a bulletproof vest in Sarajevo, as was standard security procedure for U.S. government employees, and we headed to the office's back closet to grab one. As we tried to find one my size, Tim kidded that I shouldn't take the jacket he usually wore because it was his "lucky vest." As soon as the phrase escaped his lips, Tim turned suddenly serious, "Don't ever believe there is such a thing as a lucky vest. I wear that flak jacket because it is the most comfortable. There are some people in this business that actually believe in such superstitious crap and think they are invincible. There is no law that says bad things cannot happen to you. Even if you have worked in twenty disasters, you can still get killed."

Tim described the feeling of pure terror as he and a friend scrambled to escape sniper fire in the streets of Sarajevo, crouching behind vehicles to take cover and listening to the bullets as they hit nearby. Tim did not tell me the story to brag of his exploits. He wanted to underscore the notion that Bosnia remained a very dangerous place where common sense was the best defense. No matter what you thought of your own relative intelligence, you could still get shot. No matter how experienced you were, being in the wrong place at the wrong time could be deadly.

Tim continued, "I do not know what actually happened in Chechnya, but some people think that Fred believed he had a lucky vest." The reference was to Fred Cuny, an intriguing figure in the relief community. While Tim did not indicate if he believed Cuny had gone too far, his point was not lost. Fred had acquired considerable status in Washington for helping to spearhead relief efforts in the snowy mountains of northern Iraq at the conclusion of the first Gulf War. Fred, working with a number of collaborators and backed by the deep pockets of billionaire financer Geroge Soros, had helped to restore running water to parts of downtown Sarajevo during the darkest days of the war in Bosnia. Both operations spoke volumes about the remarkable problem solving skills of not just Cuny, but relief workers as a whole, and helped save thousands of lives under the worst of circumstance.

Cuny was, by all accounts, a complex figure. Incredibly capable, he also made some needless exaggerations on his resume, suggesting a struggle to find comfort with his own identity. Fred, like all of us, was flawed, and he became a lightning rod in the humanitarian community because he took an unusually high profile in carrying out his mission. After the Iraq and Bosnia operations, Fred established an increasingly public persona, doing television interviews and speaking bluntly about events on the ground in disasters. Fred was convinced that public advocacy was crucial to get Western nations to intervene in places like Bosnia and Rwanda, and he thought he could simultaneously carry out the duties of a public spokesman and master logistician. Cuny, like everyone else in the industry, wrestled with the traditional orthodoxy that humanitarian relief efforts should remain officially neutral—particularly when one side engaged in greater abuses than the other. Cuny wanted disaster specialists to have a larger role at the policymaking table in Washington, and he thought that the people on the ground were in the best position to offer credible analysis as crises unfolded. Behind the scenes, Cuny and a number of senior diplomats pushed to create a private organization that could be fast and flexible in delivering relief anywhere on the globe while providing cutting edge public analysis of the forces driving such wars.

I understood Cuny's frustration. Even as a relatively new relief worker, I was aware that we were largely treating symptoms of conflicts rather than their root causes. No matter how knowledgeable relief workers might have been, they had little say in deciding issues of war and peace. Some even argued that humanitarian assistance extended conflicts by propping up combatants and keeping wars from burning themselves out.

Not everyone agreed that relief officials should become embroiled in politics and diplomacy. For all the practical shortcomings of neutrality, it also had clear advantages, and few wanted to be in a position where food and medical supplies were delivered on the basis of anything other than need. The appearance of neutrality was essential to ensure the delivery of assistance to both sides in a war. As soon as relief workers tilted to one side of a conflict, the more likely it was that aid itself would become a weapon of war, denied to enemies and cynically funneled to advance specific military aims. Having relief workers take sides was dangerous. The neutrality of relief, to paraphrase Churchill's comments on democracy, was a horrible system that remained superior to its alternatives.

Things ended badly for Fred Cuny. In April 1995, while trying to arrange a ceasefire in Chechnya between the Russian government and rebel forces, Cuny was kidnapped and killed. His murder was brutal and calculated. Every indication suggested that Russian intelligence services planted disinformation about Cuny knowing this would push the rebels to eliminate him. In the wake of Cuny's death, the international community walked away from Chechnya and ignored the incredible savagery with which both sides prosecuted the war. This again sent the message that killing aid workers was a good method to scare off international intervention. In a bitter second blow to Cuny's family, they never recovered Fred's body despite a long and often perilous search.

Maybe Cuny's luck had simply run out, and maybe Cuny's higher profile was an invitation for trouble. In either case, he was only trying to help those in need. Cuny's death sent shock waves through the tight-knit relief community. Many knew Fred as a friend and colleague, and wrestled with the same issues. Not knowing Cuny, and being new to the business, it was impossible to say if the seasoned veteran had crossed the fine line into recklessness. Humanitarian relief, after all, was perilous business. Hundreds of relief workers have been killed doing their lifesaving work since the fall of the Berlin wall, and this trend has only accelerated in recent years. None of them deserved to die, but all had accepted a certain measure of risk in their lives.

It was easy to understand why some felt Fred might have flown too close to the sun. Anytime someone was killed doing fieldwork, there was good reason for other humanitarians to believe they would have done things differently. Most relief workers felt that anyone who took fewer risks than they did was hopelessly timid; anyone who took more chances than them was certifiable. The reality that relief workers could simply die stupid pointless deaths, just like all those people they assisted, did not sit easily. While, as Tim argued, it would be tantamount to suicide to believe that you had a lucky vest and were invincible, it would be almost paralyzing to fully accept the vulnerability of wandering around, unarmed, in the middle of a war zone trying to provide food, medicine, and plastic sheeting to people who had been driven from their homes.

At the Zagreb airport, we waited to catch the UN flight to Sarajevo in a makeshift waiting lounge in a large tent. Military officers even issued us boarding passes, although these consisted of nothing more than small wood blocks with numbers painted on them. UN peacekeepers conducted security checks on the passengers. I watched with bemusement as UN security officials made soldiers run their automatic weapons through the X-ray machine before boarding. What were they hoping to find?

Brian Atwood was traveling with a small delegation of congressmen. They made uneasy banter as they waited for the flight. Atwood delighted in photographing a conservative Republican representative from California—known to disdain all things related to the UN—wearing a baby blue UN helmet and bulletproof vest. During the flight, everyone tried to appear casual, with limited success. As we got close to Sarajevo, the relief workers took off their flak jackets and sat on them. Greeted with a quizzical look by the congressmen, the relief workers explained that with Bosnian Serb snipers still in the hills, such a maneuver reduced the risk of getting a bullet in the backside. The congressmen scrambled to follow suit.

When we touched down, the tarmac at the Sarajevo airport was busy with soldiers, as equipment and relief supplies were hustled from planes. Several highly trained agents from the diplomatic security service that accompanied the delegation greeted us. Dressed in civilian clothes and wearing sunglasses, they carried automatic weapons and stuck close to the group. They looked ready, and almost eager, for trouble.

Sarajevo's airport was out of town, and we traveled into the city center in armored vehicles. The bulletproof windows of the vehicles were narrow and smudged, making my first glimpses of Sarajevo disjointed and almost dreamlike. Bouncing on the rutted access road to the airport, we passed sandbag and barbed-wire fortifications before going through a lengthy corridor of cargo containers, buses, and even old railcars stacked by the side of the road. The Bosnians placed the vehicles in an effort to make it more difficult for snipers to strike traffic going back and forth to the airport—one of the city's only lifelines. Thousands and thousands of bullet holes perforated the rusted cargo containers and other empty hulks.

Sarajevo was remarkably green. As we passed by destroyed buildings and war-weathered neighborhoods, every inch of available space had been converted into vegetable gardens. Tomato plants hung off tiny balconies and carrots sprouted in public parks. The Serbs had tried to starve Sarajevo by cutting it off from the outside world, and Sarajevo had responded by becoming self-sufficient. The green spaces were oddly attractive among the ruin, but also a sobering reminder of the almost medieval conditions under which people lived.

The delegation had a busy day of meetings and disaster tourism. The national library, gutted early in the war, was a mandatory first stop. The wanton destruction of the architectural gem and its multiethnic collection of literature and fine arts was a natural symbol of the senseless conflict that had torn Bosnia apart. The library was just a short distance from the bridge that was the site of Archduke Franz Ferdinand's assassination, the event that had precipitated World War I. The library was an ornate shell. Its multiple floors had collapsed into a heap. The library felt like a mausoleum, and everyone remained as quiet as if in one. The delegation also met with the small U.S. embassy staff that had continued to operate in Bosnia. Foreign service officers had slept on cots in the embassy basement and were subjected to continual power outages. In addition to meeting with Bosnian government officials in ornate but bullet-scarred offices, the delegation also tried to get a sense of daily life in Sarajevo. They met with a group of children orphaned by the war and stood outside at a public water spigot as they heard about life in a city under siege.

The visit was a whirlwind, and we were all trundled back in armored vehicles for a return trip to the airport before sundown. As much as the group had seen, it was still a carefully packaged tour. Normal conversations with Bosnians were almost impossible, and I could only wonder what they would carry away.

Near the end of my first stint working on the DART in the Balkans, I was in the Zagreb office on a wet, raw day. Winter would be wretched for refugees. I was dutifully helping draft cables for the U.S. embassies in Zagreb, Belgrade, and Sarajevo which had to again officially declare their countries as disasters to make them eligible for humanitarian relief. It was the fifth consecutive year of making such declarations, and they were sadly pro forma. It was not hard to make the case: "Based on the continuation of conflict, the onset of winter, continued movement of refugees and displaced persons, widespread destruction from war and the continuing impact on the most vulnerable populations ..." Despite all the talk of peace, there was a lot of concern that fighting would simply resume in the spring.

Tim showed me a glossy and well-produced book that Serb officials had given him in Belgrade. The book detailed the horrors committed by Croatian fascists during World War II. The *Ustashe* had allied with Hitler, and eagerly conducted a genocide against Serbs and gypsies. On one page, three decapitated heads stared out from a shelf with grotesque grimaces. A diagram explained how the *Ustashe* had invented special mallets for more efficiently crushing skulls. A grainy black and white photo captured the scene of a damp mass grave littered with empty glass bottles of acid used to speed decomposition.

That evening on CNN, I watched footage of mass graves recently discovered in western Bosnia. The wet clay looked heavy enough to bend a shovel.

Empty bottles of acid were carelessly tossed on the ground. Lessons learned by a new generation.

BACK TO BOSNIA

I returned to the DART team in the former Yugoslavia about five months later in March 1996. Much had changed. Slobodan Milosevic of Serbia, Franjo Tudjman of Croatia, and Alija Izetbegovic of Bosnia had signed the Dayton Peace accord in November of 1995. The world hailed all three as courageous peacemakers, their respective roles in Yugoslavia's tragedy swept aside in the euphoria of a fragile peace. A 60,000-strong NATO peacekeeping force, including almost 20,000 U.S. troops, had been deployed across Bosnia, and the DART office had moved from Croatia to downtown Sarajevo. The shooting had largely stopped but tensions were still high.

In the war's aftermath, Serbs fled the Sarajevo suburbs in large numbers. Because the city was reverting to Bosnian government control, militant Serbs wanted to make sure there would be nothing left for the Bosnian government in the Serb neighborhoods, not even citizens. Serb hard-liners ordered their own people to clear out, and were not above using violence to drive the point home. When senior citizens attempted to hide in the upper floors of apartment buildings, they were ushered out at gunpoint. Peacekeepers stood to the side as events unfolded.

The Bosnian government, despite offering rhetoric about tolerance, was glad to see the Serbs go. Sarajevo had survived the war as a multiethnic—although badly divided—city. But with the arrival of peace, more than 70,000 Serbs left. The animosity was so fervent that Bosnian Serbs were digging up their dead to take with them as they departed. The dead could no longer even share the same ground; what hope was there that Bosnia's living might coexist? The Serbs asked if the DART team could provide coffins and body bags. However, assisting efforts to dig up long deceased relatives had nothing to do with saving lives and was not in our mandate.

Driving through the recently emptied Serb neighborhoods, the weather was warm and sunny, a striking contrast with the leveled houses and burned out railway cars by the side of the road. As odd as it seems, destruction was fascinating in its own way. Bosnia's devastation often looked improbable. Every house and car we passed for a long stretch had been stripped to the bone. In many of the houses, not a single window, door, piece of furniture, fixture, pipe, outlet, roof tile, hinge, or light bulb remained. Even the cars were picked clean, with every window, tire, knob, and dial removed. The meticulousness was creepy. The Serbs that had left were convinced they would never be returning.

As we drove, another thing struck me as strange. In many places, washers and dryers had been dumped into the middle of the river. Dragging a large appliance into the water struck me as a bizarre thing to do out of spite. One of my colleagues explained that the Bosnians used the appliances as improvised generators. By reversing the appliances' wiring, and letting water rotate their tumblers, a beleaguered family could generate a steady trickle of power—at least enough to allow for some light in their homes. From growing small plots of vegetables on apartment balconies in Sarajevo to dragging washing machines into icy rivers, Bosnians had invented ways to survive.

Almost daily, more evidence surfaced of the atrocities that had been committed in Bosnia. A number of Bosnian Serb "collective centers" had been little more than concentration camps. Murder, rape, and torture had been perpetrated with abandon. The *New York Times* reported that at a mass grave outside of Sarajevo, investigators had found a number of notebooks containing records from a local Serbian garbage hauling company. There were invoices detailing the number of bodies delivered, and a written agreement that burials of the dead bodies should take place with no witnesses present. Had firms bid on the right to haul corpses to unmarked graves? Had government officials in Belgrade quibbled about cost overruns? These were people confident that their crimes would go undetected. Organizing these crimes required collaboration from senior politicians, military commanders, truck drivers, and accountants. The idea of squalid bureaucracies committed to eradicating people made the skin crawl.

On April fool's day, I boarded a large German military cargo plane bound for the Bosnian city of Tuzla. I was the only passenger not wearing a uniform or carrying a weapon. Despite the loud drone of the engines, I soon dozed off. I awoke as we touched down at the U.S. air base. Even though it was spring, a light snow dusted the hillsides surrounding Tuzla. At a temporary plywood office that served as a flight center, bored soldiers leafed through American magazines while waiting for their flights.

Joanne, a member of the DART team, met me outside. Joanne had previously been a successful businesswoman working for Hewlett Packard. She had driven a BMW, worn expensive suits, and religiously read the *Wall Street Journal*. Unfulfilled, she made a dramatic career change and became a relief worker.

Joanne gave me a quick tour of the large base. We passed an impressive array of tanks, humvees, forklifts, Bradley fighting machines, and cargo containers. Along a heavily guarded perimeter of concrete barricades and concertina wire, camouflage netting draped artillery pieces.

All of the soldiers on the base wore helmets and flak jackets even though they were within a secure area. In addition to wearing body armor full time, travel was tightly restricted and soldiers required special permission to venture off the base. When U.S. soldiers did journey out, it was mandatory that they did so in a convoy of at least four military vehicles, including one mounted with a machine gun. This elicited much grumbling from the rank and file. While the desire to protect the soldiers was laudable, it also made it harder for them to be effective peacekeepers. Commanders did not allow American soldiers to eat in local restaurants, drink at neighborhood cafes, or do much spontaneous mingling with Bosnians. It was almost impossible for U.S. soldiers to get to know the communities that they were charged with stabilizing. European peacekeepers operated under looser standards, and although many still viewed the U.S. as the backbone of the force, other contingents did better in establishing rapport with the locals.

The base was about fifteen minutes outside of Tuzla, and for most of our drive into the city, we crawled along behind a large convoy of U.S. military vehicles. Small children waved at the American soldiers. Their parents were considerably more reserved.

Tuzla was an exquisitely unattractive industrial city, and a spiderweb of leaky steam pipes emanated from the coal-fired energy plant at the edge of town. The soggy brown earth looked like tundra. A polluted stream wound its way through the center of the city under a smudge pot sky. Burning garbage competed with the odors from burning coal and phosphate. By the end of every day, my clothes and hair smelled, as did everything in the group house.

Squat, drab apartment complexes dominated Tuzla's skyline. A baby blue city bus sat in the front yard of a house, its decrepit frame sagging like the back of an ancient workhorse. Junked cars stripped of their parts were turned turtle along the side of the road next to wet piles of garbage.

Even though Tuzla had been near the front lines, there were few signs of major physical damage. Tuzla's old central square, which predated the communist era, did have a shopworn charm that had survived the years of pollution and neglect. But the deadliest attack against Tuzla had also occurred in the city center. A rocket struck a popular sidewalk cafe and killed seventy-two people, mostly teenagers. The impact of the explosion still scarred the cobblestones on the street. A small plaque, several wreaths, and a homemade memorial marked the spot. Wallet-sized photos of the victims hung from a wilted piece of posterboard.

While our main task in conducting assessments was to gain information about the humanitarian situation, it was inevitable that we learned a great deal about people's lives in the process. The Bosnians we spoke with were hopeful that the end of the war would allow life to return to the way it was before Yugoslavia collapsed. People spoke enthusiastically about full employment and generous social benefits. Few realized that Yugoslavia's economy had been kept afloat only by a huge debt and massive infusions of support from the West. Bosnia's economic shortcomings were glaringly evident, and Tuzla was in a particularly bad shape. The city had never received the best equipment or supplies from the central government, and its outdated heavy industries were poorly suited for modern markets.

Bosnians expressed hope that wealthy American businessmen would sweep in and buy the long-idled manufacturing plants. One man implored us that with an infusion of American money the typewriter factory in nearby Zvornick could reopen and employ hundreds of workers. I was left trying to explain why *a typewriter factory in Bosnia* might not appear to most westerners as the ideal investment, and gently pointed out that typewriters were largely a thing of the past. He was dumbfounded: "But they are good typewriters."

Along the same lines, I asked a local official in Tuzla, "Who owns most of the farms and companies around the city?"

With obvious pride he replied, "They have all been privatized."

"Well, who owns most of the stock?"

He looked at me as if I was slow, "Of course, the government owns all the stock."

We visited a center for the displaced in Tuzla housed in a public school. The school was open while concurrently serving as a home for the displaced. We walked through a throng of children playing noisily in the schoolyard before entering the rooms that served as a shelter. The aromas of stale dairy products and damp laundry hung in the air. There was still some broken glass on the floor, and plastic sheeting over the windows. The quarters were close and, as I often found it did, my breathing shortened—as if despair might be contagious. About 150 people were living in the school, almost all of them women and children. Some of the displaced were reluctant to leave, fearing that they would no longer receive help once out of the public eye, and it was a reasonable concern.

We went into the school's basement. Two women were scrubbing clothes in a wash sink. Wet clothes hung from small coat hooks meant for schoolchildren. One of the women was an attractive young mother, her daughter just over a year old. She casually brushed her bangs away from her face with a sleeve because her hands were wet. She explained that both her brother and father had been killed during the war. She was unsure where the rest of the family would go. I jotted down "brother and father" in my notebook as we concluded our interview. It would have felt rude not to. We thanked the woman for speaking with us, and we went back upstairs.

Our next stop was a small classroom that served as quarters for thirty people. It was crammed tight with bunk beds and belongings. Sacks of potatoes were stacked against a far wall. In one corner, an old woman with a scarf wrapped tightly around her head sat with her hands folded in her lap. Her recessed eyes looked like they had seen every war ever fought. We asked the usual questions. The people said they were getting enough food, but wanted more bread. There were tensions with school officials who wanted to move the displaced out of the classrooms. The UN visited frequently, but was struggling to find them new homes.

"What is your worst problem?" This standard open-ended question was quite useful in establishing priorities for assistance. An older woman replied without hesitation, "We have no men. That is our greatest problem." The other women solemnly nodded their heads in agreement, and I could feel a tightness in my chest. The women were all from Srebrenica, the one-time UN "safe haven" that had been overrun by Serb forces. Serbs had rounded up their men, led them out of the city, shot them in the head and dumped them in mass graves as UN peacekeepers did nothing. The women still hoped their husbands and brothers might be alive, but their anguish was visceral. Maybe a handful of their men had managed to escape through the countryside, but no more than a handful. Their hope was an uncomfortable emotional fiction. Srebrenica's husbands, fathers, and sons would not be coming home.

What do you say? Blankets, food, and medicine were the currency of humanitarian relief. We could not raise the dead. An adorable little blond girl with a pink plastic necklace sat on an upper bunk bed watching me. She had three coloring books and a fancy little lunchbox by her side; the trappings of a middle-class existence. She no longer had any men in her life, and her family had no home. The girl did not know where she would sleep next week or where she would go to school. No one dared to tell her that her father would not be returning. I felt like I had failed her. Walking out of the school, we passed a throng of students playing tetherball.

The next day, Joanne and I traveled east of Tuzla to conduct an assessment for an emergency housing repair program being launched by AID. Houses across Bosnia had suffered tremendous damage in the war, and many refugees and displaced could not return to their communities because they no longer had a place to live. The concept behind the emergency housing program was to fix a single room in heavily damaged houses, making them inhabitable. This would allow people to return and do the rest of the repairs on their own.

The program was controversial. Bosnia was a developed country, and fixing a single room with walls, roof tile, and windows could cost thousands of dollars. Several congressmen had complained that the U.S. government was more interested in building houses for Bosnians than their constituents.

The emergency housing program was designed to help repair more than 2,500 homes across a score of towns. While it was controversial and expensive, it did meet very real needs on the ground. It had the added benefit of generating much needed work for men of fighting age who did not have jobs. Rapidly generating employment for former fighters was one of the most crucial elements of postconflict reconstruction, but all too often, such efforts were an afterthought.

Even construction was made infinitely more difficult by the aftershocks of war. A number of saw mills producing wood for the project were badly slowed because the local trees were so full of shrapnel that they were destroying saw blades at an alarming rate. Each tree had to be carefully inspected before being cut. Selecting the Bosnian communities that would benefit from rebuilding was also a tricky affair, and it required a careful ethnic balancing act. But the strategy was sensible. The program had been designed after tireless fieldwork and hundreds of interviews across Bosnia asking people what it would take to get them to go home.

Due to security concerns, we could only travel outside of Tuzla in a convoy of at least two armored vehicles. Everyone on our team complained about the precautions. Armored vehicles were a limited commodity, handled poorly, and were highly conspicuous. Once out of an armored vehicle, the security guidelines said we were free to walk around without a flak jacket, guard, or anything else. In some rare cases, humanitarian workers did employ armed guards for their field visits, but it was always a last resort. While seemingly a paradox, armed guards usually made the situation more dangerous, not less. Having an armed person standing next to you could make you a legitimate, or at least more likely, target. Traveling with bodyguards could also invite confrontation with local militias. As crazy as it sounded, not having a weapon was often the safest course.

The armored vehicle we had for this particular trip was old and in poor shape. It looked like something out of World War I. One door handle did not work and neither did the windshield wipers, leaving us peering dimly into the gloom when it rained.

Dragin, a Bosnian staff member with a private aid group, traveled with us. Dragin had been born in Tuzla, and we inquired how locals were reacting to the influx of Muslim refugees and displaced that had flowed into the city. Dragin was diplomatic, but his sentiments reflected what others had told us: many locals viewed the newcomers as coarser and less-educated country cousins. There were complaints they burned garbage in the streets. The situation had created some tensions in Tuzla. The city's residents like so many others in Bosnia, desperately wanted things to go back to the way they were before.

Tuzla soon disappeared from sight, and the countryside was a pleasant respite from Tuzla's pollution and grime. Much of Bosnia was agrarian, and furrowed dirt roads wound through the rounded hills. Horse-drawn carts competed for space on the narrow roads with the occasional truck or Yugo. The smells of wood smoke, hay, and fresh cut timber wafted from houses with red tile roofs. Whole families worked in the fields. Many of the men still wore their army fatigues. It was a busy time in Bosnia. There were years of lost planting, plowing, and repairs to be done. People had scavenged, stolen, or recovered whatever construction supplies they could, and stacks of building blocks and roof tiles could be seen by almost every home.

We met with a group of local officials from Zvornick. When we arrived, the officials gathered around a heater, drinking Turkish coffee and smoking cigarettes. Chairs were circled for the discussion, and tendrils of cigarette smoke arched toward the ceiling. Because Zvornick was heavily damaged, these men worked out of a small house outside the city. The concrete walls of the small room held a bracing chill. Nobody took off their coats, and we all looked slightly ridiculous sitting on chairs so small that they had to have been looted from a nearby elementary school. Outside, a rooster crowed in the yard and a mother directed agitated words toward her children. We drank small, sludgy cups of Turkish coffee, a welcome ritual that came with every meeting. The warmth seeped into my hands.

We talked about the hospital, electricity, and the economy. Zvornick's factories were all closed. Farming was difficult even in the best of times. The deputy mayor argued that if we could give families even a single goat or cow, it would make a world of difference, "This area was cut off from the rest of the world. We received no humanitarian assistance, almost no food. During the war, 220,000 shells fell in this area alone. We suffered very much." I did not ask how he came up with such a precise number.

The men were unequivocal: housing was the single greatest problem. "People are very tired of being refugees," said the deputy mayor, "They just want to go home. Two thousand houses have been destroyed in Zvornick. With help from donors, we can maybe fix 300 homes. This is a small amount. People are already coming back and living in destroyed houses that have no roof and no water. The first group came back this month. Some people are even going back into areas under Serb control. People just want to go home."

Amid all the complexity of history, politics, and international affairs, it was very simple: people wanted to go home. The war and wanton cruelty that had destroyed their country was revolting. But if everything was so simple, why was fixing it so hard?

ZONES OF SEPARATION

I awoke to the sounds of a cold steady rain on the roof of the group house in Tuzla. The U.S. military was eager for us to assess the situation in the nearby self-declared Republic of Srpska, a breakaway Serb enclave that harbored dreams of eventual independence. The U.S. military, hoping to pacify the area, was concerned that more should be done to help Bosnian Serb civilians.

Joanne and I left the office to meet up with two representatives from a private charity with whom we would be traveling. We exchanged greetings standing in the rain outside a local hotel. There was a delay when we learned the interpreter they planned to bring was unavailable. Eventually, a secretary from their office, Manuella, agreed to accompany us and provide translation. We picked Manuella up at their office, and she was wearing a thin jacket and stockings. We should have insisted she change into something better suited for fieldwork.

The five of us, in two lightly armored jeeps, drove north to the U.S. army base to meet our military escort. After inquiring at the gate, a soldier pointed out four humvees parked by the side of the road. As we waited for the major commanding the detail, we chatted with the soldiers, asked them where they were from, and bitched about the lousy weather. The GIs were more upbeat than I expected, and as one explained, "At least down here we are doing something. Up in Germany, where we are usually stationed, there is not much going on. Bosnia may not be the best place in the world, but when you look around and see the destruction, you think that maybe we can make a difference. This country must have been sort of nice before. I think if we want to get the job done, we should stay a little longer." The major appeared and we ran through the day's itinerary and a quick security briefing: "If anybody starts shooting, keep up with the group."

Traveling with a four-vehicle military escort felt heavy-handed. At times, a soldier would man a machine gun mounted on the roof of one of the humvees. There was no ammunition in the weapon. Our first stop was a small house not far from the base, where, according to the major, some Muslim families from Brcko had taken up residence. We conducted several interviews, the most informative of which was with a very old woman with nicotine stained fingers. She crooked one arm behind her back and leaned against the door jamb as she spoke, cigarillo butts littering the muddy ground by her feet. Manuella told us, "She says they are from Brcko and will never return as long as the city is under Serb control. It has been four years since they left their homes and came here. This house used to belong to a Serb, and three families are living here now. Food is the biggest problem. The UN gave them some cooking oil and three kilos of flour; it was supposed to last for a month, but it is gone. They have many other needs."

The house was in bad shape, with only a few windows and a blanket for a door. Such isolated families were often the hardest to help. They survived on the periphery, and donors were reluctant to repair the house because they occupied it illegally. Their suffering was no less legitimate, but there were limits to its redress. A pair of curious teenage girls peeked out from behind the old woman. One of the girls was wearing makeup—the house had no doors or windows, and the food had run low—but the teens still had mascara. Bosnia.

We then stopped in Brka, a small, mostly Muslim, town near the border with the Republic of Srpska. We met with a group of city officials coordinating relief efforts. Brka had been on the front lines, and was struggling to deal with the influx of the displaced. As one explained, "There is no work. There are no jobs. People come here but all the houses are destroyed. We have no way to rebuild. We need materials. All of these people would go back to their homes if they could."

Near the end of the session, a middle-aged man who had sat quietly during our discussion spoke up. His words tumbled out so rapidly that Manuella struggled to keep up, "On 1 May 1992, the first grenade went off in my village. After that, every single day there were more explosions. I tried to stay at my house, but we were only two kilometers from the front line. I tried to stay to save the house, but we had nothing. No medical supplies.

No food. We had to leave. I came here because I had no choice. I lost two of my sons on the front lines." His speech slowed. The cigarette in his hand trembled visibly. "Last week, I borrowed a bicycle from my friend. I wanted to ride and see if my house had survived. For the whole war, I was only 20 kilometers away from my home, but I could not go there because the fighting was so heavy, and the Serbs controlled the area. As I got closer and closer on the bicycle, I could see many destroyed houses; the homes of my friends, my neighbors." Even after the fact, his anticipation felt like a wild, living thing.

"When I got to my house, I saw that grenades had blown in the roof. Everything was gone. My house was completely shattered." The man slumped in the chair, his eyes a red welter of despair and fatigue. He openly wept. His sons were dead. His cherished house destroyed.

Outside of Brka, we passed into no man's land. As we approached the NATO checkpoint at the "Zone of Separation"—a six-kilometer buffer separating the two halves of post-Dayton Bosnia: the Bosnian Federation and the Republic of Srpska—every house was destroyed. The area was a vast sea of mud, cordoned off with plastic tape that warned of land mines. Soldiers walked across wooden pallets in an effort to stay out of the muck. Several NATO tanks were nestled into dug-in positions, their tank barrels disconcertingly eye-level with our windshield as we went through the checkpoint. A small and inauspicious orange marker marked the dead center of the Zone of Separation. This was what people had killed for, an arbitrary line on the map. Was it worth a hundred thousand dead?

We arrived in Brod Kranank in a hard rain. The town had been largely Muslim, but the Serbs had been meticulous in destroying everything of remote value. U.S. soldiers had found increasing numbers of booby traps in the damaged houses. Serbs tied hand grenades to doors and rigged explosives to detonate when somebody picked up a stray duffle bag or piece of luggage. This too discouraged Muslims from returning. We got out of the vehicles and walked around, passing near an earthen and wood bunker constructed in the middle of the suburban neighborhood during the war. We were careful to walk on the road. Front yards promised mines.

At one point, I took a mine awareness class offered by a UN military contingent. The session was useful, but grim. Mines, which cost as little as $3 to produce, were everywhere. The young Scandinavian soldier teaching the class calmly noted that the best way to deal with minefields was to stay out of them. He made clear that if stuck in a minefield, you should wait for help. He also demonstrated how to detect mines if no assistance was forthcoming, by holding a pencil loosely between your flattened hands, and gently prodding into the soil. If the pencil hit resistance, it would slide back between your palms, indicating something in the dirt that could be a mine. Because mines were so small, this process would need to be repeated every two or three inches as one moved forward. The idea of making my way through a minefield three inches at a time while by putting my face low to the ground and poking in the dirt with a pencil was too awful to imagine.

The long row of bombed-out houses looked like a snapshot from World War II. I talked with an American soldier who took the point as we moved through the neighborhood. His gun was not loaded, but it looked menacing enough. He said, "This place makes me realize how destructive this war has been." He glanced at me quickly, with a look of sheepishness flitting across his face. He continued to scan the gutted houses for any sign of activity, "I know that sounds stupid. All wars are destructive, but these people had decent lives, and now there is this." He gestured the barrel of his gun toward the ruins.

An old man wandered out to the edge of the road. He was a Serb refugee driven out of Croatia. He did not appear intimidated by the soldiers or our questions. His nose had been broken long ago and never reset. Rail thin, he wore an army jacket that was still several sizes too small. He had stuffed his pant legs into his boots in a futile effort to keep dry. The man said that he and his wife were living in one of the few houses left standing. They had no electricity or heat and burned wood and garbage to stay warm. The man's wife stood 30 yards away looking concerned that her husband was speaking with men in uniforms.

"We left with only the clothes on our backs," as he put it. As we talked, I noticed a thin line of bloody puss dribbling its way down his ear. The man begged the American soldiers to provide several gallons of diesel fuel, but they said that would be impossible. The soldiers asked if anybody had offered to help him and his wife. "Nobody stops here," he said, "Why would anyone stop here? The trucks just go by. They do not even slow down." Dejected, the man returned to his wife.

We briefly stopped a man riding his bicycle, a Muslim who lived in the Serb-controlled city of Brcko, to speak with him. He had ridden to the Zone of Separation to meet with his family. "For me it is not too bad. There is some intimidation and many threats. It was much worse before, but I could not tell my family to come back. It is still not safe. These people are criminals." Pulling his sodden blue windbreaker tight around him, he rode off through the mud puddles and the downpour.

Our translator, Manuella, was cold, miserable, and upset. In her mid-twenties, she was quick to smoke even in the rain. "I did not even know that I would be coming today. Samir just called the office and asked if I could come, so of course I said I would. But look at how I am dressed. I am freezing. It is awful out." She added, "I am very nervous about today." It was understandable that a Muslim would be uncomfortable traveling in the Republic of Srpska, but Manuella told us that was not her main concern. "Of course it is my first time in the Republic of Srpska. I have not been here since the war broke out. But it is not that. I am from Tuzla. I am a Muslim, and my mother is Muslim, but my father is a Serb from Belgrade. My parents lived in Tuzla for many years, ever since they had gotten married. There were never any problems. But when the war broke out, my father left. He went and joined the Bosnian Serb army as a volunteer. We have not heard from him since."

"Oh," was all I managed in reply.

"I think my father is stationed in Brcko."

"Do you want to try and find him?" I asked, thinking that she might be too shy to ask us directly if we could spend a little extra time doing so.

"No. No. I will not see him," she said with venom, "We never want to see him."

We arrived in Brcko, one of only two cities in Bosnia whose fate had not been settled by the Dayton accords. Brcko was a key strategic point, the largest city in the narrow corridor that linked Serb territory in eastern and western Bosnia. Without control of this strip of land, the Bosnian Serbs in the west would be isolated and at considerable military disadvantage. Unable to resolve Brcko's disposition at Dayton, the negotiators had decided that control of the city would eventually be determined through binding arbitration.

We stopped by the city hall hoping to meet with local officials. A blasé looking receptionist sitting in a glass booth told us to try the Red Cross office. We did so. Piled into a small conference room, we met with the head of the local Red Cross chapter. He was a classic communist-era apparatchik. A heavyset man, he smoked incessantly even as he unlocked a small cupboard so a subordinate could prepare coffee. After consulting his notes, he told us that there were more than 25,000 refugees and displaced in the area, mostly Serbs from the Krajina and Sarajevo. He complained that they had received little assistance other than a smattering of private donations.

A centralized government distribution system delivered most of the relief for these Serbs, with most official support coming from Belgrade. Despite war and upheaval, the communist and nationalist system in some parts of Yugoslavia had changed little. When we asked if Muslims would be allowed to return to their homes, he replied, "All people are welcome back as long as they are not war criminals. We will be having a series of committee meetings on the issue this week." It was impossible to ignore the heavy undercurrent of propaganda and deception in his presentation. It was unfortunate that even a respected organization like the Red Cross was not immune to local politics. The Red Cross chief launched into a historical reflection, "I remember the end of the Second World War. The United States and the Serbs had defeated the fascists. It was the American soldiers that were the first people to bring us relief supplies. I remember the first CARE packages. That is when I started working with the Red Cross. I was very proud of America and how much we have in common." This was not nostalgia; he was trying to make a point:

The Croats and Muslims have always been bad people. Didn't America and the Serbs fight the Nazis and Croats together? We Serbs have done nothing wrong in Bosnia, but are now suffering terribly. Why has America betrayed its old ally? We were polite and steered the discussion away from politics.

Our next stop was a refugee center outside of Brcko that NATO officers were particularly keen to have us visit. There were more than 300 refugees and displaced living in the school gymnasium and a nearby house. Some 150 bunk beds were crowded onto the floor of the gym, including one looking oddly out of place directly underneath the basketball backstop. The manager of the center said that Serbs from around Sarajevo had been flooding into the area, and were receiving little assistance.

While having 300 people crammed into a gym was not pleasant, it was one of the nicest refugee facilities we had seen. It did not smell, the bunk beds and blankets were new. A kitchen prepared hot meals. Even the bathroom facilities, a mandatory stop during our inspections, were surprisingly tolerable. Yet, the Serbs we spoke with were quite angry, and the exchanges quickly took on a confrontational tone. At first, their complaints were no different than those of Muslim and Croat refugees: a lack of food, uncooperative local officials, and the tragedy of having lost their homes and apartments. Up above, a sparrow flitted through the rafters.

We asked people if they were willing to return to their homes.

"Yes, we want to go back," several replied, but I sensed they had more to say.

"Will you go back?"

"No. We won't go back until the Muslims leave our town," said one man.

A woman added, "My son is in the Serb army. It would be unsafe for me to live there," and her concerns were legitimate.

Another woman asked me if it was possible for the government to exchange towns. She was hoping that Serb and Muslim officials might swap villages they had conquered, allowing her to go home. I told her that this would probably not happen.

The Serbs were incensed with America, and the major was getting an earful from one woman, "I do not blame you. I do not blame these other soldiers. But your leaders make very bad decisions. Why do they bomb us? This is a civil war. Why are you attempting to destroy us? In Sarajevo, the Muslims get two-thirds of all the assistance, the Serbs only one-third. All the relief passes through Serb areas, but we do not get any of it. Why do you believe all of the Muslim propaganda? The Muslim fundamentalists are causing all the problems." It was striking to the degree which Serbs painted themselves as victims, and any suggestion that the Serb's own leadership had helped bring about Bosnia's misfortunes was conspicuously absent. The major was diplomatic, perhaps to a fault, "I believe the press has not been fair to all sides. There have been many misunderstandings. I know this is a very complicated conflict." The woman grasped the major's hand, "You are a good man."

Sitting in the bleachers, Manuella engaged in an emotional conversation with a group of teenagers. Like Manuella, they were from Tuzla, and they were eager for news of life in the city. More than anything, they wanted to know if it was safe to return. Several asked if Serbs in Tuzla were being attacked. "No," Manuella said firmly, "You will not be harmed if you come back to Tuzla. Last week, my boyfriend and I went to a concert in the park. He is a Serb, and he has not had any problems. You will not be harmed. People are at the cafes. Muslims are not killing Serbs. No one is killing anybody." One of the young women Manuella was speaking with began to cry. "I just want to leave this place. I want to go home." It was a remarkable and, for a moment, all I could see was young people eager to rebuild their lives.

Suddenly, an older Serb woman who had been eavesdropping burst forward and bitterly scolded the crying Serb girl, "Lies. Lies. Lies," she shrieked. "I do not know why you even talk to this woman. The Muslims are killing all the Serbs in Tuzla. No Serb could go there. Everywhere it is violence against our people. CNN, BBC, all these programs on the television are filled with Muslim lies."

The older Serb quickly turned her wrath toward Manuella, "You should leave here. Stop lying to these young women." The discussion had turned into an altercation, spilling out of the bleachers. The major looked apprehensive. Manuella moved by my side. She was near tears and trembling from resentment, confusion, and the cold. "Can we get out of here please?" Manuella pleaded. I walked with her into the gym's foyer while we waited for the others to finish their interviews. Manuella was shaking badly, and a bitter breeze shunted through a crack beneath the door. An old woman with a kind face briefly spoke to Manuella. Seeing Manuella shiver, she pulled the door tightly shut, and invited her back in the gym to get warm. Manuella would not go back in. The woman held Manuella's hands for a second, but Manuella was too agitated to appreciate the gesture. We walked out into the rain.

"That woman in the gym makes me so angry," seethed Manuella, "I want to punch her in the face. She tells me that everything I say is a lie. But I was in the park, and there was a concert. My boyfriend does not have problems. I am in Tuzla every day, and no one is killing Serbs. That girl I talked to only wanted to go home. Everyone here tells her that it is impossible to return to Tuzla, but it is not. All of the old people are like this. They want to fight. It is all they know. Even my mother is this way. The old people are like horses. They are so stubborn and set in their ways that they cannot learn anything new. If we could get rid of all the old people, things would be fine in Bosnia. They do not understand." With the sadness making her voice hoarse, Manuella added, "Before the war, nobody cared what you were. Everybody got along. Now, people will not even go home."

The rest of the group soon emerged from the gym. We climbed in our vehicle and Manuella, her emotions still raw, told us more about her life. "Before the war, I was studying law in Sarajevo. When the fighting started, I came back to Tuzla. I began to work as a nurse at the front lines because we needed all the people we could get. Many of my friends were in the army. Even my boyfriend, who is a Serb, fought in the Bosnian army." It occurred to me that on any given day during the war, Manuella's boyfriend and her father had been trying to kill each other.

She went on, "I heard many stories during the war, and for a long time I wanted to believe that these stories were not true. It is war, of course. People say wild things, and there are so many rumors every day. You almost need to think the rumors are not true, then suddenly, you know they are. A friend of mine was wounded, and I treated him. The Serbs had made him and his father watch while they raped his mother and sister. *Stand there and watch.* Can you imagine? What kind of people would do this? This is not human. My friend literally begged to be killed so he would not have to see this. After the soldiers raped the women, they buried them. The women were still alive when they put them in the graves. They buried them alive. I know this story is true. This is one of my best friends."

Manuella trailed off in silence. Looking through the rain-streaked windows of the jeep I could see decimated countryside all around. The jeep's heater was broken, but the chill in the vehicle ran deeper than any lack of warmth. Manuella continued to speak. "The Bosnian army went into a house. In the fireplace they found the burned skeleton of a baby. The skeleton was tiny; the baby had been maybe six-months old. How can anyone do that? I know this is war. I know that people get killed in wars, but this is too much. It is beyond war. Killing civilians, even small children, and raping women—how can anyone forget this? People talk about peace, but how can we forget? I would kill the people that have done this. I would kill them now. I know who they are."

Manuella continued, "There is a saying, it is an old proverb, 'If you give a Serb a gun, he is an animal. If you take the gun away from a Serb, he is the best man on earth.' I believe that. I do." I asked Manuella if she thought peace would work. "Not now," she responded, "This is too deep. It is too much. My mother still tells me how they had to leave their home with nothing during World War II. People in Bosnia still remember losing land after the First World War. Everybody remembers who did the killing during the last several years. These were people we knew and worked with—these were not strangers. I want it to go back to the way it was, when people just lived together. But if the troops left now, there would be more fighting."

Manuella asked us a question, "Why didn't you come to Bosnia two years ago?" She wanted to know why the U.S. had been so slow to respond to the war. It was defending the indefensible. That too sometimes came with being an aid worker. I said that more should have been done, and halfheartedly explained that Bosnia was poorly understood in America. This was not much comfort to Manuella, and she complained, "When we were finally making progress in the offensive, you came in and stopped the war." The conversation was painful.

We drove back through the wasteland of Brod Kranak where a unit of U.S. and Russian soldiers were on joint patrol, looking equally miserable in the downpour. It was striking to see American and Russian soldiers deployed together trying to keep peace in Bosnia.

We returned to the U.S. military base. The colonel in charge wanted to meet with us. He urged us to provide more assistance to the Republic of Srpska. The colonel felt that if donor assistance was spread more evenly around the country, it would be easier for his peacekeepers to work with the Serbs. He noted the genuine humanitarian needs in the Republic of Srpska, and offered military assistance if we needed help delivering aid. We thanked the colonel for the military escort and noted that the refugee center that we had visited was in good condition. We also politely pointed out that while the U.S. government was providing humanitarian assistance in the Republic of Srpska, most relief organizations had poor relationships with the Bosnian Serb leadership. Just six months before, many of these aid workers could have been killed for working in Srpska, and indicted war criminals continued to run much of the Republic's military and political machinery. Providing funding for anything beyond very carefully monitored humanitarian relief was impossible.

There was a measure of irony to the discussion. The humanitarian community had pleaded for U.S. military attacks against the Bosnian Serbs for years; now the U.S. military was beseeching the humanitarian community to provide the Serbs more aid. The colonel was not politically naïve, and he understood that the Serbs would get the bare minimum from the world until they changed their ways.

Having dutifully made his pitch, the colonel quickly changed his tone. "I know. I know. The problem with the Serbs is that they are stupid, stupid, stupid. They constantly shoot themselves in the foot. They have a terrible public relations operation. All their propaganda is clumsy and heavy-handed. They are totally paranoid. They don't even take the help they can get." As a quick afterthought the colonel added, "I hope none of you are Serbs." I shot a quick glance at Manuella, whose father was a Serb. Her face was impassive.

Leaving the military escort behind, our two vehicles headed back to Tuzla. Manuella rode in the other jeep, because its heater worked, and one of the guys from the private aid group rode with us. Darkness was approaching. We talked to kill the time. The aid worker talked about Bosnia's children and their harrowing experiences. He suggested that many of them would eventually need some sort of therapy. He was hoping the DART could fund a program to help Bosnian children care for rabbits as a form of trauma therapy. The Bosnians kids would treat the rabbits as infants as a way to work through their anguish, even to the point where they would diaper and feed the bunnies. Joanne and I were stunned into silence. After a long day of muddy decimated villages and thinking about Manuella and the tragedies she had endured, it would take more than rabbits to make some kid forget that Serbs had buried his mother alive. Joanne diplomatically emphasized that our office only funded direct humanitarian needs—programs that saved lives. There were merits to trauma therapy, but Bosnia had pressing needs such as food, water, security, and housing that had to be dealt with first. The rest of the ride was appreciably less talkative.

In Tuzla, we bumped into two people we worked with, and the four of us went to dinner at a local restaurant. We debated the merits of delivering greater assistance to the Republic of Srpska, evenly splitting on the issue. While it would be easier to keep the peace if all sides saw material improvements in their lives, it also felt like rewarding the same people who started the war. Our conversation was full of sharp edges, as if we had begun to absorb the divisiveness that surrounded us. The collective frustration was palpable, and we argued Balkan history with a passion that would have been largely absent in a similar discussion of America's past. We struggled with all the unpleasant compromises and half-truths of our work.

One of the people we were eating with showed me a book that he had purchased of line drawings by a Bosnian artist. I had seen it before. Sketch after sketch cataloged atrocities committed during the war, depicting scenes such as children being thrown off bridges, torture chambers, and drunken Serb soldiers urinating on dead prisoners. I pushed the book away. I was saturated with horror.

The next day was again rainy, foggy, and cold. A large delegation of businesspeople led by U.S. Secretary of Commerce, Ron Brown, swept into Tuzla in an effort by the Clinton Administration to encourage greater investment in Bosnia. They left after a quick visit. Several hours later, Joanne and I learned that Brown's plane had slammed into the side of a mountain during its approach for landing along the Croatian coast. There were no survivors. Official ceremonies and condolences for the twenty-seven passengers and six crew members filled the days that followed. It felt unfair. Thousands and thousands of Bosnians had died without a funeral. All the ceremonies back in Washington made it seem as if American lives were more precious than Bosnian ones. Was it unduly cynical to think such a thing? Walking through disasters was beginning to change me.

GRANDMOTHER'S WINTER

After I returned to Sarajevo from a field assessment around Mostar, the transformation taking place in the capital was striking. The dual optimism of both peace and spring filled Sarajevo. It gave the place the giddiness of a person recently set free. Shops were open, and new businesses were popping up every day. Plastic sheeting covered the holes in the roof of the mosque and the evening prayer call reverberated through the busy streets. Although the grocery store did not always have flour, it had many things that would have been hopelessly exotic a year before, like pineapple juice, imported beer, and new magazines. Workers were replacing broken windows, spending hard earned money to buy glass. People were planting flowers instead of vegetables, and putting fresh coats of paint on their houses. These were all telling signs that people thought things were getting better to stay. The cafes, the banquets of Sarajevo's soul, were brimming with people, and the women wore elegant clothes as a sign of defiant survival.

For Bosnians, war had made many everyday things, whether it was taking a tram, crossing the street, getting water, or turning on a light, impossible. While the peace agreement did not automatically make Bosnia whole, on a pleasant night in April teenagers were finally free to flirt and giggle. Neon signs were lit as beacons for customers rather than incoming fire. The ice cream vendor in a tidy white hat and jacket did a brisk business.

Many of the relief workers in Sarajevo had gone native during the long war. They had local apartments and local lovers. They had discussed political strategy with Bosnian government officials during late nights filled with countless cigarettes and cognacs. In the United States and Europe, the humanitarians tirelessly advocated for a military response against Serb forces. The international relief workers and journalists were deeply sympathetic to the tragedy that unfolded around them and they helped tug international policy down a path of intervention.

Such a loss of objectivity was troubling in that relief workers were not supposed to take sides. But, sitting in Sarajevo on a spring night, it was hard not to take a different view.

Fast forward; one week later. Suddenly spring in Sarajevo felt like a misremembered dream. Snow fell in big wet flakes and the weather had again turned damp and cold. The hills around the city were a rolling carpet of white. A few of us were sitting in the office and I recalled what one refugee had told me: "Well, of course, the war has made the weather worse. War does that." One of my local colleagues, Aldejana, commented, "Maybe so. But at this time of year in Sarajevo, it is always like this. Sometimes we get snow even in late May, like last year. We get a little spring and then it is back to winter. In Bosnia, we call this time 'Grandmother's winter.' It is always this wet, heavy snow and large flakes. It is like winter, but not quite." Just as grandmother's winter was a false season, it was very difficult for Bosnians to tell if they were in war or peace.

The morning before I left Sarajevo to return to Washington, I spent some time wandering around the city. With the hectic pace of fieldwork, I had never gotten much time to explore Sarajevo. I almost felt guilty that I was looking at the city's destruction without it being part of an assessment.

Despite all I had seen in Bosnia, the degree of damage in parts of Sarajevo was astounding. Block to block fighting in a major urban area was savage.

I walked down streets lined with yellow police tape warning of land mines and unexploded ordnance. Entire apartment buildings were collapsed in huge piles of rubble. Fire had reduced large office complexes to nothing more than charred superstructures. In some places the shards of broken glass were several feet deep. Because the war had gone on for five years, time had also taken its toll. Demolished buses with twisted metal frames were rusting in empty lots. Weeds sprouted out of the shrapnel scars on the pavement that locals referred to as "roses" because of their floral pattern.

I walked over a bridge that had separated a Serb neighborhood from the rest of Sarajevo. An oversized clock from the face of a building was broken on the ground, its hand frozen permanently at 8:58. In small shops and apartments, people were shoveling out debris and broken glass, even in areas cordoned off by mine warnings. They shoveled carefully. On the bridge there was a small bronze plaque mounted on a rusty chain-link fence that bore the name of a young woman: Suada Dilberovic. Suada had been only twenty-four when a sniper gunned her down during a Sarajevo peace rally in April 1992. Suada was the first civilian killed in the war, and her death marked the beginning of a long and terrible downward spiral. A small bunch of fresh flowers sat beneath the plaque.

On the far side of the bridge, a group of Turkish peacekeepers disembarked from their bus. Like confused tourists, the Turks posed and snapped photos of each other in front of wrecked buildings. Not even the most pessimistic would have thought that more than 100,000 people would have died after Suada. Nor would anyone have imagined that the war would conclude with Turkish soldiers helping keep the peace in Sarajevo.

It also dawned on me that a number of locals were exploring Sarajevo like they were new to the place. Faces upturned in astonishment, these people had not been able to navigate their own city for five years. They were waking up and clearing the awful cobwebs of a nightmare. The same streets they had walked down a thousand times were now impassable piles of rubble and broken concrete. There was no logic to the rocket attack that destroyed one apartment but left the one next door unscathed. There was no making sense of why.

I stopped and watched a man working in what had once been his small corner kiosk. There was little left of the structure. There were no walls or doors, and only a metal frame and a scrap of roof. The kiosk's owner was shoveling out soggy debris and picking shards of glass from misshapen metal window frames. The man then grabbed a broom and began to sweep a small corner where he could actually see the floor. The Bosnian paused for a second as he saw me observing. I said hello, and asked how he was doing. He smiled in return, offering a surprisingly good-natured shrug. Concluding our brief exchange, he returned to work, steadily, patiently. There was much to do.

CHAPTER 4

Lions and Tigers—Sri Lanka

I went to Sri Lanka in the first half of 1997 to design small aid projects that might help the country make a transition out of its long, bloody civil war. While Sri Lanka was continually rocked by suicide bombings and assassinations, I also found it to be absolutely one of the most interesting places I have ever been. Unfortunately, I was naïve about the immensity of the challenges that were ahead.

AN ISLAND DIVIDED

In the mid-1990s, AID created an Office of Transition Initiatives to help countries trying to emerge from war. Like DARTs, small transition teams deployed to the field with tremendous latitude to initiate programs that they thought would best address the local situation. In most cases, creating immediate and visible change on the ground was a key element in building momentum for peace and instilling hope in the population. While all conflicts obviously differed a great deal, there were some common elements.

The first question was what to do with the former combatants. These were young, armed men without jobs. Most were willing to start trouble because they were broke, bored, and frustrated. Transition teams helped "demobilize" these former combatants by rapidly implementing job programs in exchange for them turning in their weapons. Transition teams paid ex-fighters to build roads and clean up garbage. They gave them starter kits to help them begin farming again, with seeds, tools, and small amounts of credit.

Sri Lanka

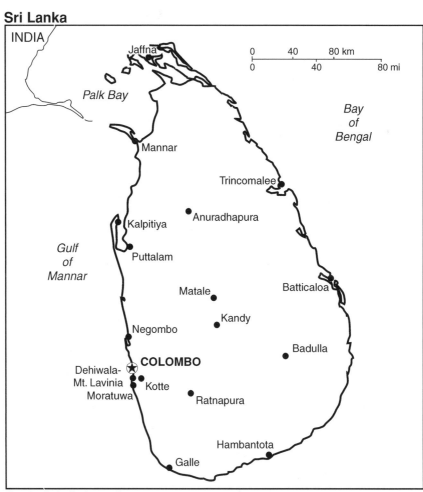

INDIA

Jaffna

Palk Bay

0   40   80 km
0   40   80 mi

Bay
of
Bengal

Mannar

Trincomalee

Anuradhapura

Kalpitiya

Gulf
of
Mannar

Puttalam

Matale

Batticaloa

Kandy

Negombo

Badulla

Dehiwala-
Mt. Lavinia
Moratuwa

COLOMBO

Kotte

Ratnapura

Hambantota

Galle

Cartography by Bookcomp, Inc.

In addition to encouraging the demobilization of soldiers, the office also handled rapid reconstruction efforts. It also aided local journalists to promote tolerance, and offered training for new political parties learning how to function in a democracy. Transition work was, by its very nature, far more explicitly political than traditional relief efforts. Unlike humanitarian assistance, transition programs were not neutral. They dealt with the political, economic, and social forces driving conflict. The world was starting to do some of the very same things that Fred Cuny had argued for before his needless death in the wastelands of Chechnya. Instead of simply treating symptoms, the world was trying to come up with a more creative cure for the disease.

AID assembled its transition teams from a hodgepodge of relief specialists, career development experts, contractors, and others. A friend of mine had moved over to become the new office's chief of staff, and I leapt at the chance to put together a new program in Sri Lanka. I was particularly intrigued because, not only was it a chance to get back out in the field, but because the work demanded learning a great deal about Sri Lanka.

Sri Lanka was the teardrop of land that almost touched the southeast coast of India. The country was small and tropical. It was only 270 miles from one end of Sri Lanka to the other at its longest point. The country was split primarily between two ethnic groups, the Sinhalese and the Tamils. The Sinhalese made up about three-quarters of the population, with the Tamils most of the rest. The Sinhalese practiced Buddhism while the Tamils were Hindu. Despite cohabiting the same small island for years, the two languages were strikingly different, and the divide between the two cultures was considerable.

The Portuguese first colonized Sri Lanka in the 16th century, then later the Dutch and, still later, the British. The British developed large tea and rubber plantations on the island, and they made the island's name at the time, Ceylon, virtually synonymous with tea. Like India, Sri Lanka maintained many of the vestiges of the British colonial bureaucracy.

Tensions quickly erupted in Sri Lanka after independence was achieved in 1948. The newly empowered Sinhalese majority flexed its political muscle and embraced leaders and policies that were baldly nationalistic. Sinhalese replaced English as the official language, and the new government declared Buddhism the state religion. The Sinhalese spurned calls by the Tamils to have Tamil declared a second national language. Widespread riots and pogroms against the Tamils claimed thousands of lives, and the government did precious little to protect its own Tamil citizens.

In many respects, both the Sinhalese and Tamils viewed themselves as an endangered minority: the Tamils in Sri Lanka felt the majority Sinhalese treated them as second-class citizens; the majority Sinhalese perpetually feared that the huge Tamil population just across the straits in India would overwhelm them and their culture. This sense of mutual aggrievement and misunderstanding provided much of the tinder for the conflict to follow.

With repression against the Tamils continuing on a steady burn, the tensions erupted into a full-blown civil war by the early 1980s. In the city of Jaffna, the heart of Tamil culture in Sri Lanka, government-backed thugs burned the Jaffna library in June of 1981, destroying one of the most important historic collections of books and manuscripts in Asia. A small Tamil guerilla group, the Liberation Tigers of Tamil Ealam, better known simply as the Tamil Tigers, began calling for independence for Tamil regions in the north and east of the country. The Tigers killed thirteen government soldiers in an ambush in 1983. This, in turn, triggered more Sinhalese riots and violence against Tamils. The conflict soon spun out of control.

The Tigers quickly developed from a minor insurgency into one of the toughest and most ruthlessly inventive guerilla forces on the planet. First, the Tigers, and their leader Velupillai Prabhakaran, systematically eliminated rival Tamil military groups. The Tigers then turned their attention to the government. In many ways, what took place in Sri Lanka was a preview of the tactics that would become all too common in the Middle East during the years that followed. The Tigers trained an entire wing of fighters to conduct suicide attacks, including a group made up of teenage girls, the *blackbirds*. The Tigers went after both the powerful and the innocent. A bomb in a bus stop in the capital of Colombo killed more than 100 people. A suicide truck bomb crashed through the gates of a makeshift army camp and killed forty. The Tigers assassinated scores of parliamentarians, civil servants, religious leaders, businessmen, and others.

In 1987, India tried to calm the violence by sending over 40,000 peace-keeping troops to Sri Lanka. The Tigers were undaunted, and led a series of spectacular attacks against the Indians. In an embarrassing failure, the Indians ultimately withdrew, and the civil war in Sri Lanka again intensified. Demonstrating their reach, the Tigers exacted savage revenge on India, assassinating Prime Minister Rajiv Gandhi when a woman suicide bomber blew herself up while laying a garland of flowers at his feet at a campaign rally. Following the assassination, seven Tamil Tiger suspects committed suicide after police surrounded them. The Tigers also killed Sri Lanka's president in 1993 as a woman suicide bomber rode a bicycle into the reviewing stand at a May Day rally. Police later recovered the woman's head atop a nearby building.

The violence was outlandish, exotic, and disturbing. Most Tamil Tiger fighters wore cyanide capsules around their necks because they would rather kill themselves than be captured. The Tigers perfected tools such as suicide naval attacks using high-powered speedboats packed to the waterline with explosives. In field battles, the Tigers often employed human-wave attacks, sending soldiers, some of them little more than children, to certain death—but overwhelming army positions in the process. The year before I arrived, the Tigers overran an army base at Mullativu and killed 1,500 government soldiers—they did not take a single prisoner. The Red Cross also complained that government forces had taken virtually no prisoners during the same stretch. The government, while expressing sympathy with the Red Cross, stressed that most of the wounded Tigers killed themselves by taking cyanide, and one sensed that the government actually did wish they had more prisoners—so they could torture them.

The Tigers were quick, mobile, and able to blend into the civilian population. When I interviewed a UN staffer who had worked and lived on the front lines for some time, he noted that a short time before a group of about only ten or fifteen tigers, mostly teenagers, were able to hold down an entire battalion of Sri Lankan government forces before being killed. "Incredible, really," he said with a mixture of fatalism and admiration as he sipped his afternoon tea.

Sri Lanka's island geography, instead of isolating the rebels, made it easier for them to employ speedboats to move troops behind whatever lines government forces established. The Tigers were a textbook guerrilla insurgency. Their leader had avoided capture on an island only slightly smaller than West Virginia. They had beaten back the Indian army, one of the most powerful military forces in the region. They continually employed high-tech and low-tech weapons with fiendish ingenuity. It was an almost over-the-top Hollywood version of a guerilla group: fanatical, well organized, financed through a shadowy and complicated international network of drug money and smuggling, and with an elusive leader who loved Clint Eastwood movies.

In late 1995, the government captured the Tamil stronghold of Jaffna after a major offensive. This was an important victory for the government, but it posed many challenges. Jaffna remained largely cut off because the Tigers controlled a belt of territory between Jaffna and the rest of the country. The Tigers also made clear that the loss of Jaffna would not mean the end of the war. In January 1996, they blew up the central bank in Colombo killing almost hundred and wounding more than 1,400.

Like many conflicts, you could cast Sri Lanka's characters and their ambitions on the back of a napkin: Buddhist Sinhalese versus Tamil Hindus; a majority population versus a minority population; a separatist group labeled as either terrorists or freedom fighters depending on your point of view. It was also easy to focus on the sensationalism of Sri Lanka—but amid the brutality, there were also remarkable threads of compassion and sophistication. Unlike most countries in conflict, Sri Lanka was still a functioning democracy, with voter turnout levels that put most Western democracies to shame. The country also had quite a good health system and literacy rates over 90 percent.

Even though considerable swathes of the country remained under the control of Tigers, fighting would virtually stop under a ceasefire so that all the school students could take the same national exams on certain test days. As people fought and killed for a separate state, no one wanted to jeopardize the educational prospects of kids in schools. The combatants observed a similar ceasefire so that Sri Lanka could conduct a nationwide polio immunization campaign.

When I arrived, Sri Lanka's fourteen-year war had already claimed more than 50,000 lives. While it might have seemed an unlikely candidate for a transition program, there was real hope that by providing more aid to the beleaguered citizens of Jaffna, the world might be able to sap Tamil public support for the deadly insurgency.

BENEATH THE SURFACE

Sri Lanka's capital Colombo gave the illusion of calm, and the city tended to move at a more sedate pace than many of its bustling neighbors in South Asia. Out in the harbor, large container ships slowly plied their way north, making for an almost tranquil scene. The scorching tropical sun left young women soldiers on guard duty seeking refuge from the heat in the slender bits of shade cast by light poles. Although the women looked professional as they cradled automatic rifles with burnished wood stocks under their arms, vigilance and boredom fought equally hard for their attention. Checkpoints were scattered throughout the city, but much of the traffic was simply waved through. Slow-eyed soldiers kept half their attention on the ships in the harbor and dreamt of confrontations that proved elusive.

The general absence of bomb attacks in Colombo since the large ones of the year before had not left people feeling reassured. Instead, the public continued to wait for the next shoe to drop. No one I spoke with expected the army to be able to stop the Tigers. The city was simply too large, and too open to commerce and travel. It did not take much to keep a country off-balance: a few strategically fired mortars; cleverly concealed land mines; a hand grenade at a public market or army post; the assassination of a cabinet member or senior police officer. These were the methods that even a few could use to terrorize the many, and the Tigers were very good at it.

Colombo was caught in an awkward normality, and much of the country was resigned to the war. The sandbags, closed roads, and checkpoints felt halfhearted. While the president, the U.S. ambassador, and a handful of prominent citizens were safer, the government left average citizens to their own devices.

Life in Colombo went on despite the periodic high-profile incidents. With the actual front lines of the war well removed from the capital, the conflict was often out of the minds of most in the government. Sri Lanka was in denial about its civil war, and wealthy and well-connected Sinhalese families remained insulated from its effects. They kept their sons and daughters out of military service, leaving the deadly grind of combat to poor families with few economic alternatives. The business community made good money from arms sales and the profiteering that always took place in a wartime economy.

In contrast, Tamils in Colombo had a very different existence, and they had adjusted to the uncomfortable realities of being a minority laboring under constant suspicion. Most Tamils in Sri Lanka could get by in Sinhalese, while most Sinhalese could speak almost no Tamil. So while Tamils could navigate the society, they still had to deal with daily distrust and discrimination. I chatted with a number of Tamil staffers who worked at the AID office, and it was telling that they always shared their insights in hushed tones—even when we were alone in a vehicle or well out of the capital. The Tamils had learned to tread lightly, and they understood that even reasonable complaints could spark a violent backlash.

Rani, who was Tamil and Christian, complained that the police in Colombo treated all Tamils as criminals and Tiger sympathizers. Not long before, the police had broken into her home in the middle of the night. Rani had woken up scared and bewildered as the police ransacked the premises looking for Tiger cadres or incriminating information. She was never told why they came. Rani was far from radical, and the fact that she worked with AID, and had done so for a number of years, made her an unlikely suspect.

Rani also explained how it was a regular occurrence for the police and army to search and grope Tamils on buses. Often times, the police searches were an excuse to solicit bribes or engage in petty theft. Most Tamils understood that to deny a policeman a bribe could quickly lead to them being labeled as terrorists. The constant and often arbitrary nature of these police crackdowns and harassment only further alienated most Tamils.

One of the Tamils who worked in the car pool explained to me, "In 1997, the Sinhalese burned down my house outside of Kandy. We went to the police, but they would not do anything. That is when we moved to Colombo, because the security is better. We were very poor after that." He talked about how the blaze had destroyed almost all of his family's belongings. He knew the identities of the people who had set the fire. The driver continued, "Not all the Sinhalese are bad people. When they burned down my house, some of the Sinhalese helped me and my three sisters by hiding us in their houses with their families." The driver also shared his perspective on the Tigers: "The people in the north, they always like to fight. And many of us do not blame them. They only want their human rights, which is correct. But still there are many times when I cannot say anything. Even in Colombo, if I speak up on a bus about my rights, maybe then all the people will start hitting me."

A colleague and I were to travel to Jaffna, and I would make repeated trips to the north over the following months, but we also wanted to conduct numerous discussions in Colombo. The best way to get a sense of the situation was to talk to a wide array of Sri Lankans and international experts, and not just rely on Sri Lankan government officials and the U.S. embassy. In Colombo, we held a lengthy meeting with a group of Sri Lankan journalists at the AID office. The journalists agreed on several points. They all felt that Sri Lankans, to a remarkable degree, had become desensitized to the steady undercurrent of violence and corruption. Human rights abuses and "disappearances" were so commonplace that they had stopped being news. Readers had grown distrustful of journalists, in no small part because the government owned much of the media. As one reporter put it, "I know people who read the state-owned Lanka House papers just for the obituaries, classifieds, and a good laugh. That is part of the problem; people just assume papers and news are biased. They think all reporting is partisan and has a political agenda."

It was hard to deny that Sri Lankans were war weary. Numerous rounds of peace talks had collapsed over the years, with so many false starts, dead ends, and lurches back into violence that few people allowed themselves the luxury of thinking the war might end any time soon. It was not easy for local journalists to ask hard questions about the war, and there was very little in the way of front lines reporting from Sri Lankans. Most reporters were afraid to take on their editors or military censors to report stories from a war that was so capriciously violent.

At first, the discussion was polite and nonconfrontational, but it did not take long to heat up. The shortcomings of those in his profession clearly angered one journalist: "Why isn't there reporting from the front lines anymore? We sit in army press conferences and wait for the foreign journalists to ask the questions we want to. Even the Sri Lankans who get on the helicopter and get to go to Jaffna or ask the hard questions, it is always the Sri Lankans working for the foreign papers and channels."

His outburst angered an older reporter who did not appreciate being challenged, "I must disagree. After the Indian peacekeepers arrived, five local television journalists went to Jaffna. The Tigers attacked these reporters and burned them alive. We knew these people. Being burned alive is not a very nice way to go, you know, literally burned alive. How many foreign journalists have the Tigers killed in this war? None. We have families. Who will take care of them if we are killed? The army or the Tigers would not think twice if we disappeared."

The reporters did not disagree on the facts. They expressed their mutual frustration. The journalists were asking if they collectively lacked courage or if the media, like everyone else, had simply lost their way in a self-perpetuating war. Few readers wanted to read about the more complicated issues, such as regional power-sharing proposals, that would be involved in a lasting peace deal. "All this material on devolution and constitutional reform, none of that sells newspapers," one editor observed. "It is all deadly boring and only an academic could wade through it."

Another journalist chimed in, "The people just do not see how any of this will change their lives. The parties who now advocate devolution opposed it before. The party who opposes it once proposed a similar package. No one is serious about peace. It is all seen as political posturing and efforts by politicians to improve their own position. No matter what goes through, it will just be a way for politicians to line their own pockets." He continued, "The other day, a teenage boy was mauled and killed by a lion down in the south. Now that was what people wanted to read. But even that reporting said a lot about the war. The headline read, 'First ever Sri Lankan killed by lion.' It was a play on words, because everybody knows only the Tigers kill people in Sri Lanka. But our work should not be just about selling papers. We have a duty as journalists to get stories out and be more aggressive."

While all the journalists had problems with government censorship, they acknowledged that things were far worse in Tiger-controlled areas. "As bad as the media can be here, at least it is something. There is nothing other than the Tigers on the other side." I asked if radio broadcasts reached the Tiger-controlled territory. "They don't have batteries," explained the reporters. The army and police confiscated batteries from Tamils in the conflict zones because they feared they would be used in improvised explosive devices.

We also discussed a minor item I had read before I had arrived, the fact that Sri Lanka had the highest suicide rate in the world. The report had blamed this trend on Sri Lankans' tendency to internalize their anger and frustrations until it pushed them over the edge. One of the reporters laughed when I brought up the topic. "The government has taken a bold step to combat this problem. We can no longer report if someone had died by suicide. They have banned the word suicide from print—unless the victims are Tigers. I am not sure that this will entirely fix the problem."

Sri Lanka had all the traits of an island, a place that was both insular and worldly at the same time. The nation's ports had brought a host of different foreign influences to its shores over history. However, Sri Lankans assimilated these influences while still going their own way. It did not take me long to realize that Sri Lankans understood much more about the outside world than the outside world understood about Sri Lanka. You learned quickly that although Sri Lankans were very good at presenting things with a Western face, this often concealed an internal logic of astrology, families, history, and caste. It was very hard for a foreigner to penetrate.

In our meetings with government officials and local activists, everyone agreed on the importance of bringing aid to Jaffna. We met with government minister after minister that insisted Jaffna's reconstruction was the highest priority, and that mobilizing resources to improve the living situation for the Tamils in the North was imperative. While I was skeptical, it did seem like there had to be practical steps that could be taken to improve life on the ground.

As we began to plan the details of the trip to Jaffna, I was shocked to learn that U.S. embassy officials had traveled to Jaffna only once since it had been "liberated" by government forces fifteen months before. No one from AID had been to Jaffna during that entire period. Military flights went into Jaffna on a daily basis, and the war was the single biggest issue in Sri Lanka, but many in the embassy had fallen into the trap of looking at the country solely through the eyes of Colombo.

JAFFNA

As I prepared for the trip to Jaffna, I got a call from the embassy the night before our flight. The political counselor informed me that there had been an assassination attempt on the president. He said the attempt had failed only because the would-be bomber had accidentally set off the bomb. Subsequent information revealed that it was a hand grenade and not a bomb. Later still, the government revealed that it was not a suicide bomber, but a teenager who had found a hand grenade in a bush. Wild rumors were a constant part of the landscape.

Our van wheeled through the darkened streets of Colombo at five-thirty in the morning as we headed for the military airport. The streets were refreshingly free of traffic as we swept by dusty eyed police at checkpoints.

In the Spartan air force waiting lounge, we waded through throngs of soldiers killing time before their flights. There were considerable delays and confusion as we explained who we were and where we were going. We passed through one of the most sophisticated X-ray scanners I had ever seen, and it was another reminder that Sri Lanka was on the cutting edge of both making and detecting bombs.

The military cargo plane on which we were flying was an outdated craft bought second-hand from the former Soviet fleet. The Sri Lankan air force pilots were crisp and professional in pressed white uniforms as they walked across the tarmac. They were accompanied by two hung-over Ukrainian pilots wearing ill-fitting Hawaiian shirts and flip-flops. I was sure the Ukrainians would do the actual flying. The safety record of the Sri Lankan air force was horrendous, and it had lost multiple planes due to both crashes and sabotage. The Ukrainian pilots were in a foul mood as they slammed the cockpit door.

The plane was a relic. Where there had once been window curtains, there were only faded and bent hangars that rattled terrifically as the pilots started the engines. The fabric on all the seats was torn. The shredded carpeting exposed grungy sheets of plywood underneath. Several seats lingered permanently in the fully reclined position, and bags of supplies were stacked in the aisle. It was obvious that many of the soldiers were flying for the first time. I watched as soldiers tied their seat belts in knots while others contemplated getting sick. Because of the warmth outside and the heavy cooling system inside, the plane soon filled with a thick fog as we prepared to take off. Condensation hung heavy on the smudged windows.

As the plane approached Jaffna, the pilots went into a steep dive about a half-mile from shore in an evasive maneuver. We skimmed along only 100 feet above the ocean below, and I could see the face of a fisherman in a boat clearly as we approached the runway. It was only possible to reach

Jaffna by plane or by boat because the Tigers still controlled all the roads into the north. This made moving supplies and people into Jaffna expensive, time-consuming, and difficult. Under government control, the Jaffna peninsula was even more isolated in many respects than it had been under the Tigers.

We were met by a colonel who would serve as our military liaison during the visit. He apologized that the regional force commander was not able to greet us. It quickly became apparent that we would conduct our fieldwork under trying circumstances: a pickup truck full of Sri Lankan soldiers brandishing automatic weapons would accompany us. We hopped in two vehicles, and headed out of the heavily guarded military base.

The military had leveled a number of houses and removed a great deal of brush around the base to create a buffer zone between themselves and the Tigers. The military had bulldozed thick red clay berms along the side of the road, and barbed wire stretched far into the distance. In a number of cases, villagers were living in makeshift huts across the street from their houses awaiting approval from the military to return. It was the first time that I had seen people displaced such a short distance, but it looked every bit as desperate as being a thousand miles from home.

We rolled through the dusty, hot streets, over jarring roads pitted by war and fifteen years of neglect. Military checkpoints were everywhere, and the sections of the peninsula which the military base occupied were a no-go zone for most civilians.

The local hospital was one of our first visits. The woman in charge of the facility toyed with a large ceramic aspirin on her desk as we talked. It seemed fitting. The Sri Lankan soldiers milled about, and we knew it would be difficult for people to speak their minds given our armed guard. We appreciated that the people we spoke with would have to deal with the military after we left, and the last thing we wanted to do was place them in greater jeopardy. At first, we kept the discussion strictly operational, discussing hospital equipment, the availability of doctors, and the patient load. Shelling had heavily damaged two of the hospital's wards.

We continued to talk as we walked around the hospital. This gave us more breathing space. Near the hospital's generator, I spoke with a doctor that worked in the maternity ward. A score of pregnant women sat and laid uncomfortably on wire beds that lacked mattresses in dim rooms. "Many of the women have to come to hospital very early before they need to deliver, because they are not sure they will be able to get through checkpoints when it is time to have their babies. Many of them came here on bicycles. It is not a healthy situation. Because people are staying in the hospital longer, it is getting more crowded and sanitation is getting worse." The doctor was a thin, middle-aged man. He wore horn-rimmed glasses and was well put together. He looked like someone you would trust to deliver babies and make fair decisions. Our conversation masked by the sound of the generator, I asked, "Are there still many disappearances here?"

He looked nervous. "I really should not talk about that here. The military is good to us here in the hospital. They let us do our work. But yes, there are ... problems."

"How do people feel about the army?"

He warmed to the topic. "It has been fifteen months and there are no visible signs that things are improving. Moving about is very difficult. To get from my house to the hospital I have to go through at least three checkpoints every day. Sometimes soldiers treat us very badly. I have no political agenda; I am a doctor. At night, we have only the internists at the hospital. If there is an emergency, we cannot even come here because of the curfew. How are people supposed to carry on with their lives? Some nights, if I am a little late, I have big problems."

Our conversation trailed off as the rest of the group wandered back toward us. As we made our way to different meetings in Jaffna, several things were apparent. First, the government was eager to declare that all was well on the peninsula and saw our visit as an important opportunity to present their side of the story. Second, even after being in control of Jaffna for fifteen months, security was still tenuous and the military exerted a remarkable degree of control over daily life. In some parts of the city the military almost outnumbered the civilians.

Jaffna must have once been an elegant city. The old colonial homes maintained a glimmer of former attractiveness despite pocks from small arms rounds and the creeping vines that worked their way up the walls. Large gaps in red tile roofs exposed the interior of numerous buildings to the elements. Most of the windows were barricaded up or shot out. There were more bicycles on the streets than seemed imaginable. Vehicular traffic was comparably light. Because the war had dragged on for so long, Jaffna had done its best to adapt to its isolation. Bikes had replaced cars, and the peninsula still managed to produce an agricultural surplus—even with incredibly tight security measures in place.

Because we were trying to figure out what type of assistance would make the most impact, we talked to a broad cross section of people. It made for a very different experience than only focusing on refugees or the displaced as I had usually done with the DART teams. At the local university, we sat down with the vice dean and several professors in a whitewashed classroom. Although restrained, the professors were aggravated. As the vice dean argued, "If Jaffna is part of Sri Lanka, why is it so different? Why can't we move about? Why are things so expensive? Why are there checkpoints everywhere? And I am not blaming anyone."

As the vice dean explained, "When there is one incident on the peninsula, a grenade or a shooting, tensions rise everywhere and the people are afraid to come out of their houses. If you heard a single shot, this campus would clear within minutes." The government was keen to hold local elections in Jaffna as a means to weaken political support for the Tigers and legitimize their own presence in the process, but most locals saw elections as badly beside the point. "How can we talk politics or elections when people cannot even make a living? It is impossible. We cannot move about, and we have no electricity. There are no communications. It is a very bad situation. There cannot be politics when people cannot even make their lives."

One of the professors lamented, "You ask the local government officials, they will tell you that there are as many people leaving Jaffna as returning. People here have no way to get messages to their families. For Tamils to travel to Jaffna even for a single day, sometimes it will take a month of waiting before you can get back out by plane or ship. There is only one phone in the area, and that is in the government office. Even then we can only call Colombo, not the other way around. We are very isolated and frustrated."

Most of the professors worried that the Tigers would try to retake the peninsula. "How can we expect people to rebuild their homes in this environment? Things are very uncertain. Nobody knows what the security situation will do next. I had to do repairs to my own house, and I only made the repairs necessary to make it habitable. Who is willing to invest here? The banks do not want to make loans, and the people are afraid to take them."

The vice dean praised the army, which probably was smart since one of the officers was eavesdropping on the conversation. "The military has been very helpful to us, particularly these gentlemen. Relations between the university and the military are good. This is not the problem. For example, the army cleared the land mines from the playground. But if people are taken into custody, it is still very hard to find out where they are. It always has to go to a higher level, or through the International Red Cross, and that takes time. This is particularly bad in the areas near the front where neither side is in full control. The trauma of the families is great. In many ways, it is not fair to the army. We need to have the military doing less and the government doing more. The military is doing transportation, telecommunications—everything. That must change if we are to get back to normal."

We heard similar comments from people all over Jaffna. In rich red fields, we visited with small family farmers. They complained that there was no way to get their crops to the market. Before the war, it was only a several-hour drive from Jaffna to Colombo. Farmers used to wake up early in the morning to take their produce to the capital. Now it was almost impossible to get goods to the market. When the farmers loaded up bags of onions or tomatoes into bags to take to the ferry, soldiers at checkpoints would thrust their bayonets into the bags looking for contraband or simply out of spite. It would literally take days for the produce to reach the market, and the vegetables were often sufficiently damaged that they were worth only a fraction of their normal price. It was understandable that the army was struggling with security against a foe as tenacious as the Tigers, but in doing so they were strangling Jaffna's economic life.

The army also imposed a number of mandatory stops on our tour. The soldiers took us to a large Hindu temple to show us that they had not damaged it during the war. They then, entirely predictably, took us to a Buddhist temple to show us how the Tigers had damaged it ten years before. We asked to see the Jaffna Library, and one of the soldiers shrugged noncommittally, "It is not working now." After some additional prodding, and explaining that we knew the library had been destroyed, the soldiers took us out to the area surrounding the library.

The entire area was abandoned and overgrown; a forsaken landscape of broken cement slabs and decimated buildings. Overlooking the ocean was the old Dutch fort, which dated back to the 1600s. The Sri Lankan army had made their last stand at the fort in 1994 before the Tigers had first driven them out of Jaffna after an extended and brutal combat. The fort's interior was almost completely destroyed, and only the massive outside walls were unperturbed. Nearby were the remains of the Sri Lankan Telecom building. The Tigers had dynamited the main communication tower and gutted the building in the late 1980s. The 200-foot tower lay coiled around the building in a twisted mass. Many of the homes in the neighborhood had only a single wall left standing. Jaffna's community college, another fine old building, was also demolished.

The Jaffna library was in equal ruin. The library's graceful onion-shaped dome was still intact, although marred by artillery holes. The whole area was a terrible monument to the folly of a war where every side had lost. One of my colleagues lamented the library's destruction. This was true. Yet, I could not help but feeling callous; destroying books and buildings was almost tame in comparison to the human costs.

At the end of the day, we were hustled back to the military barracks in the no-go zone. Despite the array of Sri Lankan army personnel deployed around the peninsula, the Tigers moved actively after dark. As we returned to the military base, we bumped into the same Sri Lankan major who had briefed us that morning. He was wearing white shorts and a polo shirt. He had just finished his afternoon game of badminton. He told us not to worry about the sounds of shelling in the distance.

That evening we dined with the general in charge of the base, and had a long conversation with him over a drink after dinner. The general did not get many visitors, and he welcomed both the company and the opportunity to hold forth on his philosophical views. The general was a career military man, and sported a thick mustache and a slight paunch. He viewed Sri

Lanka as a natural wonder, "You tap into the ground you find a well and you can just drink the water. In Sri Lanka, you can find something edible on eight out of ten trees—seeds, leaves, fruits, even the roots. This outfit I am wearing right now, I can wear 365 days a year. This place is a paradise. We have everything we could need right here, but we have lost it. We are fighting because of greed, because of the rupee, because people want what their neighbor has. A man sees his neighbor with a new jeep and he says, 'I must have one'—even if this other man has sweated for fifteen years to earn it and the other man has done nothing. We have no morals today." The general tried to explain why the violence in his country had become so calamitous: "An assassination in the United States is a drop of ink in a large barrel. But in Sri Lanka," he held up his half empty water glass, "such a drop of ink turns the water very dark. Here, assassination has become like a child's toy."

There was a heavy element of nostalgia in his comments. "We used to have great leaders as politicians. They went to Oxford and Cambridge. Now anyone can be a politician. Any floor sweeper must take a test to get their job, but not a member of parliament. They are power hungry. It is just a way to make money. Our old leaders had money, so they did not have to steal from anyone." I resisted pointing out that some of those old leaders, despite their wealth and English education, had led the country down the path of ethnic division and war.

I asked about the continuing reports of civilians disappearing while in military custody and a recent high-profile rape case involving the army. The general responded testily, with a flash of temper that I had not seen before. "I don't remember any human rights monitors during the Gulf War. The U.S. army literally bulldozed over Iraqi soldiers, and I do not remember anyone in the U.S. government calling for an investigation." The general tried to explain that some of those who disappeared had not been victims of violence, but were simply Tamils that had left the area to escape unhappy marriages or debts. He suggested that other Tamils alleged to have been disappeared were really Tiger fighters that had been lost at sea in boating accidents. None of it had the ring of truth.

The general was resentful that he appeared on several international watch lists because of his own human rights record. "I did not go to attend this conference in Korea because I was in the south during the JVP uprising," he said, referring to a violent leftist Sinhalese revolt that been crushed by the government several years before. "Now they say I am some abuser of human rights. I did nothing wrong. It was a hard time, and we were fighting against our fellow Sinhalese. I got three field promotions in eighteen months. They sent me to the worst places. But I did not get promoted for human rights abuses. I got promoted because I did my job."

The general went on: "Yes, there have been a few rape cases that have gotten a lot of attention in the press and Tiger propaganda. These are very bad things, and these men must be punished. But they are two cases out of 40,000 soldiers and 500,000 people. These are not very many cases for the number of people here. Every day in the south, in Colombo, Kandy, and other places, these things happen. But in Jaffna here it gets a lot of attention."

STRANGERS IN A STRANGE LAND

Over the weeks and months that followed, I gained a much better understanding of why the situation in Jaffna was so difficult for all involved. The government was in the dubious strategic position of holding down large amounts of territory in a place where its soldiers did not even speak the local language. Most of the soldiers were poorly educated and trained for less than three months. Instead of being welcomed as liberators, they were seen as an occupying force. The Tigers had become quite good at provoking tensions between the public and the army. Relations between the military and the local Tamils had badly deteriorated after a suicide bombing that took place not long after I first visited, and in many places throughout the city, there were checkpoints every several hundred meters.

The army felt it had no choice but to deal with every person it encountered as a potential threat. I spoke with Guillermo, an official working with a UN relief agency in Jaffna. He said, "They are trying. The other day I saw one of the soldiers talking to a local and he called him 'tamblo,' which is Tamil for 'little brother.' I see some of the soldiers playing with children at the checkpoints." But Guillermo also recognized the inherent difficulties, "It is just a bad situation. Let me give you an example. The locals were complaining that just to make the eighteen-mile trip from Point Pedro to Jaffna they had to pass through thirteen separate checkpoints. So the force commander says, 'Ok, here is my plan. Every day we will run an express bus from Point Pedro. We will search the people as they get on the bus, have two soldiers ride along, and then the bus will go straight to Jaffna."

Guillermo smoked quickly and efficiently between broad hand gestures. "So the first week they do this, the Tigers string a claymore mine in the trees along the bus route. The explosion kills the two soldiers and a bunch of civilians as well. The Tigers then put out an unofficial announcement that basically said, 'This is the risk you take for cooperating with the government in Jaffna.'"

"You can see that the soldiers are just boys, and they are scared. I do not blame them. They try hard to get along. But as soon as there is an attack, they freak out. And then the disappearances start all over again and the whole situation gets worse. The people who came back," said Guillermo in reference to those Tamils who had returned to Jaffna after the government had retaken the peninsula, "just want to get on with their lives. They thought change would come quickly. The slow pace of everything frustrates them. It takes all day to get anywhere."

The dynamic was not much better for the Tigers. Not only had they suffered the indignity of losing their stronghold and would-be capital, they had little strategic choice other than to antagonize the same Tamil civilians they claimed to defend. Because they no longer controlled Jaffna, they desperately tried to squeeze the peninsula however they could: attacking incoming supplies; destroying aid projects; killing soldiers and using violence against local Tamils who cooperated with the government. This meant killing Tamils with mines and booby-traps and doing everything they could to provoke renewed violence and trouble. Ultimately, the government had to improve the quality of life for Tamils in Jaffna if they wanted to break the cycle of violence.

In Jaffna, I met with the government agent, the highest-ranking civilian official in Jaffna. The government offices were dim, and hardly the bustle of activity you would expect for a place facing such immense reconstruction needs. In a bit of a curiosity, the government had actually maintained a government agent in Jaffna when the Tigers had entirely controlled the peninsula. The government had routinely paid civil service salaries and even provided some modest government services in entirely rebel-held areas—even though these benefits clearly aided the Tigers to a large degree. This allowed the government to claim that it had never lost control of the country—despite the fact that the government agent had served at the pleasure of the Tigers. The Tigers usually killed those officials who they viewed as disloyal. The life spans of government agents in Jaffna were particularly short.

The government agent insisted, "The entire peninsula is currently cleared of Tigers," and he initially did his best to put a good face on the situation. He told me that about 1,000 people a week were returning to Jaffna via the ferry from eastern Sri Lanka, with an equal number headed out. The peninsula was in an uneasy stasis, and the area's population remained about half of prewar levels. Basic reconstruction materials such as cement and roof tile were hard to find, with cement fetching at least twice the price it did in Colombo. More than one-third of Jaffna's houses were destroyed. The assistant government agent pulled out a thick ledger with desiccated pages. "These 600 people are dead," he stated simply. Page after page listed the names, age, and occupation of those killed.

The Tigers had assassinated the Sri Lankan Minister of Housing in an attack in Jaffna about eight months before. As a result, senior government officials—other than those in the military—had stopped going to the peninsula. I recalled the comments of one Sri Lanka army officer who grumbled that the military was stuck with all the reconstruction efforts. "These ministers sit in Colombo and make up fairy tales. That is why we have such a hard time getting them to do things up here. They don't know what it is like, so the government agent has become little more than a glorified reporter." The government agent was well-intentioned, affable, and ineffectual. Toward the end of our discussion, he confided that both his son and daughter had gone back to Colombo because they did not like dealing with all the military checkpoints.

The checkpoints were the most constant and visible reminder that Jaffna was still unstable. Long lines of bicyclists lined up at checkpoints like cattle herded through a shoot. In some cases, the checkpoints were less than a length of a football field apart. The entire peninsula faced a curfew from eight until six, and being on the roads at anytime after curfew was a terrifying experience for all involved. Only a tiny fraction of the population had electricity, and even those people could only use their very limited power for part of the time.

Over a subsequent dinner conversation, the base commander explained his dilemma. "Yes, I know the problems people face going through checkpoints. But we also have many problems. Last week my men found 2,800 grenades in an abandoned latrine pit. There are false bottoms put in bullock carts, to conceal weapons and explosives, all of these things. We find many oiled and polished T-57s wrapped in plastic and buried in the ground here in town, ready for use. We have incidents where Tigers have filled entire bicycle frames with explosives. Then, they leave the bicycle in the market and 'boom'. Even if we check people when they come into town, we need to check them when they come out. Every time we let our guard down, they hit us hard, every time. This is not a war where I can send tanks to overwhelm the Tigers. This is a war where we must root out those hardened cadres one-by-one."

The Tigers were adroit at using churches, temples, and mosques as sites to cache weapons, medical supplies, and personnel. When the government raided or attacked these positions, the Tigers were able to claim that nothing was holy to the government. In return, the army desecrated known Tigers' cemeteries, striking a deep nerve. It did not leave much room for compromise.

The irritations of occupation were constant, and they served a cancer undercutting any possibility for reconciliation or reconstruction. The army seized fertilizer because the Tigers used it to make bombs, but this meant that farmers had an even harder time growing crops. The inability to move goods to markets in Colombo ensured a glut in the local market and lousy prices. Fishing was restricted because the Tigers smuggled in people and weapons with boats. The navy frequently seized even modest skiffs, robbing poor families of their only source of income. It took months for letters to arrive. It was hard to have much confidence in rebuilding when you could not even get cement. The problems all fed each other in a cascade.

The gregarious Father Leo, who I met with several times, was an avid gardener, and Jaffna's Tamil Christian minority had been outspoken on issues of war and peace. Father Leo had to resort to hiding his sprinkler heads under the bed when soldiers searched his house because they kept confiscating them for no particular reason. Every checkpoint, every delay, and every obstacle to going about life as normal left the army more estranged from the people whose favor it was trying to gain.

An officer stopped our vehicle at a checkpoint. Ten soldiers armed with automatic weapons on five motocross motorcycles passed us and headed into the heart of jungle. The motorcycles were not camouflaged. They looked like they could have been purchased at any Western sporting goods store. It was a *Mad Max* vision of a counterinsurgency campaign. Sri Lanka's was an unconventional, dirty war, and there was not even the illusion that anyone was playing by the rules. As a local bishop explained, "There are still a great many roundups by the troops. The military will surround a village and herd everyone into the temple. They make everyone go. Little children, old men, everyone. The soldiers then bring in someone who used to be a Tiger, and this man has a hood over his face. The man then points out this person or that person and these 'suspects' are taken away. We report all of these disappearances to the military, but they say they do not have a single one of these people."

Numerous people we spoke with mentioned the white minivans used by the government to snatch people from their homes or off the street. A van would stop suddenly, someone would be thrown in and then they would never be heard from again.

Civilians were constantly in the crossfire, as the Bishop made clear. "There was an incident last month where the boys," most Tamils still referred to the Tigers simply as 'the boys,' "had put a claymore mine up in a tree. It killed two soldiers. So the army starts shooting into the crowd, killing seven people. The army says the claymore killed these people. But you could see very plainly, two bodies were obliterated; seven had single bullet wounds."

"In another incident, the Tigers threw a grenade that killed two soldiers. The army then shot two men, but they were not Tigers, they were fathers; one with three children, one with two. Then to cover their tracks, the soldiers set off a grenade by the chests of the two dead men. When the family went to recover the bodies, the army said it would only release them if the families signed a statement declaring that the men were Tigers. The families refused, so the army is still holding the bodies."

As we talked over tea, the bishop looked tired. "People are fed up with both sides. They don't want to be seen with either side. If the Tigers come to your house, then the army will come later and think that you are a sympathizer and you will be in grave trouble. People want to get back to their lives. People do not support the Tigers any more either. The boys only care about power now and the attacks on civilians make people very angry."

"But mostly," the bishop added with a sharp tone, "people here are angry with the Tigers because they ran away when the military came. They feel betrayed. Fighting for fourteen, fifteen years and they have nothing to show."

A PERFECTLY REASONABLE PLAN

I visited several towns on the very northern tip of the Jaffna peninsula, starting with the port at Kankesanturai. The port was a good one, with a deep draft and decent shelter. It was entirely under the control of the Sri Lankan navy. The port was badly underutilized by commercial traffic, and it occurred to me almost immediately that improving the flow of goods in and out of the harbor would do a great deal to improve the quality of life on the peninsula for all involved. The greatest obstacle to using the port more widely for commercial traffic was two sunken ships that lay near a jetty at the mouth of the harbor. Both ships were large and had sunk long before.

The navy officers I met with said they were unable to properly raise the ships or otherwise remove them, and suggested that companies to do such work could be found in both Colombo and neighboring India. Because of these conversations, I spent more time than I ever thought I would talking to salvage experts and divers about potentially raising the sunken hulks. Raising the wrecks would not be a traditional aid project by any means, but it did have real potential to deal with the problems that almost everyone I spoke with identified. Removing the ships and upgrading the off-loading facilities would make it possible to bring in 250 more tons of cargo to the peninsula every day.

At nearby Point Pedro, I inspected the small dilapidated jetty used by most commercial traffic. The jetty itself was makeshift. It had been constructed by sinking old barges and filling them with rocks. All cargo was off-loaded by hand.

The Tiger leader, Prabhakaran, had been born between Kankesanturai and Port Pedro. It was difficult to talk with the locals given the Sri Lankan military still insisted that I travel with an armed guard, but a number of people said that the commander in their area had been doing a good job. Business was still difficult, and ambulances were unable to run at night, but most credited the local commander with taking a surprisingly enlightened approach.

I met with Brigadier Larry Wijeratne, who was the local commander in charge of the area, and I was impressed. He struck me as one of the few government officials I met who understood that brute force alone would not win the conflict. He had made a real effort to reach out to the local community. He was one of the most liked army officials working in Jaffna, and his name had not been associated with many of the abuses I had heard elsewhere. He too was incredibly frustrated that the military was generally the only branch of government doing reconstruction work. I shared my concerns that a relatively new backhoe that I had come across earlier in the day was sitting unused because it needed a few spare parts from Colombo. The locals had been waiting months for the government to bring in the parts, which were not expensive. I was encouraged about the plan to help repair the port in part because Wijeratne thought it would go a long way toward addressing local headaches.

I visited a small local hospital with Jennifer, who worked for the relief group Doctors Without Borders. Jennifer was from St. Louis. On the front of the small hospital was a sign indicating that guns were not allowed in the facility. Jennifer shrugged as we passed, "You know that's a lie. When a soldier gets wounded, their buddies will usually come into the hospital and guard him." I asked her about security in general. "There are still roundups and disappearances, but the military has gotten much more measured in its responses. Even after Tiger attacks, they have not been totally out of control." In the time since my first visit to Jaffna, I noticed that people were moving about better, and the checkpoints were more professional.

The relief community in Sri Lanka was much smaller than other conflicts in which I had worked. Sri Lanka was a largely forgotten war. Only a handful of organizations were truly expert in dealing with the situation on the ground. All of the successful relief workers had worked out mutual accommodations with both the military and the Tigers to be able to do their jobs. This was not always easy, and most of the aid workers spent a great deal of their time negotiating so that they could do their work.

In many ways, the Sri Lankan government was eager for donors and aid groups to do the work that it should have been able to do itself. Equally problematic, the Tigers were willing to veto projects that they thought would undercut their chances for success on the battlefield. The first question for relief workers should have been: "How can we best improve conditions so that people will support peace and stability?" Instead, after discussions with the Tigers and the government, it was clear that we were trying to improve conditions for civilians without fundamentally altering the military or tactical playing fields.

The Tigers used careful logic in negotiating with donors who wanted to work in Jaffna. They understood that it was dangerous for them to be purely obstructionist, so they allowed humanitarian supplies such as food and medicine. But the Tigers also sent the message that nothing in Jaffna should improve too much compared to the period when they had been in control. For example, the Tigers tolerated a few generators, but large-scale electrical repairs were deemed off limits.

The donors were in a difficult corner. In essence, they had to get a permission slip from both sides to do any work in largely Tamil areas. It was difficult to see how any assistance, other than humanitarian aid, could be effective when delivered under such conditions. This was in part because nobody doubted the willingness of the Tigers to blow up any person or project that they did not like—something which cast my own work in a difficult light. The absurdity of a separatist movement, supposedly motivated by its love and respect for the Tamil people, detonating public work projects in Jaffna that would serve only Tamils was difficult to swallow.

Back in Jaffna town, I toured a local vocational school. The grounds and lawns were well tended—other than those areas that were roped off because of mines. The classrooms were bare of equipment. I got judicious answers when I asked who had done the looting. The technical college needed equipment, and there was a tremendous local need for workers skilled in carpentry and masonry. The Tamils in the area were well educated, and I never ceased to marvel that even in the middle of the war, teachers still held classes outside under a tree when they needed to. That said, there were still very few young people that had the practical skills needed for reconstruction.

After several months of work, I had put together a modest plan that I thought was sensible. There were several elements. First, we would contract with a salvage company to remove the sunken ships from the harbor to allow more goods to flow into the area. Second, we would provide funding for small teams of human rights monitors, including some expatriates, to investigate disappearances and other abuses in the north. Lastly, we would work with the United Nations to get the technical college up and running again so that it could move forward with an expanded program of vocational training.

I was realistic in understanding that these actions alone would not magically bring peace to Jaffna. But we designed the projects to deal with the problems that were most pressing: the inability to move goods and people in and out; the need to create jobs and income for young people; and the continuing human rights abuses by the government that alienated the public.

In Jaffna, I met with the editor of the lone local newspaper. The paper was printed on an ancient offset press. The editor proudly told me, "The only other place you can find this press is in a London museum." The paper had been operating since 1984, and the editor described how the staff had "hid in the basement during air strikes." The editor had to be very careful in his reporting. "It was easier when it was just the Tigers; now it is more complicated. We have the Tigers, the army, militia groups. I get phone calls every day. We are walking a very fine line. Not everybody is happy with what we are writing." Both the government and the Tigers were quick to use selective reporting for their own political purposes. For example, the Tiger propaganda wings in London and Australia quickly picked up editorials condemning disappearances by government troops. A piece critical of Tiger attacks against civilians appeared in government-owned newspapers in Colombo equally quickly.

"We deliver all of our newspapers on bicycles," said the editor. "Some of our boys are getting problems at the checkpoints. The soldiers cannot read Tamil, so they think that this is a paper published by the Tigers."

The editor pointed out a short story in that day's paper. I was alarmed, but not surprised, when he said that I appeared in the article under the headline: "U.S. says Tigers losing support." The selective quote came from a discussion I had with several local human rights activists the day before. While I had said that attacks on civilians had cut into support for the Tigers, I had made equally tough comments about the slow pace of government reconstruction efforts. It was rarely useful to be part of the story, but reporters often wrote whatever they wanted in such settings. What we saw as a modest assistance program could quickly become viewed by others as part of some grand nefarious plot by the U.S. government to tilt the balance of Sri Lanka's conflict.

It was not long after the story appeared in the newspaper that I began to get messages passed to me from the Tigers through intermediaries. They told me in direct terms that it would be better to travel without military escort. "If you are with the army, the Tigers see you as a fair game. It may take you a little longer without the soldiers, because of the checkpoints, but you will be much safer." It was discouraging that the Tigers were watching me, but welcome that they did not view me as a direct target. They also told me that because of a number of recent battlefield losses, the Tigers were in an "inflexible mood" and were concerned about some of the projects that we were considering. While they fully supported assistance to the technical college and human rights monitors, they viewed any port improvements as a "problem."

DISASTER JUNKIES

Fast forward another month. The war was raging as the government tried to reopen the road to Jaffna and reunite the peninsula with the rest of the country in a physical, if not a political, sense. The numbers of dead continued to spike with little territory changing hands; twenty-five killed one day, seventy-eight the next, seventeen the day following. For a country as small as Sri Lanka, the death toll was appalling. The mutual propaganda campaigns droned on. The Tigers claimed the government was bombing civilian positions and destroying entire villages in the north. The government accused the Tigers of hiding food from civilians and using the handicapped in suicide bomb attacks. It was hard to wade through all the layers of bullshit and come up with something approaching reason.

Back in Jaffna, I was alone in my room at the guesthouse in the middle of the night. The generator was off. A heavy rain was about to fall, and the shutters and doors in the house banged against their frames in anticipation. The noise was more soothing than disturbing. The air was sticky and un-comfortable, and I shifted on the bed to move closer to the breeze. I could hear the offbeat rhythm of steady small arms fire. Plink, plink, plink; as if that too was part of the local weather pattern.

A government minister had arrived in town—to rededicate a Buddhist temple. With so much work to do, the religious provocation felt point-lessly unwarranted. I could hear the first heavy drops of rain falling outside, splashing in the red dust of the streets.

Looking up at the ceiling, I wondered if I had become a disaster junkie. It was hard to avoid. When I returned to Washington after my time in the field, sitting at a desk felt listless and bureaucratic in comparison. War zones provided a steady rush of adrenalin and new experiences. Walking near the edge was enthralling like an exotic narcotic. It pulled me back despite all the incredible cruelty and misfortune. This was how people got in too deep. Being a disaster junkie was what pushed normally sane people into doing stupid things as they looked for the next big high.

The disaster business ruined more than its fair share of people. I had met far too many people that were left alone, lonely, and bitter after years of wandering fieldwork. There were the drunks and misanthropes, people who were reduced to a husk of their former selves by cynicism and personal and professional estrangement. The stress, coupled with the constant moving from place to place, left them burned out and listless as they hunched over at hotel bars complaining about their lack of a car and driver, or the bad contract they had signed five years ago. These were the people quick to say that any effort was doomed to failure while no longer being willing or able to suggest alternatives. They were casualties every bit as much as refugees or the displaced.

This was not to even mention the crazies, of which there were more than a few. Those attracted to field disaster work were not always the most stable to begin with, and as one of my colleagues put it, "If they were screwed up to start out, how do you think a year or two in a war zone will treat them?" I did not want to end up a victim, even while understanding that to become a disaster gypsy was to enter a landscape where all too many things were out of your control. The sounds of the rain were relaxing, but at that moment I felt absolutely alone.

The next day I visited an area on the southern edge of the peninsula. Jaffna had several large lagoons, and there had been a steady exodus of displaced Tamils coming out of the Vanni, a large region below Jaffna still controlled by the Tigers. The Vanni had traditionally been rich in agriculture, with its export crops destined for India. Families with money or good connections were able to buy their way out of the Vanni—past the Tigers, soldiers, and mid-level government bureaucrats. Some headed to Colombo; others left the country entirely. The poorest stayed behind, wandering from village to village as the conflict's front lines shifted. The Tigers strongly discouraged people from leaving areas under their control, and as one Tiger banner hanging over a main road in the Vanni ominously intoned: "If you leave, your family remains."

I visited a jetty and met with families coming across the lagoon from the Vanni as they headed into displaced camps. Small fiberglass boats were low in the water as they carried the fleeing families and their meager possessions. Rows of thin, wooden, open air fishing boats bobbed in disorderly rows. The displaced families that had already made it to the shore sat under a tin pavilion waiting. They would be detained for several days in a transit camp until they were cleared by government security. The local fishermen looked as poor as the displaced. Their houses were run down and families stretched out fishing nets on the dirt road for repair. The transit camp had the density of a refugee camp, but malnutrition was not a severe problem. No one in Sri Lanka's war would starve to death, but many would still die.

A colorful plaster Jesus, slightly worn by time and weather, was perched at the head of the jetty, welcoming all. An old man confronted me, "The army broke my hand," he said, as he showed me his ugly swollen appendage. What was I to do? It felt ridiculous. I was trying to design an aid program and I was helpless to fix everyday problems. I felt overwhelmed.

The fighting in Sri Lanka intensified in the months that followed, and my efforts to put together a transition program were ill-fated. I got everything wrong. In my eagerness to put together projects that could help the people of Jaffna, I never took a deep breath and pieced together all the obvious signs that Sri Lanka was simply not ready for peace. No amount of money or goodwill from donors would substitute for a willingness by the government and the Tigers to forge an agreement. Making progress on reconstruction or a hearts and minds campaign was impossible. The government had a willful disregard of the situation in the north and the Tigers remained willing to kill anyone who stood in their way. It only took a matter of months for the proposed projects to fall apart because the violence quickly got out of hand. Looking back, I was stupid to think I could make real progress without the conditions on the ground being right. I was new, enthusiastic, and determined to produce something that would look like success. I lacked the wisdom to stand up and say that I did not think the time was right.

On May 14, 1998, a Tiger suicide bomber jumped into the jeep of Brigadier Larry Wijeratne, killing the general and two of his guards. It was Wijeratne's last day at his post as the commander of Sri Lankan forces in Point Pedro area before a scheduled transfer to Colombo. At the time of his death, he was returning from a farewell lunch hosted by local Tamils. His replacement was reported to have told local Tamils that they should expect to pass through ten checkpoints a day until he could guarantee the safety of his troops.

Afghanistan

Cartography by Bookcomp, Inc.

CHAPTER 5

Taliban in the Basement—Afghanistan and Pakistan

After working for two years in the State Department, I joined a small, but well-regarded, conflict prevention organization, the International Crisis Group. The community of people who dealt with conflict for a living felt the aftershocks of September 11 acutely. Shortly after Afghanistan and the Taliban fell to coalition forces, a colleague and I traveled to Afghanistan and Pakistan in February and March of 2002 to look at the future of a troubled region.

BLOWBACK

After a long series of invasions and tribal conflicts over the years, Afghanistan gained a reputation as both a difficult country to conquer and even more difficult place to rule. For most Americans, Afghanistan lurched from the front pages of the news to largely being forgotten, with no small cost for Afghans and Americans alike.

In December 1979, the Soviet Union invaded Afghanistan, as Moscow looked to prop up a faltering allied government and expand its reach further south. The Soviet invasion was a disaster. Some 100,000 Soviet troops were largely able to control the cities, but a fierce Islamic guerilla resistance of *mujahideen* fighters (those who engage in holy war or *jihad*) led a growing rebellion. The U.S. government, and its allies in Pakistan, directly fed arms and money to these guerillas, including foreign fighters such as Osama bin Laden.

The war with the Soviets was ferocious and, by 1982, more than 4 million Afghans had fled their country. At least 700,000 Afghans died during the

Soviet occupation. After enduring a painful military quagmire of their own making, the Soviets withdrew from Afghanistan in 1989, and many attribute the misadventure for hastening the Soviet Union's ultimate demise. However, Afghanistan's misery did not end with Moscow's departure. Competing, and well-armed, Afghan warlords quickly set upon each other in the wake of the Soviet withdrawal, and the country descended back into bloodshed and anarchy.

Cynically, Afghanistan's neighbors and the world at large continued to supply weapons to the respective factions in an effort to ensure that no militia would gain an upper hand and unify the country. The suffering in Afghanistan was grievous, but the world turned a blind eye. These factors, coupled with Pakistani support, helped lead to the creation of the Taliban— a group of largely ethnic Pashtun hardcore Islamists who vowed to bring the country under strict religious control. The Taliban secured numerous battlefield victories and controlled much of Afghanistan by the mid-1990s. The lone effective holdout against the Taliban was a loose group of *mujahideen* forces known as the Northern Alliance led by veteran fighter Ahmed Shah Masoud.

The Taliban instituted draconian Islamic law: hands were amputated for theft; adulterers were stoned; and even watching videos was forbidden. The Taliban also gave shelter to Osama bin Laden from 1996 onward as he evaded U.S. pursuit for his role in masterminding a number of terror attacks, including the first World Trade Center bombing in 1993. On September 9, 2001, Osama bin Laden and the Taliban orchestrated the assassination of Ahmed Shah Masoud. Masoud, who had held out for years against Soviet occupation and survived countless battles against the Taliban, was killed when two men posing as journalists detonated a bomb hidden in their camera equipment. Two days later, on September 11, al-Qaeda launched the devastating terror attacks in New York and Washington.

U.S. forces, working in conjunction with the Northern Alliance, soon launched military operations against the Taliban and al-Qaeda as Osama bin Laden fled into hiding. By early December 2001, Afghanistan's capital, Kabul, had fallen to the U.S. coalition. By early February 2002, I headed to Afghanistan and Pakistan as part of my work with the International Crisis Group. A collection of former diplomats and foreign policy experts who were appalled by the international community's failure to stop the terrible loss of life in Somalia, Bosnia, and Rwanda established Crisis Group in 1995. Crisis Group was independent of any government, and designed to help the world prevent and contain deadly conflict by deploying small teams of political analysts on the ground in countries at war to provide practical recommendations on how best to end the violence. Field research was the core of our jobs, and we regularly met with an incredible variety of local and international actors—from warlords and peacekeepers to journalists, international diplomats, and politicians. Fred Cuny had originally been slated to head Crisis Group's operations before he was killed in Chechnya, and I suspect that he would be pleased that the world had finally found a voice for those working on the ground to prevent deadly conflict.

Unlike relief agencies, Crisis Group did not deliver assistance, so we were free to speak bluntly about the forces driving war and the best solutions for addressing them. Crisis Group's tough assessments did not always make it popular. Some of my colleagues have been declared persona non grata in Zimbabwe, Indonesia, and Sudan, weathered lawsuits in the Balkans, and been subjected to death threats by extremist groups. I found working for Crisis Group a very good fit—it mixed the immediacy of being out in the field with a very thoughtful approach to understanding conflict. In one of those odd quirks of fate, I had originally planned to make a trip to Afghanistan in September 2001 to meet with both Taliban and Northern Alliance officials. I was quite fortunate that I was not on the ground in Afghanistan when the September 11 attacks occurred.

THE NEXT BIG THING

It was hard to shake out the cobwebs as we drove along the arid stretch of highway outside of Islamabad, Pakistan after twenty-five hours of flying. Day laborers toiled by the side of the road, and garishly decorated buses honked their horns. The smell of roasting meat wafted from street vendors. An overturned bus at a clumsy angle blocked most of the road. Its broken windshield was crumpled on the pavement. Gawking onlookers peered into the front of the bus, stepping gingerly as if bad luck might rub off on their hands or clothes. As traffic crept by on the dusty shoulder, a small knot of motorcycle policemen discussed the situation without urgency. It was a disturbing way to start the trip.

I was traveling with Bob, a New Zealander, who was a longtime Asia hand. A former journalist, Bob was a pleasure to work with because of his brutally incisive sense of humor and general contempt for pomposity.

We were looking at the security situation in both Pakistan and Afghanistan, where we had established operations in the wake of September 11. Although Pakistan was not at war in the same way as most countries in which we worked, it was a key player in the new war on terrorism and inextricably wrapped up in the situation in Afghanistan. Pakistan was a deeply troubled country, and it had repeatedly switched back and forth between military and civilian governments since partition from India in 1947.

General Pervez Musharraf had ousted the democratic government through a military coup in 1999, shortly after both India and Pakistan had openly tested nuclear weapons. Musharraf declared martial law and suspended the constitution before naming himself president. September 11 had placed Musharraf in a tricky spot. Pakistan's military and intelligence services had long backed the Taliban, but Musharraf, understanding the depth of the

U.S. outrage over September 11, very publicly declared himself an ally of the United States and a partner in the war on terror.

We were staying at the Marriot Hotel in Islamabad. As soon as we arrived, it was abundantly clear that Afghanistan was the next big thing. With just a few short months passing since September 11, Pakistan and Afghanistan were the places to be. The disaster industry worked that way. Every new conflict or disaster generated a virtual stampede of relief workers, journalists, and diplomats leaping into action. New disasters brought more money for aid groups, higher ratings for the networks, and the chance to be on hand as history was made. It was a completely different matter when attention faded and the disaster gypsies trampled out just as quickly as they came.

An odd collection of expatriates filled the hotel lobby. A battery of television cameras had been set up on the roof so that reporters could film their segments with dramatic pictures of the mountains in the distance. It was illusion: the footage looked remote and wild even though filmed from the roof of a comfortable international hotel. We mimicked the lead we knew reporters would use: "In mountains like those you see behind me, hardened Taliban fighters . . ." The fact that we were in Pakistan and not Afghanistan meant little to the miracle of television.

The hotel was crawling with international reporters. As we got a cup of coffee in the lobby, I noticed the reporter Peter Arnett sitting at the next table with a young woman. Arnett had become famous for his reporting with CNN during the first Gulf War, but his career had subsequently fallen apart. It made me wonder if Arnett still had some vestigial instinct that naturally pulled him to wherever in the world was "hot"—this was the downside of becoming a disaster junkie.

Bob and I made our way across town to meet with a Pakastani journalist. The journalist was a slight man in his mid-fifties. His tweed jacket gave him the kindly air of a doting academic, and his hands shook with a mild palsy. Earlier in his career, he had been publicly flogged and jailed because the government took exception to his reporting. The harsh treatment had not broken his spirit, and he was adamant that a free press was Pakistan's only hope for salvation, "If there are no courts, no parliament, no rule of law, how can you have freedom of the press?" He observed that more and more papers engaged in self-censorship because they relied on government advertising revenue and feared running afoul of the authorities. The Pakistani intelligence services also regularly planted news stories, bribed reporters, and threatened others that were deemed "too independent."

The reporter was sincerely baffled why the United States had been so quick to lavish praise—and more than a billion dollars in aid—upon General Musharraf in the wake of September 11. He was sharply critical of the conventional wisdom that Musharraf had changed his stripes. "Musharraf was posted in Quetta," a large Pakistani city near the Afghan border, "in 1995 when the Taliban was created. He helped establish the Taliban." One reason Pakistan's military had backed the Taliban was its desire to keep Afghanistan weak and unstable so it would not pose a strategic threat. The journalist was exasperated by the fact that the international community was taking Musharraf at his word. "The military gave the Taliban money and direct support. On 9 September, two days before the towers fell in New York, Musharraf was giving speeches defending the Taliban." He noted that a nearby fourteen-story building had recently burned, and that it not-so coincidentally had housed financial records regarding Pakistani military assistance to fundamentalist groups.

Even after September 11, General Musharraf had advocated working with the Taliban, declaring, "The moderate Taliban are willing to bring about change. They should be accepted in a future administration." It was only after intense pressure from Washington that Musharraf adjusted his rhetoric. Even during the U.S. military campaign against the Taliban, there were credible reports of Pakistani military flights evacuating Pakistani intelligence services and Taliban elements escaping the fighting.

Since I was the lone American in the room, he asked me why the United States preferred Pakistan to be led by soldiers rather than civilians. I wished I had a better answer. He compellingly argued that despite the bright spotlight on Pakistan since September 11, the Pakistani military view of the world had changed little. The journalist, like many we spoke to in Pakistan, maintained that the military had a highly symbiotic relationship with Islamic militants. The military had used concerns about Islamic extremism and tensions with India as a means to justify their hold on power—even as they provided direct support to Islamic hardliners. By quietly supporting extremists, while paradoxically warning of the threat of a fundamentalist revolution, the military was able to insist that Pakistan was too dangerous for democracy. The West had always been willing to swallow the argument, although most of the evidence suggested that Pakistan would be less radical if allowed to return to civilian rule. The military government always portrayed itself as the best defender against the same extremist groups that it nurtured—an effort one of my colleagues compared "to the man who murdered his wife and then pleaded for leniency as a widower."

Greed also drove the military, and the security services consumed about 40 percent of the country's national budget with no oversight. The journalist argued that most Pakistani military officers had three desires: to be granted a nice piece of land by the government; to secure a good pension or plum government job after their posting; and to send their children to school in America. "If the military were to give up their grip on power, all of those perks would be in danger. With a civilian government in place, the military could no longer skim all the cream off the top."

We later had tea with a retired Pakistani lieutenant general at his nice home in Islamabad. An older man, the general still held himself with a military carriage. He fondly expressed hope that he would be able to get out for tennis later in the day. He looked fit. Even though he considered President Musharraf a friend, he casually used the terms "dictatorship" and "junta" in describing the government. Even as a former military man, he was concerned that Washington had given Musharraf a green light to consolidate his hold on power. The general joked that the Pakistani military's only problem with democracy was "not being able to guarantee who wins." The general admitted that the military has long worked with *mujahideen* fighters in Afghanistan and in Kashmir to advance its strategic goals. The general was surprisingly progressive in his views, and he pointed out that it would be difficult to rebuild the country's economy or education system as long as the military consumed such a large part of the budget.

A senior editor of one of Pakistan's large English daily newspapers also asked me, "Why does your country always prefer my country to be run by the military? If we are going to have bad leaders, why shouldn't we be the ones picking them?" While I resisted the notion that U.S. foreign policy was the only reason Pakistan was a mess, it was discouraging to speak with so many people who supported democracy but did not see Washington as an ally. Most Pakistanis we spoke with were disturbingly resigned to the fact their leaders, both military and civilian, were corrupt and shortsighted.

As we made our rounds in Islamabad, there was a great deal of media coverage regarding the kidnapping of a *Wall Street Journal* reporter, Daniel Pearl. A little-known group of Islamic extremists had reportedly abducted Pearl, and the news stories were odd and full of strange inconsistencies. There were e-mail demands for $2 million ransom and calls for the United States to release F-15 fighter aircraft the government of Pakistan had purchased years before—an unusual request for terrorists. Pearl had been working on stories that explored the links between the Pakistani security services and extremist groups, such as the Taliban. Predictably, Pakistani officials claimed that the kidnapping was a plot by Indian intelligence services to make them look bad. Much of the local reporting on the case was full of disinformation. The more I read about Pearl's disappearance, the more quickly it became apparent that the war on terror was anything but black and white in Pakistan.

KABUL

I was excited and apprehensive about going to Afghanistan. Even though I had traveled to numerous bad places, Afghanistan had always held a place in my mind as one of the roughest—it was mountainous, lawless, and it was the dead of winter. The UN and the military ran the only flights going into Afghanistan, and we spent the better part of a day in the hurry-up-and-wait game of getting on a UN flight. We started at the UN flight office in downtown Islamabad, which was really just a small house with a desk set up in the driveway to process passengers. They weighed our bags and we filled out paperwork. Then, like everyone else, we stood around.

A scruffy crew of internationals filled the yard: reporters, a few UN officials, some relief workers, a couple of businessmen looking for high-risk returns, and several people who were probably spies. The faces were worldly, a mélange of Europeans, Asians, Americans, and Africans. Conversations were carried out in a low singsong of accented English interwoven with a smattering of other languages. Almost all of these people were familiar with war and disaster, but few knew Afghanistan well. Eventually we piled into a small convoy of minibuses and headed for the airport. Officials at customs and passport controls waved us through.

The entire group of expatriates waited in a large lounge at the commercial airport, and it made for a surreal scene. One entire end of the waiting lounge was filled with old Pakistani men and women, most of them dressed in simple white robes, all waiting to board a flight to take them on their religious pilgrimage, or *hajj*, to Mecca, Saudi Arabia. A cleric made his way around the room leading loud prayer chants. Most of the pilgrims had saved for years to be able to afford the flight, and it would be the first time out of the country for many of them.

All the passengers on the UN flight clustered at the other end of the lounge. Anticipating the cold weather of Kabul, the internationals were swathed in a colorful splash of expensive gortex outdoor gear. The internationals kept expensive laptops, backpacks, satellite telephones, and briefcases close by their sides. All of them carried significant amounts of cash. They too were on their own sort of pilgrimage. The waiting lounge was perfectly segregated by nationality, by color of clothing, and by worldview. The fact that the two sides could have been divided by a wall did not speak well about the potential for mutual understanding in the post–September 11 world.

The wait for the flight was considerable, and the long series of prayers that rang out across the charmless waiting lounge left me strangely exhausted. Finally, after the last pilgrim to Mecca had long since departed, we boarded our plane. I had expected that we would be traveling on a battered cargo plane, but I was mistaken. The aircraft, chartered out of South Africa by the UN World Food Program, was brand new. There were even flight attendants. The actual flight was short, only about an hour, and for much of our flight we were enshrouded by dense cloud cover.

I did not get a sense of the landscape until minutes before we set down. Banking out of the clouds, one of the first things I noticed was the color of Kabul. There was no hint of green, not even a single blossom, breaking the dun-colored landscape. It was like being thrust into a sepia-toned photo from the 1880s. Snow-dappled mountains wrapped around the valley and a jumble of low mud buildings stretched out below. The winter season and years of drought had drained the hills of pigment. The homes that were stacked on the hillsides looked like they were carved from the earth itself. Kabul was frozen in time.

As the plane touched down, I finally saw a few scraps of color: the garishly bright carcasses of wrecked fighter jets littered at the far end of the runway. The airfield was an elephant's graveyard of dilapidated and destroyed fighters, cargo planes, and transports from different countries and eras. Afghans had long since cannibalized many of the larger aircrafts for parts before dragging them into the fields just off the runway. Because most of the military aircraft were using the nearby landing strip at Bagram airfield, the armed presence at the airport was light. There were a handful of sandbags and machine gun nests separating the airport from the windswept surrounding fields. I suspected that a heavy blanket of mines covered the fields, making any approach almost suicidal. It was cold outside.

Kabul's air terminal was a grim affair. The glass was gone from most of the doors and windows, and a few pieces of plastic sheeting did little to keep the wind out. The terminal's barren concrete interior, devoid of either heating or lighting, held a cave-like chill. The afternoon light had started to dissipate, making it colder still. A few Afghan soldiers stood around with guns, but no gloves. They looked miserable. A guard pretended to check passports, but the effort was desultory, a charade to pretend that government was functioning.

Hewad, who would serve as our Afghan "fixer," met us at the airport. "Mr. Bob? Mr. John?" Having a good fixer was essential to navigating an alien situation well. In our case, Hewad would be both translator and guide. He would help arrange meetings and he would give us the inside scoop on some of the Afghans with whom we would meet. As we waited for our luggage to be dropped on the immobile and long-broken baggage carousel, Hewad explained that he had recently worked for the reporter Dianne Sawyer, "You have heard of her? She is a very nice woman." Hewad was an ethnic Pashtun, but had grown up in the city of Mazar-e-Sharif, a city in northern Afghanistan that was largely ethnic Uzbek. Bearded and compact, Hewad had an easy smile. He had worked for the BBC Uzbek-language service as a correspondent, and had lived in Moscow, Prague, and Pakistan earlier in his life. He had a great deal of experience working with journalists.

Kabul in February felt like a place where you could get a chill that stayed with you until you left. We trundled into a yellow and white taxicab that Hewad had arranged. There were many cabs and cars on the street because, as Hewad explained, all the drivers had come to Kabul looking for work.

Although there had been daily street battles in the early 1990s between factions hoping to control the capital after the Soviets left, Kabul had not seen intensive combat in years, and most of the subsequent fighting had taken place outside of the capital. Large sections of Kabul had been decimated over a decade before and left in lingering decline since that time. Bob had worked in Kabul as a reporter during 1992, at the height of factional fighting in the capital. Rocket attacks had raged between the forces of such warlords as Ahmed Shah Masoud, General Rashid Dostum, and Gulbuddin Hekmatyar. On some days, hundreds of rocket attacks pounded the southern part of Kabul. Bob's time in Kabul was a horrible experience; much of it spent in terror and confusion.

Despite the Taliban's fall, hard living still defined Afghanistan. It was the dead of winter and people were walking around in thin plastic shoes with no socks. Children wore ratty old jackets whose cheap stained fabric was shiny from years of use. It would have been easy to think the Afghans were simply resistant to cold, but this was given lie by the way people gingerly warmed their hands over a cup of tea. People had gotten used to being cold all the time. As kids played outside their small houses, you could see the bitter weather etched in sharp shades of oranges and reds on their wind-burned cheeks. Elderly war widows plied the slushy sidewalks with outstretched hands begging for alms. Again and again, we would see men and boys who had lost limbs to land mines; the lucky ones were outfitted with clunky prostheses. No one turned a head when a baby cried loudly.

Later, when we traversed the dirt roads in the hills above the city, the scene quickly passed from relatively urban to a desolate, bleak, and rural landscape. Small headstones tilted in disarray filled a sprawling Muslim cemetery, with green banners slapping in the wind. In the villages that were only minutes outside of Kabul, the 21st century unraveled to reveal the 12th amid extreme poverty and neglect.

Afghanistan was home to a myriad of ethnicities, and the faces in the streets of Kabul were an incredible collection: one distinctly Mongol, the next strikingly Persian, a Slavic profile, a Tajik, a Pashtun, an Uzbek—everything under the sun. The multitude of civilizations that had washed across Afghanistan had left a fascinating flotsam of language, dress, and intermarriage. The loyalties of ethnicity, language, and family played a powerful role in both politics and violence.

There were many people with guns in the street, some in uniform and some not. We passed jeeps and armored personnel carriers with British and German troops. The peacekeepers came from a host of different nations, and the mix of uniforms, hardware, and insignia gave the place a frontier feel. However, there were few checkpoints, and people were in the streets although there was still a curfew at night. The city was not on edge, but the calm was illusory.

Outside the capital, U.S. warplanes were still bombing Taliban elements in Pashtun areas of the south, making it difficult for Pashtuns to feel like they were welcome in the new Afghanistan—particularly because there continued to be civilian casualties from these air strikes. Armed carjackings and banditry were persistent across much of the country. Friction between rival militia factions also continued to run high, and Afghanistan remained one of the most heavily mined and armed places on earth. The country's economy, other than the opium trade, was in ruins.

As we drove, it started to snow. Kabul was a city of compounds: the U.S. embassy, the headquarters for the peacekeeping force, and other official buildings. Almost every structure of import was isolated within high, gated walls, and it gave the city an impersonal feel. With the influx of internationals, local hotel rooms had become a commodity. Fortunately, Hewad had booked a place for us. My expectations were minimal, and I imagined that we had secured a place on a cold cement floor in an Afghan house. Our taxi took us down a narrow back alley, and we walked through a low metal gate. As we walked into a remarkably nice, and contemporarily decorated, house, Peter, the proprietor of the new guesthouse greeted us. A fire blazed away in the grate, and a stereo played in the background.

Hewad, having gotten us to the guesthouse, excused himself and informed us, "I have to go read the news." It turned out that in addition to his work as a fixer, Hewad was also an evening news anchorman on one of the local television broadcasts. The fact that there were local news broadcasts after Taliban rule was testament to how rapidly things were changing.

Peter showed us our room, and offered tea. Peter was a British national and former military man. He had worked and lived in Afghanistan on and off for the better part of twenty years, usually employed as a cameraman for the BBC. Peter knew Afghanistan very well and had a genuine affection for the place. He had helped to get the very first BBC crew into Kabul after the Taliban had been toppled. He had also filmed an interview with Osama bin Laden the year before, and he wondered why Western intelligence services found locating Osama so difficult. "He was quite eager to do an interview. If we could arrange it, you would think the CIA would have been able to do the same."

Peter, although calm and very collected, was clearly a conflict junkie, and cameramen had long enjoyed a reputation as some of the most gonzo of journalists. He liked working in war zones. The money was good and capturing the right picture with bullets flying around was a very specific skill. Given his long Afghanistan experience and his vast network of contacts, Peter's services were in considerable demand. He made good money by providing referral services to journalists who needed help on the ground—he had become a fixer of fixers.

Peter had rented the guesthouse shortly after Kabul's liberation and had it quickly repaired. He knew there would be a sharp increase in need for places to stay. The house's previous tenant had been one of Osama bin Laden's wives, who as Peter complained, "left the place a perfect mess." Peter was gregarious, and he knew how to do business in Afghanistan: officials were bribed, armed guards were hired, deals were made, and militia leaders were given a piece of the action. There were a thousand tricks to get a reporter closer to a story, and Afghanistan felt much like Rick's Café in

Casablanca—everything was possible for a price. It wasn't that Afghanistan did not have rules; it was just that these rules had nothing to do with the law. Peter was happy that we brought him two bottles of whiskey. Alcohol was still hard to find around town.

I sat by the fire and talked to a part-time cameraman and aspiring artist, Jake. Where Peter was calculating, Jake was unguarded and scatterbrained. Rolling his own cigarette, Jake talked about his recent assignment around Tora Bora, the rugged mountain stronghold where Osama bin Laden had slipped away from U.S. and Northern Alliance troops. Jake spoke with melancholy about how quickly the huge influx of Western journalists, aid workers, and militaries was changing Afghanistan. These new arrivals were spreading around suitcases full of cash, and Jake believed that the Afghans were becoming increasingly rapacious in response. Armed Afghans were resorting to extortion, threats, and robbery, and Jake thought the environment was making everyone uglier.

In many ways, a whole new value system had been dropped on Afghanistan almost overnight. The Taliban's Islamic Puritanism had disappeared, replaced by an approach to the military and politics that was democratic in name but often highly mercenary in practice. The differences were apparent to Afghans both young and old. An elderly Afghan herdsman had approached Jake while he was at Tora Bora and told him: "You must be a very poor man. You have no fixer. You have no guards. You have no car. You are a very poor man, very poor." Even a goatherd was able to parse Afghanistan's new status symbols. "The funny part," Jake added with a raspy cough, "is that the old man was exactly right."

Jake had also done some teaching in the city of Jalalabad, and the pent-up thirst for education amazed him. Several Afghans had pulled him aside on the street—entirely out of the blue—asking him if they could get lessons. Jake also shared a warm-hearted, but fuzzy-headed, plan to get schoolbooks to Afghans. He wanted to exhibit his charcoal drawings in New York City, and have people donate books that would be shipped to schools in Afghanistan. I suggested that it might be cheaper to buy the books in Asia. Jake nodded slowly in response.

Jake's other project involved finding keys to an armored vehicle owned by CNN. He had been with the CNN crew when the truck blew its clutch in Tora Bora. Some locals promptly stole the truck. The vehicle was later seen in Jalalabad and then in Kabul. The truck was reportedly in the possession of a minor warlord who was trying to sell it for cash. Jake thought he could negotiate a favorable deal for the truck's return: the minor warlord would make some money, he would as well; and CNN would get its vehicle back.

That evening we had a meal along with Peter and two guests who were also staying in the house, both of whom worked for a security firm and were former British intelligence. The conversation started slowly, but it was not long before Peter produced a bottle of whiskey and a box of Cuban cigars. The group around the table had worked in a who's who of trouble spots: Angola, Vietnam, Tajikistan, Nigeria, and beyond. One of the security guys had been working in Sudan helping the government design defense perimeters for its oil fields just before going to Afghanistan. Peter had been arrested in Sri Lanka, and deported from Uzbekistan.

Leaning back in his chair, Peter explained that in the days before Kabul fell, allegiances on the ground rapidly shifted with the tide of the military offensive. Afghan militias were notorious for preferring to switch sides rather than lose a fight. A number of local fighters in Kabul seized foreign members of the Taliban and took them hostage. The armed kidnappings were far more economic than political. The kidnappers hoped for generous ransom from either the families of these foreign-born Taliban fighters or the CIA. A number of negotiators hired by families began to appear around Kabul.

Peter knew one Afghan family that had kept an Arab fighter locked in their basement for several weeks. They attempted to find someone willing to pay a ransom, "but nobody wanted the guy." Making matters worse, the Arab Taliban fighter complained about both his captivity and the quality of food he was getting. "I guess he didn't like rice that much," added Peter. The Afghans, fed up with the nagging, and with neither the U.S. forces nor family stepping forward to pay for the man's release, "simply shot him in the head."

Keeping Taliban in the basement was more difficult than it appeared.

HEWAD'S BROTHER

Several days later, during a break in our meetings, Hewad gave me a tour of southern Kabul—the neighborhoods of the city that were most heavily damaged during the civil war. What had once been Kabul's main shopping street was devastated. Thousands of rocket attacks and a steady stream of 50-caliber machine gun fire had whittled every building down to a nub. The ruined structures looked like dribbled wet sand; what a child would mold on the beach.

Because the destruction was a decade old it had an almost ancient feel; as if southern Kabul was the crumbling skeleton of a forgotten city. Squatters lived precariously perched in many of the bombed-out buildings. Only one or two new structures, including a large Mosque built several years before, stood out among the obliterated landscape. We also passed the large public stadium. The Taliban had punished and executed prisoners in front of crowds at the stadium. As Hewad described, a group of teens that had gone to play soccer on the field found a 50-gallon barrel sitting in the middle of the grass. When they went to move it, they discovered the metal drum was filled with the severed hands of prisoners that had been punished for theft under the Taliban's harsh interpretation of Islamic law.

As we drove, Hewad explained how his brother, Kochai, had run afoul of the Taliban the year before. Apparently, Kochai had gone to another town hoping to sell off several goats, which he did. The exchange left him carrying more cash than he normally would, and he tried to find someone with whom he could change money. In the process of changing money, several Taliban—in what was a case of mistaken identity—accused Kochai of harassing a woman. According to Hewad, even the crowd that gathered at the scene insisted that the Taliban had the wrong man. However, the Taliban were suspicious because Kochai was still holding the cash that he had gotten for the goats. The Taliban dragged Kochai off to jail, and subsequently transferred him for imprisonment to the interior ministry in Kabul.

While in jail, the Taliban repeatedly beat Kochai. At one point, they hit Kochai on the back of the head with a brick, and he lost a great deal of blood as a result. The serious injury also left him somewhat deranged. After about a week in jail, Kochai was able to get a letter out through another prisoner to Hewad. Hewad lobbied the Taliban for his brother's release, and they were reasonably cooperative knowing that Hewad worked for the BBC. After six more days in jail, the Taliban released Kochai, who was in very bad shape.

Hewad continued, "Kochai was very, very, paranoid of the neighbors. He was even afraid of me. We took him to a number of shrines in the country hoping that he could be healed, but nothing worked. Eventually, I took Kochai to Peshawar," a city in neighboring Pakistan. "In Peshawar we gave him shock treatment. That helped. He is better now than he was." It was still clear that Kochai suffered from trauma and that he probably had lasting brain damage. Hewad did not tell the story with a sense of pity for his brother, himself, or his family. He spoke of the incident with the irritation you might associate an American describing an undeserved parking ticket.

An inch of snow fell overnight, with more accumulation on the mountain slopes that rose sharply out of the valley. On the snow-slicked street, a bus collided with a taxi, crumpling its hood and setting off much angry arm waving. The U.S. embassy was our first stop. Outside, an Afghan soldier stood post at the embassy's perimeter. Concerned about potential car bombs, he told our taxi driver to park on the other side of the street. I handed our business cards to a U.S. marine standing guard behind the main gate. He was young. We hoped to meet with some of the senior diplomats on the U.S. team, and the marine disappeared to talk to his superior. We loitered in the driveway, stamping our feet to stay warm.

After a short time, the marine returned and let us in. I felt bad for him. He was stuck with guard duty standing in the cold in some country he probably knew nothing about a few months before. He relaxed almost instantaneously upon seeing that I carried an American passport. As he waved over us with a handheld metal detector, I noticed five more marines dressed in full combat gear manning a machine gun nest inside the entrance of the gate. They ushered us through to the next checkpoint.

Layers of bright new razor wire festooned the high compound walls of the embassy. The place looked impregnable. As we approached the next checkpoint, we passed a massive heap of rusting debris that had recently been dragged out of the embassy for disposal. The embassy had been empty for twelve years since its personnel had evacuated in 1989. Afghanistan had largely been off Washington's radar before September 11. Then, in the span of a single day, Afghanistan became the epicenter of U.S. strategic planning. Many Afghans wondered whether Washington's renewed attention would be an unmitigated blessing.

The marines waved us through a roadblock toward the embassy. The embassy was run down, but not heavily damaged. All things considered, it had survived well enough. Workers repaired communications equipment on the building's roof, where several more machine gun nests only added to its fortress-like appearance. A lanky marine, wearing a black turtleneck and jeans, jogged by with an assault rifle slung across his back. He said hello with a distinctly southern twang. He was all business.

Another cluster of marines stood next to the bullet-scarred doorway of the embassy's front entrance. The commander led us into the lobby. A secretary scurried down the stairs, appointment book in hand, and her footsteps echoed across the cold stone of the lobby. "It is a little crazy here, and apologies for the confusion. I'm here from Paris for two months to lend a hand." I respected a Foreign Service secretary who volunteered to leave a cushy post in Paris to sleep on a cot, eat military rations, and be confined to a compound. We scheduled a meeting with a senior official in the embassy for several days later and departed back through the multiple layers of security. The entire process of going into the embassy—even just to set up an appointment—reinforced the notion that American diplomats were incredibly isolated amid such tight security.

There were very few women on the streets of Kabul. During the course of a usual day, I only saw one or two women who were not wearing full-length *burkhas*, the long, loose garments that covered women's entire bodies save for the small veiled holes around the eyes. However, I did notice that all the women we saw wore surprisingly elegant footwear despite the cold and mud. It was as if they wanted to take pride in the one feature where they were allowed to display their femininity.

We stopped by the headquarters of the peacekeeping force, and Italian troops guarded its perimeter. A small group of soldiers strung barbed wire. We passed through several checkpoints before stopping at the main gate. A group of local workers were cleaning up garbage and repairing an abandoned building nearby. The Italians animatedly bossed around the Afghans, the Afghans moved at their normal pace and nobody understood much of the exchange. This was the new Afghanistan.

As we waited for someone to emerge from the base, a series of military vehicles stopped at the main gate for a mandatory weapons check. The soldiers included British, Germans, Italians, and Austrians. A number of the men were not wearing uniforms, and they were either CIA or U.S. Special Forces. The vehicles were equally diverse: Toyotas, Defenders, jeeps, an armored personnel carrier, a Land Rover with Dubai plates, and troop transports. A tall British soldier with a rifle strung across his back emerged from an armored vehicle carrying a huge stack of *naan*, the local bread, and I could not help but laugh. Given the diversity of the peacekeepers, it was amazing they could even keep each other sorted out, much less the Afghan factions. There were at least eighteen different nations involved in the peacekeeping effort, and coordination was a serious problem. The peacekeeping force was also remarkably small—only 4,500 soldiers to patrol a huge, lawless country. While the United States had led the military campaign to topple the Taliban, it had largely refused to contribute men to the peacekeeping effort, leading one European military officer to complain, "Washington wants to do the cooking and then leave all the dirty dishes for us."

A British captain appeared and suggested that we meet with his superior, a colonel, the following morning. Setting up meetings in Kabul was a challenge. Most of the normal telephone lines had long been out of service, and there was no directory for satellite phone numbers. We literally had to go knock on the gates at different compounds around town to arrange interviews. Arranging meetings in Kabul was a lot like dating in the 14th century. You made a long journey, banged on a gate, and asked to speak with the master of the house. Outside of the British embassy as we waited for a meeting, a very old man walked up and shoved a dog-eared slip of notepaper in our hands. He asked in halting English, "Is this ok?" The note, in English, was crisply penned in a woman's handwriting. The letter of reference declared the man to be a first-class dobie, or houseboy, and added that he was "very good at ironing." The letter was dated 1975.

The streets of Kabul were bustling. There was food and goods in most of the markets, and the Afghans were quickly adapting to the altered economic realities. Under the Taliban, the Afghans grew beards, hid their alcohol behind false walls, and held clandestine viewings of *Titanic*. With the United States military victory, the locals were handcrafting satellite dishes and trying to figure out how to set up Internet cafes. There was a newly booming business in the local manufacture of satellite dishes crafted from scrap metal. Although entirely functional, the different shapes, patterns, and colors of the dishes looked like a form of installation art dropped down in the middle of Kabul.

There was a particular flurry of enterprise in those activities formerly banned by the Taliban. The local movie theater had reopened after years of being closed, and its high marquee was emblazoned with splashy banners advertising salacious Hindi films. The movies were doing brisk business.

Along narrow back streets, portrait photographers had set up shops on the sidewalk. The Taliban had forbidden all but passport photos. The tall red box cameras used by the photographers looked like they could have come from museums. Families proudly sat their sons down for long-awaited portraits. The boys were rigidly uncomfortable and unsmiling as they posed. It was endearing.

In the snowy fields around Kabul, children flew kites with dour determination despite a temperature in the twenties. In one of their more ridiculous excesses, the Taliban had outlawed kites as well, and U.S. Special Forces had been handing out kites to kids to help generate goodwill. A small, inexpensive gesture could make a difference. Flying a kite on a near-frozen string was an elegant symbol of defiance against the way things had been. It was not all progress though. Less savory elements of local life had also sprung back. I cringed when asked if I wanted to attend the dog fights scheduled for the next day.

We met with a senior relief worker, Simon, who had been in Afghanistan for years. Despite periodic hassles from the Taliban, his aid group had been able to deliver humanitarian assistance almost continually through Afghanistan's times of trouble. After September 11, the organization had briefly left the country when the Taliban had indicated they could no longer guarantee the safety of its staff. After the rapid progress of the allied military offensive, the group returned.

Simon had a gentle manner, and he spoke both thoughtfully and with a certain worn resignation. He was worried that the international community, and particularly the Americans, had gotten into something that was more complicated than they understood. When I questioned Simon about the general situation, he stroked his beard and hesitated before answering, "You know to be blunt, this country will not be sorted out until all the old leaders die. One or two already have. The rest are still a problem." He smiled wanly and carefully explained that his organization, a very respectable charity, was not advocating violence against the handful of warlords that still controlled much of the countryside—despite the U.S. military presence. Simon's sentiments had been expressed to me more colorfully by a Kabul taxi driver who declared, "Afghanistan is ready for peace; anyone not ready for peace should be shot."

Simon was alarmed that the United States was working with the same warlords that had done so much to wreck Afghanistan, and the small size of the peacekeeping force meant that Northern Alliance warlords were still the de facto leaders of many of Afghanistan's larger cities. Controlling Kabul was important, but it did not necessarily give the new government legitimacy outside the capital, and Afghan history was replete with examples of those who were unable to extend their rule of Kabul further into the countryside.

Simon offered a balanced view, and he highlighted both the dangers and opportunities in the current climate. He was frustrated with how the West, and particularly the Western media, approached Afghanistan. He gently mocked the confusion of many reporters who thought Afghan women would run through the streets ripping off their *burkhas* immediately after Kabul fell. As Simon noted, "Reporters do not understand that these things take time. This is a dangerous place. If a pretty woman shows her face, maybe a local commander tries to rape her. Women are scared. What woman wants to be the first one to take such a risk? What guarantee can a foreign soldier, who will leave in several months, offer to a poor woman?"

We had a late lunch in a local café, and there was not a single woman in the restaurant. Given the speed with which Afghans had again embraced dog fighting, kite flying, and music, such attitudes toward women would probably shift over time, but certainly not easily. What comfort did Western opinion provide these women if men—infuriated at seeing merely a patch of exposed ankle—whipped their legs with sticks?

GOOD INTENTIONS

Late one afternoon, we headed out to meet with the Afghan general in charge of the national police force. We had seen a number of police on the streets directing traffic, and this was somewhat surprising given that the country had not had a functioning police force in years. It had been more than a decade since any police had received formal training. As we approached the police headquarters on the outskirts of town, gusts of wind spiked across a frozen muddy field that stretched out nearby. A teenager in an ill-fitting uniform guarded the front gate. He proudly gripped his gun and stood at attention. I glanced down and noticed he was wearing old tennis shoes without socks.

The headquarters were bleak. There was no electricity. The building's drab cement Soviet era interior was freezing cold. The general was out on patrol, so we sat with several policemen crouched around a wood stove in one of the offices. There was no paper on any of the desks. There were no books on any of the bookshelves. Wads of cotton peaked through the torn fabric of the broken-down couch. A rubber stamp on one of the desks appeared to be the last vestige of a working bureaucracy. No one in the office was doing anything other than brewing tea and trying to stay warm. The general's assistant noted that the police force had not been paid in months. Most of the cops only showed up at work in the hope that some Western donor would eventually pay back wages. His police uniform was homemade. The assistant, like most officials, spoke in rhetoric left over from the era of the Soviet invasion—the last time Afghanistan had a fully functioning police force. During the Taliban era, the incredibly Orwellian sounding Ministry for Promotion of Virtue and Prevention of Vice had replaced the police. Not only did Afghanistan need to resurrect an entire police force and army, it also needed to throw out the Soviet model under which most Afghan security officials originally had been trained.

The general arrived. We were ushered into his office. It had a few token symbols of status: the office was larger than the others, there was a small plastic vase with paper flowers in the corner, and there was a phone on the desk. However, there was no pen or paper and the shelves were empty. There was no tangible sign that any work took place at all.

Years of fighting in Afghanistan's wars had left the general's face incredibly weathered. His eyes were sunken. Slouching back in his chair, he lit a cigarette with shaky fingers before thrusting his hands deep in his pockets in an effort to keep warm. An officer stepped in the room and saluted smartly before starting a small fire in the stove. It was late afternoon and the light was starting to falter. Darkness filled the room like a creeping tide. The general gave us a rambling lecture on the evils of the Taliban before launching into an extended plea for resources. The police had no official uniforms, few weapons, and almost no radios. In 1990, the police had more than 300 vehicles, now they had a handful of borrowed trucks. As I glanced around the shabby office, it was difficult to accuse the general of overstating the sorry condition of his force.

The general continued to talk in muted tones, and despite the small stove, the room was very cold. The general described ambitious plans to restore a police force of 70,000 men, but he looked exhausted and unconvinced. The gathering dusk made it feel like our conversation could simply trail off. There was almost an unimaginable amount of work to do to get Afghanistan back on its feet.

We were subdued during the drive back into town. Pictures of the late Northern Alliance military leader—Ahmed Shah Masoud—were plastered on the walls of compounds and in the windows of businesses. With the fall of the Taliban, Masoud had become more popular in death than he was in life. He was a martyr, the one Afghan fighter that was never fully beaten on the battlefield by either the Soviets or the Taliban. The posters of Masoud in the windows were also a sign of fealty to the new political order. Every shop that displayed a portrait of Masoud was distancing itself from any links to the Taliban. It reminded Bob of all the Middle Eastern taxi drivers in New York and Washington who displayed American flags on their cars after September 11.

During dinner at the guesthouse, the power blinked out as Peter described his plan to open a pizzeria in Kabul. He had found a suitable location, and was investigating how best to oust the squatters that were living in the building. Peter's dream was to create a restaurant that would serve international workers at international prices, "I want people to step out of Kabul when they come through the front door. I would probably bring waitresses in from Tajikistan. I would not make them wear mini-skirts or anything, but they would be more open than local women. If you sit down, you will have to buy something. That would keep the Afghan men from gawking." He had already located pizza ovens in London, and he thought he could get all his ingredients, other than mozzarella, locally.

An interesting cast of characters continued to make their way through the guesthouse. I talked with Chris, who was also former military, and was working on a documentary tracing the story of a Pakistani Brit who has been trying to get his brother out of jail in Afghanistan. Apparently, the brother had been in and out of trouble and had developed a drug problem while living in England. He had gone to Pakistan hoping to quit his habit, and eventually he had fallen in with the Taliban. He went to the front lines in a battle between the Taliban and the Northern Alliance in 1998. After only six days of fighting with the Taliban, most of the men in his unit were killed. The Northern Alliance captured and jailed him. He was imprisoned for three years, with most of his time spent in hard labor, the only benefit being that he did manage to kick his drug habit. His brother appeared to be on the verge of finally getting him released from jail after the minister of defense had intervened. Chris was wrapping up the documentary, for which Peter had served as a cameraman. His producers were eager to rush the feature to release because of the intense interest in all things related to the Taliban and terrorism.

The next morning we returned to the peacekeeping headquarters where the Italians were again standing post. We stood waiting in the cold for thirty minutes. I killed a few minutes talking with a British reservist who had been called up to serve in Afghanistan just ten days before. He normally worked as a graphic designer in London. His assignment in Afghanistan was to design propaganda for a psychological warfare unit. He was proud to be part of the effort in Afghanistan, which he thought was much more important than the work he had been doing in London. It was good to see such enthusiasm. I wondered how his experience on the ground would shape him.

We met with a British lieutenant colonel in a small mess tent on the base with a packed dirt floor. The colonel was brisk and no-nonsense, and he offered us a quick, but thorough, political, and security briefing. He was in charge of intelligence at the headquarters, and he projected a reassuring sense of seasoned military efficiency. Like many of the people with whom we spoke, the colonel was adamant that the peacekeeping force needed to be significantly expanded. It would take more troops to genuinely exert control over the unruly provinces and counter the influence of well-entrenched local warlords. He argued that without a stronger peacekeeping force, trouble-makers from both Afghanistan and neighboring countries would quickly reemerge. There were already signs that Iran was aggressively inserting it-self into Afghan politics. Stories abounded about the Iranians doling out money to Afghan ministries and local warlords. Some feared that the Iranian overtures in Afghanistan would prompt Pakistan—another longtime med-dler in this country—to step up its own covert activities. The colonel felt the Iranian threat was overestimated, but he did feel that unless Western governments moved quickly, Iran would fill the vacuum.

The threat of continued proxy wars was on our minds as we visited the Foreign Ministry. Set within a cluster of government buildings, the ministry was busier than the other official offices we visited. Most of the staff were wearing business suits, and there were files folders on many of the desks. Afghanistan's urbane Foreign Minister Abdullah Abdullah had become a media darling, and his large entourage milled about in the hallway. Minister Abdullah, an excellent English speaker, was quite good at understanding what Western audiences wanted to hear about democracy and the respect for human rights.

We met with a different senior official in the foreign ministry; an older diplomat with an aristocratic bearing. He smiled and apologized for the lack of heat in the building. The diplomat was a loyalist to the former Afghan king, and he had worked with the monarch during his long exile in Rome. When we asked about the role of foreign countries, particularly Pakistan and Iran in his country, he responded with an excessively diplomatic explanation: "Afghanistan's neighbors want peace and will stop meddling in Kabul's internal affairs." However, he soon dropped the pretense, and complained about the adventurism from Tehran and Islamabad. The Afghan diplomat wanted more U.S. troops on the ground, and he felt this presence was crucial not only to deal with local militias but also to discourage other countries from becoming involved in Afghanistan's internal affairs.

The diplomat, having only recently returned to Afghanistan, was living at the local Intercontinental Hotel. While the Intercontinental usually evoked images of posh living, that was not the case in Kabul. The Intercontinental was wildly overpriced, and lacked both heat and hot water on most days. It was also striking that some of Afghanistan's senior diplomats had been out of the country so long that staying at a run-down hotel was their best lodging option. As we walked out, I wondered if this dignified man would be able to wind down his years with a sense of optimism or be greeted by another wave of bitter disappointment and treachery.

We stopped by the UN offices, and met with a European who was help-ing to organize the *Loya Jirga*—a grand council that would decide on Afghanistan's future government. Thin and neat, Jorgen carefully smoked a cigarette he had rolled himself as he ushered us into his office. He was an old Afghan hand, and unlike most on the UN team, Jorgen knew the intracacies of Afghanistan well. There were lines of fatigue and frustration stenciled around his eyes. He was doing much of the heavy lifting in a very difficult political process, and trying to help the Afghans forge a consensus government on a short timetable was a gargantuan task. His knowledge of Afghanistan was deep, and he understood the myriad fault lines that ran between regions, commanders, and ethnic groups. Like everyone we talked to, Jorgen wanted a more robust peacekeeping force more widely deployed around the countryside. As it was, the peacekeepers largely stuck to Kabul, giving the warlords a great deal of latitude everywhere else.

Jorgen was working very hard, but he feared that the situation was sliding off the tracks, and the slow moving UN bureaucracy exasperated him. He wanted to be able to deploy field staff and monitors in the provinces to work with local religious and political leaders to facilitate the *Loya Jirga* process. It was a sound idea. However, UN headquarters in New York took months to approve any candidate—even though the *Loya Jirga* was to be held just four months later. The warring parties continued to view the UN the same way students approached a substitute teacher: everybody could get away with everything. UN security officials had also forbidden Jorgen from walking to work, a decision that was maddening for a man who navigated Afghanistan safely for years. In general, Jorgen felt that the UN's decision to leave a "light footprint" in Afghanistan was exactly the opposite approach they should take in a country where almost all government institutions were in shambles.

On a personal level, I wanted Jorgen to succeed. I wanted him to overcome the petty bureaucracy, crazed warlords, and disinterested superiors to help the people who need it. Given modest resources and the right people, a guy like Jorgen could probably get the job done. Yet, even though there was stirring rhetoric about freedom and liberation in Washington, New York, and London, nobody cared quite enough to give him the tools he needed to succeed. As we left, the afternoon sun slanted through the window and sharply illuminated the thick curls of cigarette smoke around Jorgen's head. The compound below his office was filled with freshly painted white UN vehicles. Jorgen turned back to his word processor and the countless battles of stubborn bureaucracy.

BUZKASHI

There were many hopeful signs in Kabul, and on every morning other than Fridays, I woke up to the sounds of construction. People were painting houses and storefronts. There were more goods in the market. People were replacing broken glass. The signs of confidence were distinct, and just as animals sensed a change in weather, humans could detect the shifting winds of violence. While optimism alone was not enough to bring peace, its absence could quickly lead back to war. For example, at the Ministry of Defense, long lines of people waited at the front gate, and all were hoping for jobs. Those soldiers that had not been on the front lines had not been paid in months. Many of the soldiers we spoke with were willing to leave the military if they could find employment, but most had limited skills.

The sudden inflow of foreign aid, peacekeepers, and journalists grossly warped the local economy. The word around town was that CNN was paying $10,000 a month in rent for the house they were using as an office.

This was in a country where the per capita income was still around $200 a year. The distortions rippled through the economy. We paid Hewad $150 a day for serving as our fixer—not bad money even in the West. (It was half of what he charged Dianne Sawyer.) We paid $50 a day for our driver and full-time use of his vehicle, the same amount we paid for our room in the guesthouse; a relative bargain by comparison. Local policemen and assorted gunmen were available for $35 a day to serve as armed guards. Everything was paid in cash; crisp U.S. twenties and hundreds, and every westerner was traveling with a small fortune of hard currency.

Cold, hard cash was the new language of Afghanistan. At the UN flight office we booked passage out of the country. We had the ill fortune to get in line behind a pair of Chinese diplomats buying tickets for a large official delegation from Beijing. The clerk painstakingly went through the fifteen forms the Chinese had filled out, stamping each in quadruplicate. One of the Chinese diplomats pulled out a stack of $100 U.S. bills, the currency of choice, and counted out $9,000. The Afghans had to be stunned by the sums of money foreigners had at their disposal, and it was small wonder that local perspectives were quickly getting warped. The Afghans must have thought that everyone in the West normally carried thousands of dollars in their pocket.

War-torn countries were often incredibly expensive, and people would charge whatever they thought they could get away with in an environment where there were not many choices. Some of the worst hotel rooms I have ever stayed in have also been the most expensive. With no real economy in place, profiteering made sense—particularly when many westerners did not even try to bargain. Unfortunately, this also meant that much of the money that flowed into countries in conflict went to people that already had resources—such as hotel owners and people who could organize security guards and transport—leaving much less for the people who actually needed support. There was also a small elite of well-trained and educated locals who easily found well-paying jobs working for international aid groups. This also meant that some of the most talented locals were reluctant to take government jobs when there skills were desperately needed because they did not want to take a pay cut. A local driver for the UN was often better paid than a government lawyer or civil servant.

The sea of loose money had created a climate of unreality. As long as Afghanistan was the flavor of the month, Afghans could name their own price for goods and services. However, it would only be a matter of time until the money dried up: CNN would head for the next war, donors would get tired of footing expensive bills, and the country would still be very, very poor.

We stopped back by the Foreign Ministry to get an exit visa—Afghanistan being one of the rare countries where you need official authorization to leave. Hewad assured us getting the exit visa would not be much of a problem, because the people in the office were "all from my home town." Hewad drafted a letter requesting permission for me to leave the country. Several officials inspected the document and one of the economic officers signed the letter, which was then taken to another office to be rubber stamped. We walked outside to another building, sat in another waiting room and got another signature on the document. While Hewad got expedited treatment in every office, the process was time-consuming. We then drove to the passport affairs office, where the policeman in charge greeted Hewad warmly. He too signed the letter. We then went to a downstairs office, but the man who could actually stamp my passport with an exit visa was at lunch. We left and then came back. A few foreigners—three Germans and a Japanese man—were sitting in the office. All of these people had fixers as well. Hewad was again able to leap to the front of the queue, and the man stamped my passport in short order. Hewad took my passport back upstairs for initialing by the passport chief. It had taken us visits to seven different offices to get a legitimate stamp in my passport *allowing me to leave* Afghanistan. Hewad smiled, "Seven offices, no bribes; it is good."

We piled in the small taxi and drove back out to the headquarters of the peacekeeping force. At the brigade headquarters, we met with a British intelligence officer in charge of liaison work with the Kabul police. The captain was understated but sharp, and he spent most of his waking hours dealing with local police issues—everything from people getting their cars stolen to trying to figure out how police could deal with warlords. He rattled off crime statistics from across the Kabul, and I noticed that he had a deep windburn, not the mark of someone who spent most of their time behind a desk. His main point was simple: the police would not function properly until they felt empowered to take on all the other factions running around with guns. As it stood, the police were just another militia, and a rather poorly equipped one at that.

By Friday morning, several inches of snow covered Kabul, a welcome development given Afghanistan's long drought. The city was quiet because it was Friday, and the snowfall made everything appear peaceful as the city slowly went about its routine. A young man hung loaves of *naan* outside of his store. A kabob vendor smokily fanned the first coals of his fire. On Chicken Street, Kabul's closest approximation to a tourist trap, carpet salesmen unshuttered their doors. Other than a few greetings, no one paid me much mind. Part small town, part wild west, Kabul made Islamabad seem impossibly staid in comparison.

We again lunched at the Herat café. Hewad made the rounds of the dining room with a relish worthy of a local political candidate. Hewad admitted that since he started working as an anchorman more people recognized him around town. It also made his work as a fixer easier since more government offices were willing to set up meetings. Over kabobs, Bob and Hewad traded horror stories from the early 1990s about one of the most feared militia leaders, Gulbuddin Hekmatyar. "If he was smiling when he talked to you, you knew you were in trouble," said Hewad shaking his head. Hewad recounted that a friend of his who was a fellow reporter had written a story in 1992 about a battle that Hekmatyar's militia had lost. Hekmatyar was worried that the news story would make it more difficult for him to recruit more fighters, so he had the journalist dragged from his vehicle and summarily executed. Hekmatyar, who was in exile in Iran, had been making noises about the "U.S. occupation" and his desire to return to Afghanistan, a prospect that filled most Afghans with dread. There was almost no popular support for a militia leader like Hekmatyar, and a real sense of fatigue and disgust with the old guard military, but there were still forces willing to bankroll him as means to create general havoc.

It was a Friday, the Islamic weekend, so there was not much we could do in the way of official meetings. Hewad informed us that there was going to be a *buzkashi* match during the day. *Buzkashi* was a traditional Afghan sport, consisting of two teams mounted on horseback dragging a goat or calf carcass around a field in an odd mix of polo and rugby. I had seen similar games in northern Pakistan, although they were smaller affairs. We agreed it was worth going to see the match.

A large crowd turned out to sit in the cement open-air stands and observe the festivities. About twenty horses and riders milled about, and a flag was stuck in the ground at both ends of the field. The riders wore an interesting mix of traditional garb and modern outdoor gear. The horses looked strong, but some had seen better days. Hewad did his best to explain the rules: basically you tried to drag the goat carcass a full length of the field without someone snatching it from your grasp. The niceties of strategy and scoring eluded me. The proceedings were delayed as the crowd waited for several government VIPs to be seated. Hewad and I joked that some things were the same the world over.

A light coating of snow blanketed the field, and a backdrop of mountains stretched high in every direction. General Mohammed Fahim, the head of the Afghan army and the new Minister of Defense, turned out to be the VIP for which the crowd was waiting. He took a seat near the action and it was only fitting; one of the teams of horsemen was from his home area of the Panjshir Valley. The area had long been a Northern Alliance stronghold, and Fahim and several other key Tajik ministers were from the Panjshir.

Small boys with cigarettes and sweets hawked their wares, and even a few girls attended. Several guards in mismatched uniforms stood post, happy to have gained free admission. The action got under way in a scuffle of men and horses, with the riders pushing to position themselves to grab the carcass off the ground. Steam exploded out of the nostrils of the horses, the riders whipped their steeds, and the men and horses met in a bruising crush. Scooping a dead calf off the ground while mounted on horseback demanded great strength and remarkable riding skills. A few riders were knocked from their saddles and fell roughly to the ground.

The knot of men and horses repeatedly threatened to trample into the concrete stands, sending spectators scurrying for cover. Two riders broke out of the pack. The horseman with a better grip on the carcass tried to tuck it under his leg to make riding easier. The competing horsemen raced across the pitch trying to pull the calf from each other's grasp. The men rode in precarious positions, with one leg draped across the saddle and their bodies dangling near the frozen ground. Holding their whips in their teeth, carcass in hand, they played to the cheers of the crowd. As the riders thundered across the snowy turf, a Chinook helicopter swooped low overhead as it headed to an adjacent military base in a bizarre juxtaposition of ancient and modern. The Afghans stared intently skyward, not with awe, but with the keen eye of men who knew their military hardware.

The sight of the helicopter sparked Hewad to share a thought. For the most part, he had steered clear of discussing politics, although he had some well-formed opinions. "When you go back to Washington and when you talk to people in power, you tell them that the best thing the world can do right now is to have an American B-52 fly overhead once a day. It doesn't need to drop anything; everyone just needs to know that the Americans are still here and paying attention."

Many Afghans shared the sentiment. People felt that only the United States could provide the security to keep the country from sliding back toward civil war, and we were repeatedly told that the only logic that many Afghans would respect was that of superior force. Given such a perspective, it was understandable that the United States had gotten a respectful, if not always warm, reception. Everyone was surprised by the speed of the U.S. military victory and the limited casualties they had suffered. Most Afghans who were not involved in the military simply wanted the Americans to be strong enough that they could return to normal life, and thought an expanded peacekeeping force was essential to creating the political space for them to work out their differences. In contrast, many of the militia leaders thought they would not really have to change their ways as long as they swore loyalty to the new boss in town. The warlords seemed convinced they could run out the clock, and hold their positions until the United States became distracted elsewhere. It was a mixed blessing for the United States. As a dominant military power, it could exert its authority across much of Afghanistan if it was willing to do so. By the same token, any sign of weakness or disinterest by Washington would mean that others would quickly rush in to fill the void.

BROKEN CLOCKS

We met with a senior diplomat at the U.S. embassy. The secretary, still on detail from Paris, came down to escort us from the gate. Despite the recent flurry of activity at the embassy, much of the building was unchanged from the late 1980s. Although most U.S. embassies look like nothing has changed in more than a decade, this was one of the rare cases where it was true.

Although there were eighty U.S. marines living in the embassy compound, and several handfuls of technicians working to restore communications, there was a very small diplomatic presence in Afghanistan. The imbalance between resources for U.S. military and U.S. diplomacy felt ill-advised. The American diplomat was blunt about the situation facing Afghans, "I don't know how some of these people get out of bed in the morning given the problems they are facing." Even the currency was an issue. Several powerful warlords and politicians were hoarding large caches of local banknotes they printed for their own purposes—a charge that had also been leveled at a Russian printing house that formerly held the contract to manufacture the currency. The banking system was a total mess and until several weeks before, the head of Afghan's banking system, "had been a branch manager of a Bank of America in McLean, Virginia."

I was impressed that the American diplomat did not shy from the hard questions. "Expand the peacekeeping force? That is what I hear from every single person I talk to. I cannot tell you how many times we have repeated that back to Washington. I hope they do expand the troop levels. I am not sure they will." The diplomat was frustrated with his superiors in Washington. The administration wanted to avoid anything that looked like nation building despite the fact that was what Afghanistan needed more than anything else. Just a short time before, the White House press secretary had almost proudly dismissed the request for more U.S. troops in Afghanistan: "The President continues to believe the purpose of the military is to be used to fight and win wars, and not to engage in peacekeeping of that nature."

None of us realized until later that a good part of the Bush administration's reluctance to expand the peacekeeping force in Afghanistan was a direct result of its desire to move forward with planning the invasion of Iraq. It was a very short period after Afghanistan's toppling that the U.S. military began diverting some of its most important assets away from Afghanistan and toward the Persian Gulf.

The travel of U.S. diplomats in Afghanistan was tightly restricted, and most of the embassy's staff were not permitted to leave the embassy compound. It made for an odd mix: shadowy teams of U.S. Special Forces slipped through the south of Afghanistan while the diplomats were essentially confined to quarters. In Afghanistan, the United States relied on the military to direct reconstruction programs to a remarkable degree. The military established small teams of U.S. soldiers, accompanied by an aid expert, to implement rebuilding projects in rural areas.

These reconstruction teams were fast and flexible and did generate a measure of goodwill for the military. In many ways, they built on the lessons learned through transition programs, such as the one on which I had worked in Sri Lanka. In addition, they provided security as much as they were a means to aid rebuilding.

However, this approach was not without serious pitfalls. First and foremost, the teams effectively obliterated any distinction between humanitarian organizations and the military. For Afghans at the village level, aid groups and the U.S. military were all seen as part of an occupying force, and many relief workers rightfully complained that this made them legitimate targets for the Taliban and others. Indeed, scores of aid workers would be killed in Afghanistan in the years that followed. Because the reconstruction teams were led by the military, it also meant that they were far better at dealing with security issues than they were at relief or development. The U.S. military does many things brilliantly, but humanitarian work has never been its forte, and the army was probably better left to what it did best. The need to have aid workers accompanied by military teams also spoke of the larger problem: there was not enough security on the ground for people to go about their normal business.

It was hard to escape the feeling—whether it was among U.S. diplomats, UN officials, military officers, or others—that there were many good, competent people trying to help drag Afghanistan forward but who were trapped within bureaucracies that refused to do the right thing. It made Afghanistan feel like a Shakespearean tragedy in the making.

While at the embassy, we also met with a senior AID official, who gave us a tour of the grounds. The guy wore a bright red sweater that would have fit in at any office Christmas party. He spoke in a loud and bracing manner that was incomparably American, but he was also very well regarded professionally. Boxes of prepackaged military rations were stacked in the embassy hallway. Offices had been converted to sleeping quarters and narrow cots crowded the walls. The AID official showed off the ramshackle living conditions with an almost boyish enthusiasm. He liked a difficult mission.

He also took us down to the embassy's cafeteria, or the "time capsule," as he called it. The small lunch counter and kitchen had literally not been touched since the day the embassy staff evacuated twelve years before. Empty plates, thick with dust, graced the tables. A sign still advertised 60-cent hamburgers, a daily special that had lasted more than a decade. Badly yellowed newspapers and magazines from the 1980s fanned out across the counter. The floor tiles had all buckled and cracked, littering the floor with loose debris. Huge black cobwebs that could have come from a horror film draped the kitchen.

Walking around the grounds, the American explained that staff morale has risen considerably now that people could occasionally take showers. As we walked out, the AID official bantered with the marines, and encouraged us to keep in touch. The happy warrior was at his post.

At the Interior Ministry, we met with a senior official who was one of the most powerful Tajiks in the Northern Alliance. The Interior Ministry had control over the national police and internal security, a key plum in the new government. We were ushered into a waiting room filled with a scruffy collection of fighters from the Panshjir Valley also awaiting a meeting. The men were a rough lot, and they were the people that had been running parts of the country over the past decade as their own militia fiefdoms.

Oddly, another westerner in the waiting room went out of his way to lavish praise on one of the guys sitting next to Bob and I, "You are the real *mujahideen;* the *mujahideen* who stopped the Soviets." This westerner, like many outsiders, still had a romantic view of the *mujahideen* as the plucky fighters who felled the Soviet giant. The attitude was also common among some journalists who put fighters like Masoud on an almost saintly pedestal. It was telling that few locals shared this view. It was hard to maintain romantic illusions about the *mujahideen* when you had to live with them. After the guerillas left the room, laughter convulsed Hewad. "The man that he called the 'real' *mujahideen* is known by everyone as the biggest crook in Afghanistan—in all of Afghanistan."

Well dressed and slick, the interior ministry official struck me as someone with higher political aspirations. Sophisticated enough to please Western diplomats, but more than willing to engage in the hardball practices needed to get ahead in Afghanistan, he was a formidable force. The official did not speak to us in English, but from time to time he carefully corrected Hewad's translation. It was a sign that he was in control. Much of the discussion was dedicated to figuring out how to get the police up and running, and addressing international concerns about accountability of aid dollars.

The official said all the things he knew we wanted to hear about accountability, ethnic relations, and the need for reform. He was shrewd. Afghanistan was entering a very different phase, where being a successful commander in the field was no longer enough. Successful politicians would have to be both ruthless and presentable. For example, President Hamid Karzai certainly was presentable to the West, but it remained to be seen if he was tough enough at home.

Right around the time we prepared to leave Afghanistan, a series of incidents made clear that reshaping Afghanistan would be a long slog. The tourism minister was beaten to death at the Kabul airport as pilgrims awaited flights for Saudi Arabia to make the *hajj*. President Karzai was quick to label the killing an assassination. At a local soccer match, police violently clashed with fans angered at the lack of available tickets. In Kabul, British peacekeepers came under fire at their checkpoint from unknown assailants. No single event was a sign that the place was falling apart, but all made clear that Afghanistan's violence simmered barely below the surface.

Before flying back to Pakistan for further research, we said our goodbyes and paid Hewad, our driver, the guesthouse, and the cook. At the airport, the local customs officials were doing a thriving business in shaking down travelers that had bought carpets and other local souvenirs. Maybe it was a sign of life returning to normal.

On the UN flight, the two South African women flight attendants received a very warm welcome. The plane was filled with men who had been working in Afghanistan and only saw women in *burkhas*. The men were all perfect gentlemen, but I don't think I had ever seen an entire flight behave as if they were smitten before.

Pakistan felt very different upon return, mainly in comparison with Afghanistan. The airport seemed newer, brighter, and more modern. The laughter of women and little girls in the parking lot felt easy and infectious. The picture of the woman on the Lipton Tea billboard did not have her face covered with a veil. It was the first time that Islamabad felt like an island of women's rights. I greatly appreciated a long hot shower that evening.

Many of our meetings in Pakistan were held in private houses in Islamabad's sprawling suburbs, and although most of the meetings were with retired generals, party members, and government officials, almost every home was beyond what these people should have been able to afford on an official salary. While both the political parties and the military spent a lot of time pointing fingers and arguing about who was more corrupt, it was clear that everyone in power had a hand in the till.

We met with representatives from the major political parties. All were urbane, well spoken, and sharply critical of the military government. All offered compelling analyses of what had gone wrong in Pakistan, yet no one admitted even the slightest degree of culpability. All of the party officials lambasted the new Washington consensus that General Musharraf was "a courageous man" taking on the terrorists. As one noted, "Is this the same courageous man who said that we needed to work with the Taliban after September 11? Courageous? Please." They had a point. Even one of the retired generals we spoke with expressed fears that the United States had gone too far in backing a military government, "For god's sake, please don't give us any more fighter planes."

The stories on missing *Wall Street Journal* reporter Daniel Pearl had largely disappeared from the local media, although the case still drew international attention. A short time later, video of his execution, by beheading, appeared on the Internet. While the government claimed to have apprehended those behind the crime, substantial unanswered questions remained. It was difficult to think that the government was not lying.

We endured a very unpleasant meeting with an urbane, but noxious, Pakistani foreign ministry Afghan expert. He cheerfully lied to us, and grew upset when we suggested that Pakistan's direct military and intelligence assistance had been key to many of the Taliban's early military successes. "You show me the proof, not one Pakistani prisoner was captured by the Northern Alliance. Not one Pakistani soldier was involved with the Taliban. Maybe some boys who are studying religion at the *madrasses* got involved, but that is it." His comments were all the more irritating because the Pakistani military officials we met with openly admitted the scope of their earlier activities in Afghanistan.

General Musharraf was in Washington as we concluded our trip. Sitting in the Islamabad Marriott I watched a joint press conference between President

Bush and General Musharraf. President Bush kept coming back to a common theme: General Musharraf shared America's values; President Bush thought General Musharraf was a good man with a good heart. On television, the two presidents were full of bonhomie as the praise for Pakistan's latest military dictator came on uncomfortably thick. I could not help but wonder what General Musharraf would do with the Taliban in his basement.

CHAPTER 6

The Fourth Ostrich—Liberia

When a colleague and I and traveled to Liberia for Crisis Group in June and July of 2002, that country's conflict was a forgotten misery far from the headlines or any international attention. But to those involved in Liberia's civil war, the stakes were high and intensely personal. Unfortunately, it did not take long before we became part of the story.

THE RIGHT HAND MAN

Touching down in Monrovia, the signs of Liberia's ongoing civil war were not immediately apparent, but the sense of decay was pervasive. Creeping mold stained many of the buildings shades of black, and the entire city looked like it was in slow motion collapse. Liberia had once had its turn as the next big thing, but it had slipped very far from international attention. With the focus on Islamic extremism, Afghanistan, and the gathering storm over Iraq, few cared about another seemingly intractable African conflict.

President Charles Taylor, one of Africa's most ruthless and colorful warlords, had dominated Liberian politics for years. Despite widespread condemnation and even UN sanctions, he ruled the country like a feudal lord, relentlessly exploiting Liberia's resources, terrorizing citizens with fearsome militias, and eliminating all those who stood in his way. The story of his ascension to power read like fiction: a jail break in Massachusetts, rumors of CIA involvement, revolutionary training in the desert of Libya, and a protracted civil war launched on Christmas day. With Liberia's leaders increasingly viewed as pariahs, Western foreign aid dollars had dried up. The economy had collapsed back to a barter system. Only a few war profiteers close to Taylor grew rich from black market trade in diamonds, timber,

Liberia

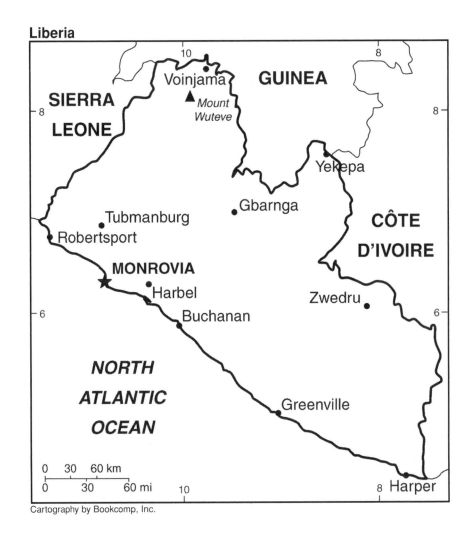

Cartography by Bookcomp, Inc.

and guns. Liberians were left fighting for smaller and smaller scraps, and an insurgency in the countryside was gaining tempo.

I was conducting an assessment of the political and security situation with my colleague, Comfort, who ran our office in neighboring Sierra Leone—a country trying to emerge from its own civil war. Comfort was an exceptionally smart and talented West Africa expert. We were staying at the Mamba Point Hotel in Monrovia. The hotel was a local legend, as was its sister establishment in Sierra Leone. Both hotels had stayed open even during block-to-block fighting in the respective capitals. The hotel's owner, a short, stout Lebanese man with a shaved head and thick mustache, grumbled that guests only occupied five of the hotels forty-five rooms. The fact that he was even then ready to keep the hotel open implied a willingness to grease the right government palms.

The hotel was a stone's throw from both the beach and the American embassy compound. I could see the U.S. flag fluttering behind the embassy's high walls. The beach was indescribably filthy. It was the same spot where Liberian security forces conducted summary executions during the 1990s, leaving dead bodies to tumble in the surf.

How had Liberia come to such horrors? The history of the place was singular, and it was one of the few countries in Africa deeply shaped from its onset by America. Indeed, Liberia sprang from both the best and worst of American intentions during the early 1800s. Prominent Americans including Henry Clay, Daniel Webster, and James Monroe formed the "American Colonization Society" in 1816. The group coalesced around the idea of transporting freed black slaves back to Africa from the United States. Some of the American Colonization Society's founders were idealists who felt that freed blacks would fare better in Africa than in a deeply prejudiced America. Others had more insidious motivations, and many southerners in the group felt that repatriating freed blacks back to Africa was the best way to keep them from inciting those who were still slaves.

Whatever its merit, the plan moved forward in fits and starts. Negotiating at gunpoint with local chiefs in West Africa, agents purchased small tracts of land in what later became Liberia and Sierra Leone. By 1820, the first ships brought settlers back to the shores of Africa. Although yellow fever and tribal assaults devastated these resettlers, they clung to survival in their new home—which they rather loftily dubbed Christopolis. Some 11,000 freed blacks ultimately returned to what is now Liberia, whose capital was renamed Monrovia—in honor of U.S. President James Monroe. Liberia achieved independence by 1847.

The dream of a society where Liberians could "rise to be a people" was subverted in ways that the American Colonization Society never imagined. The freed slaves (or Americo-Liberians as their descendents are known) soon evolved into a privileged, almost colonial, class that gave indigenous

Liberians no say in national affairs. Propped up by revenue from a long-term lease to the Firestone Company for a massive rubber plantation, and aided by their "special relationship" with the United States, the political party of the Americo-Liberians, the True Whigs, ruled Liberia for more than a century.

The Americo-Liberians created a curiously stylized version of American life in Africa. English speaking men with names like Taylor, Johnson, and Roosevelt built Freemason halls and Christian churches. They wore topcoats and tails for official ceremonies. The Liberian flag, with its lone white star in a field of red and blue, resembled the state flag of Texas.

Over time, Americo-Liberians also blended their ways with native customs. Liberia's elite began to consult with *zoes* or shamans, and practiced periodic animal sacrifices. Reports of ritual cannibalism were too widespread to dismiss as myth. Superstition abounded in Liberia, and militia fighters often wore face paint, wigs, and even women's clothes into battle, believing that a disguise would protect them from harm and free their spirits from culpability for their crimes.

When Master Sergeant Samuel Doe seized power in a bloody coup in 1980, he became Liberia's first indigenous president. In one of his inaugural acts, he had a drunken firing squad execute the presidential cabinet on a Monrovia beach. While President Doe proved to be as corrupt and power hungry as any of Liberia's other presidents, fate shone upon him for a time. Liberia was one of America's most important cold war outposts in Africa, and American largesse flowed into the country. Everyone knew Doe was a despot of the worst sort, but he was Washington's despot.

By 1989, and with the logic of the cold war fading, Charles Taylor entered the scene. By way of history, Taylor was an Americo-Liberian who had previously served in the Doe government, before being accused of embezzling $1 million from the Liberian General Services Administration and fleeing to America. Taylor studied in Massachusetts at Bentley College. He was subsequently arrested and jailed in the Plymouth County House of Corrections. After fifteen months in jail he escaped, sawing through the bars of his cell window and climbing out on a knotted sheet. (Other conspiracy theories maintain that the CIA freed Taylor as part of a plot to overthrow Doe's government.) Taylor then somehow made it to Libya where he trained at Libyan president Moammar Qaddafi's "World Revolutionary Headquarters"—an academy for aspiring international insurgents and would-be terrorists. After a bout of nasty bloodletting between Taylor and other Liberian rivals hoping to unseat Doe, Charles Taylor launched a guerilla war into Liberia on Christmas day 1989.

The civil war was protracted and lethal. Monrovia became a key front, casting Liberia into chaos for much of the 1990s. President Samuel Doe met a grisly end. A rebel commander was filmed torturing Doe in the Executive Mansion, cutting off one of his ears and proudly eating it. Videos of Doe's macabre last moments were still for sale in markets in Monrovia when I was in the country. Nigeria inserted a peacekeeping force in Liberia, but it did little to abate the fighting. Eventually, the Nigerians became fed up with trying to keep the nonexistent peace, and brokered a deal with Taylor: the peacekeeping force would depart if elections were held. With Taylor having the strongest military force, the results of the election were a foregone conclusion. A local campaign slogan explaining why people were willing to back Taylor during the presidential election was devastatingly insightful, "He killed my ma. He killed my pa. I think I'll vote for him." Many war-weary Liberians threw their support behind Taylor because they believed that if lost he would plunge the country back into civil war. Taylor had successfully fought his way into the presidency of the small resource-rich West African state.

Hopes that Liberia would return to normalcy under President Taylor were short-lived. After a few token gestures of reconciliation, Taylor cemented his control over the security services while stirring up trouble across the region. Taylor funneled guns, money, and fighters to Revolutionary United Front (RUF) rebels in neighboring Sierra Leone, driving that country into a whirlpool of carnage. RUF fighters were infamous for amputating the arms of anyone—man, woman, or child—who they saw as sympathetic to the government. Despite repeated denials from Taylor, it was clear that he had a heavy hand in Sierra Leone's war. The UN slapped sanctions and an arms embargo on the Taylor government. But with substantial diamond and timber revenues, Taylor proved difficult to shake from power. His rivals had steadily disappeared or were killed; many fled the country. Liberia slowly imploded. A new rebel group, the Liberians United for Reconciliation and Democracy, or LURD, sprung up and began to fight against Taylor in the countryside.

One of our first meetings was with Cyril Allen. Allen was a long-time Taylor confidante and, until just before our arrival, Chairman of Taylor's National Patriotic Party. He was widely rumored to be one of Taylor's key money men, but there had been something of a falling out between the two. Allen had raised accusations of corruption against some in the government, and subsequently offered to step down as party chair. The charges of corruption were bizarre because everyone knew the government was completely corrupt, from Taylor on down. Taylor, Allen, and those who ran the country systematically stole whatever they could find. This suggested that the reports had more to do with political maneuvering than anything else, and Allen appeared to be complaining that the wrong people were skimming too much off the top. He was also trying to protect himself from charges of the same. The spat sparked a great deal of speculation in Monrovia, and it was a place where political disputes often proved fatal.

Driving in a taxi through the industrial park where we were to meet Allen, every building we saw was abandoned and in an advanced state of decrepitude. Rusted steel beams were askew at odd angles, and the warehouses and factories had all been looted. The area was empty save for a knot of militia men wearing t-shirts who guarded the entrance to the industrial park. The place was ominous. Comfort and I were quiet. Allen's factory—which produced plastic wares such as buckets, wash pails, plates, and cups—was the lone oasis among the ruins. The building was clean, freshly painted, and operating with a full staff.

Allen spoke with the easy, rapid-fire ebullience of a veteran politician and a seasoned con man. His office was deeply air-conditioned, and it was a welcome respite from the thick humidity outside. Allen spoke animatedly. He laughed and churned the air with his hands. When trying to make a point with extra sincerity, he would place his palms flat on the desktop. It was an almost religious gesture. Allen rarely broke eye contact. It was disconcerting.

An attractive young Thai woman strolled into the office to borrow one of Allen's several cell phones. "Visiting for the week," smiled Allen. His mistress was bored and petulant. Like others in the Liberia's small ruling elite, Allen proudly maintained his multiple liaisons in public view.

Allen spoke as if he and Taylor were still fast friends. When we asked if he was concerned that most government militias had not been paid for six months, he insisted, "These boys, our fighters, are so loyal to President Charles Taylor that they do not mind not being paid. They would risk their lives for him even for nothing. That is how much they love the president." Allen was adamant that reports of new fighting within Liberia between the government and the shadowy LURD insurgents were greatly exaggerated, "Liberia is the safest country in West Africa."

Allen also insisted that the United Nations had been unfair in imposing sanctions that included an arms embargo and a ban on travel by senior government officials. "President Taylor's only fault is his generosity and closeness to the people. He doesn't have a single international bank account." Across Monrovia, the government had erected large billboards depicting cartoon elephants (the United States and Great Britain) cruelly crushing ants (the Liberian people). Allen also weaved religious themes into his soliloquies and noted with pride, "I do not drink. I do not smoke. I do not do drugs. I have never been drunk a moment in my life. I am a good Christian. President Taylor is a good Christian. I am filled only with my faith in God." Behind Allen's desk, a large portrait of Jesus Christ hung next to an equally large framed picture of Allen warmly shaking hands with Libyan President Moammar Qaddafi.

Allen was a survivor. He had played an important role in three successive governments in Liberia; a remarkable achievement given that Taylor's two predecessors were both slain in office. Local lore has it that Taylor's immediate predecessor, President Samuel Doe, once paid Allen $100,000 to fix the results of a presidential election. When Doe allegedly learned that Allen had pocketed $60,000 of the funds, he flew into a rage and threatened

Allen with castration—a warning that pushed Allen into joining Taylor's nascent rebel movement.

Allen was nattily attired, comfortable but professional in slacks and an expensive powder blue European button-down shirt. In a casual show of status, a handless attachment for his cell phone was clipped near the collar. His office was his nerve center. It did not take long before he jabbed at one of the buzzers below his desktop to summon assistance. Allen introduced us to his son, who managed the factory in which we were sitting. Allen made embarrassingly clear that he was still the boss. Allen even showed us payroll records to underscore his generosity. He wanted us to believe that he was just a plucky entrepreneur doing his best during tough times. It was bullshit, but he mixed fact, rumor, and half-truth in a fascinating web.

As a veteran of the scene, Allen has a thorough scorecard on Taylor's often-fractured political opposition. He happily recited the laundry list of their flaws. He also made clear that President Taylor would go to great lengths to retain power, "President Taylor will totally destroy Monrovia before he would ever let the LURD take control." Coming from Allen, who once advocated using chemical weapons on the rebels, the threat was not to be taken lightly.

Toward the end of our conversation, Allen leaned forward in his chair, his still eyes locked upon mine. Any trace of a grin disappeared from his face. "My friend; my brother," he told me. "You could go to the presidential palace. Right now, you could go to the presidential palace. You could kill President Charles Taylor. My brother, you could stand there and cut Taylor's heart out of his dead body. You could eat his heart right there on the spot. You could do this my brother. But let me tell you: you would be a dead man. The president's boys would kill you within seconds. Seconds. You would be a dead man."

Allen delivered his comments earnestly and with shimmering menace. Cyril Allen was not speaking metaphorically. He spoke as if he was certain that I had come to Liberia to kill Taylor, carve out his heart, and seize the presidential palace. Many Liberians still believed that eating the internal organs of a fallen foe allowed the capture of that warrior's strength. There were many Liberians who would happily eat Taylor's heart.

Allen's mood quickly lightened as we concluded our conversation. He once again flashed his Cheshire cat smile, "My brother, my sister, come see me any time." As we left the factory and climbed into our small taxi with its badly ripped plastic seats, we watched Allen's Thai mistress glance at her watch and wait impatiently for Cyril in his brand new SUV. Welcome to Monrovia.

WAITING FOR THE DELUGE

In the evening, Comfort and I met with Roosevelt, a Liberian who was active in what was left of the local human rights community. His work made him deeply unpopular with the government. Roosevelt spoke in low tones and his gaze continually darted around the room as a caged parrot squawked loudly in one corner of the hotel's veranda. It was not paranoia. He was under government surveillance. Roosevelt and his circle of friends had been helpful in the past, arranging meetings with a broad network of people willing to discuss the security situation. A friend of Roosevelt's, Paul, who also worked on human rights issues joined us.

Roosevelt passed on several local press clippings from government-controlled newspapers that had appeared after the release of our last report on Liberia. The accounts include personal attacks on Comfort and another one of our colleagues. It maintained that Crisis Group was part of an international conspiracy bent on destroying Liberia. The articles were fabricated, and although we laughed, it was unnerving to land on the government enemies list. The government had arrested Roosevelt not long after Comfort's previous trip to Liberia, detaining him for a number of days. Consequently, Roosevelt rarely slept in the same place more than two nights in a row. The government had also arrested a prominent local newspaper editor, Hassan Bility, shortly before our arrival—although it continued to deny holding him.

Roosevelt compared the situation in Monrovia to that of an angry sea tossed by conspiracy and fear. Neither government soldiers nor the LURD rebels wore uniforms, and it was very hard to tell who was fighting who in the countryside. Liberians had taken to calling the insurgency a "shadow war." There were also persistent rumors that Taylor's own militias frequently staged fake battles as a pretext to loot towns. Further complicating matters, nobody really knew much about the LURD. The group's only stated political goal was to remove Taylor, and its leadership was underground. With the government doing its best to eliminate the last vestiges of a free press, most Liberians had no choice but to rely on gossip. Roosevelt complained that disinformation had become so rampant, "that if the government says to you, 'Good morning,' you want to check your watch to make sure what time it is."

Roosevelt was one of the few Liberian human rights activists not forced into exile or prison. He was taking incredible risks. There was nothing to stop the government from threatening his family, throwing him in prison, or simply making him disappear. There was a court system in Liberia, but verdicts were for sale to the highest bidder and Taylor rarely got a verdict of which he did not approve. Despite all that, Roosevelt was still willing to take a public stand for the often abused constitution and for the rule of law. It was remarkably courageous.

Roosevelt had a sharp, dark sense of humor, and he even smiled when accounting his own arrest. Roosevelt and Paul would do what they could to assist us during our fieldwork, and they departed with the usual Liberian salutation: a handshake followed by a casual snap of the fingers. Comfort noted that Roosevelt was more withdrawn than in the past. The government pressure was starting to take its toll. She thought he should leave the country. I had never worked anywhere where there was such a strong malicious undercurrent, and it was evident in everything from people's body language to the ruined city itself.

The people we spoke with were hard-pressed for solutions. When we asked people what to do, they trailed off in uncomfortable silence. Many saw getting rid of Taylor as the logical first step or, as one local activist described, "First you must kill Dracula." But nobody thought getting Taylor out of Liberia's Executive Mansion would be easy, and most were terrified that any attempt to remove the president by force would trigger wholesale bloodletting. Several Liberians spoke optimistically of an international peacekeeping force led by the United States coming to the country. It was hard to tell people that with the invasion of Iraq waiting in the wings, the White House cared very little about West Africa.

We stopped by the European Union offices to meet with Carlos, a longtime Liberia hand. Carlos chain smoked, and he periodically punctuated the conversation with a wildly distracting giggle. Carlos believed catastrophe awaited Liberia, and he ticked off a compelling series of reasons why. Rebel attacks were getting closer to the capital. Most government soldiers had not been paid in months. Expatriates and the Lebanese business community were clearing out their dependents. Taylor had reactivated some of his most feared militia commanders who were recruiting child soldiers. All of Monrovia was nervously awaiting the next bout of destruction.

Carlos grumbled about trying to deal with the EU bureaucracy while working in a place as chaotic as Liberia. "They are updating our evacuation plan. It is a big joke. I've been through four evacuations here in Monrovia. The evacuation plans never get used. When people start shooting, all hell breaks loose. You don't get out a file and see where you are supposed to go." Plans to use the building's parking lot as a helipad in case of an emergency particularly irritated Carlos. "You've been out there, a helicopter won't fit. It is crazy." He laughed his strange laugh as he mused about "having a helicopter crash in the middle of an evacuation." Liberia had exhausted Carlos's capacity for surprise, but not amusement. He was pleased that we brought him a bottle of whiskey. Carlos had been in Liberia too long, and the country's constant dysfunction and despair had sapped him of any optimism. I was perplexed when Carlos insisted that we golf with him over the weekend.

On the fourth of July, we met with a senior official in Liberia's Foreign Ministry. She ushered us into her comfortably appointed office. Although most of Monrovia continued to suffer without electricity or running water, her air conditioning was on full blast. Much of the discussion was formulaic.

We asked her, "Is your government violating the UN arms embargo?"

"We have a right to defend ourselves," she responded. "Rebels are entering our country with guns given to them by foreign powers. We have every right under international law, including the UN charter, to protect ourselves."

We inquired if the government would lift the state of emergency and numerous other security restrictions. "There is a war going on," she said. "After the war we can lift the state of emergency, but not before."

We noted that many opposition politicians complained that they faced government harassment and had little freedom to engage in public debate. "It is not the government's fault that President Taylor's opponents want to stay in exile," the Foreign Ministry official maintained. "How can they compete in elections if they don't come to Liberia? There is nothing stopping these people." She also mentioned Ellen Johnson Sirleaf, an opposition politician, who went into exile after a failed bid for the presidency, "Ellen came several times and was very critical of the government. Nothing happened to her. You must live among the people if you want their support."

Every answer was heavily scripted and delivered as if by rote. It was not until we asked her about her own safety that she displayed a more thoughtful side. She was very nervous that violence would soon break out in Monrovia. She lived on the outskirts of the city, in an area called Riverview, not far from the large UN compound. The UN had recently announced that it was moving operations from Riverview to downtown near the Mamba Point area, setting off a flurry of speculation that even the UN was bracing for the worst. She joked that her neighbors wanted to post signs advertising the UN's new address so the looters would leave them alone. She also knew that if LURD rebels started to infiltrate Riverview, everyone in the neighborhood would be vulnerable to reprisals by government militias trying to root out "collaborators."

There was lament in her voice when she talked about her own government's fighters, wishing they would demonstrate restraint, but knowing full well they would not: "It is bad. The boys in the pick-up trucks roaring up and down the streets with guns. They all act like it is a big game. Everybody knows it will be the civilians that get killed. The soldiers hardly ever fight each other. Our troops should be stationed at key strategic points. They would still be able to do their job. Everyone would feel much better if they were less visible. But ..." Her voice trailed off. She shrugged.

We then met Rudolph Sherman, the head of the True Whig party. Sherman was also the nominal leader of a loose coalition of opposition parties hoping to form a unified front against Taylor. Liberia's opposition parties were notoriously splintered. In the 1997 presidential election, the opposition parties made an agreement to coalesce behind a single nominee but soon reverted to mutual squabbling in their quest for power. It was very difficult to find a Liberian politician without significant baggage, but as one Liberian described, "If you are drowning, you will reach up to grab even a snake."

The True Whig Party headquarters was housed in an immense building. It must have once been quite impressive. But like many official buildings in Monrovia, it was gutted. When we asked for the party chief, a couple of guys loading cases of empty soda bottles in a truck directed us behind the building toward a small shack. All twelve floors of the office building were derelict, and we met with Sherman in an old tool shed furnished with several broken school chairs. The True Whig Party had been Liberia's dominant political party for more than a hundred years, but the party, like its building, was reduced to a shell. The party had few members or resources and almost no grassroots structure—a common problem for opposition parties that feared to tread in the countryside where Taylor's militias ruled with a free hand.

Sherman had a kind face, and was candid in describing the shortcomings of the opposition. Constant bickering, inflated egos, leaders reluctant to give up comfortable exiles, and a lack of funds had made it easy for President Taylor to continue to divide and conquer his opponents. There were allegations around town that Rudolph himself was on the Taylor payroll, and given Liberia's dire economic situation, it was easy for Taylor to buy off those he could not intimidate.

Rudolph used his ornately carved walking stick as an armrest as he spoke, "The biggest problem with Liberia is that everyone wants to be president. It is winner take all politics where your tribe, party and region get everything if you are president. They get nothing if you are not. Nobody wants to be a senator or a judge because these positions do not have any power. You still have to go to the president with your hands open asking for a car or a salary." The fact that the True Whig Party went from totally controlling Liberia to operating out of a shed provided all the evidence Sherman needed for his argument.

"My own party did a very bad job. We forgot that we originally came to power as an opposition party. In the 1920s and 1930s, other parties gave us a good run for the money. But we began to squeeze them out and took everything for ourselves: the jobs, the money, everything. It was the same thing under Samuel Doe, who only favored people from his region. Taking, taking, taking. Now it is this way with Taylor." Rudolph was concerned that even if Taylor was ousted, his successor would be little improvement. Nevertheless, Rudolph did feel that Taylor was vulnerable to pressure, particularly from the United States, "He wants to be respected. He fought a war and won. He also won a presidential election. But he craves legitimacy. If President Bush sends a message directly to him, he will listen."

Rudolph was likable enough, and Comfort asked him why he stayed in Liberia. He laughed, "I am too old to go somewhere else. I travel to other countries almost every year, but I like the pace in Liberia. I am a lawyer. I have a small rubber plantation that allows me a comfortable life. Here, that is enough. In another country, I would have to be working all the time just to get by. I'll stay here. This is my home." A gentle breeze worked through the open door of the shed. I could see the ocean waves breaking in the distance.

ISLANDS IN THE STREAM

The Mamba Hotel Point was a curious scene on the night of the fourth of July. The bar and lounge were about as elegant as Monrovia got, albeit in a tired tropical way. The rattan furniture and overstuffed red couches were dingy, but comfortable. The staff was nervously attentive, the by product of too few guests and the constant scrutiny of the Lebanese owner. In one corner, a ruddy overweight Dutchman discussed the best way to smuggle exotic animals to Macedonia with the owner. The owner was well-versed on the subject: "It is much harder now, not like it used to be. There are all these people involved: customs officials, Interpol and even Greenpeace. The animals are considered endangered. You could not even take that parrot over there without problems."

A few international relief workers drank beer and talked among themselves. Two Ukrainian pilots were on the couch and drinking heavily with their new Liberian "girlfriends." I would later learn that the pilots were delivering an illegal shipment of weapons from Serbia in violation of the arms embargo. The Ukrainians looked happy with their work. There were also a few better-paid Liberian government officials drinking and smoking cigarettes. Keeping an eye on the internationals was part of their job, and little at the Mamba Point avoided official scrutiny. An old tape of Kenny Rogers singing *Islands in the Stream* played on the stereo in an unending loop.

We had dinner with Mario, a thirty-year-old Lebanese who ran the only store in town that sold cell phones. As in many parts of Africa, the Lebanese business community was vibrant despite the chaos. Mario's business was a cash cow given that the regular phones rarely worked. Mario was a big man; and he oscillated between gruff and graciousness as he dispensed off-color humor and shared his view of life in Monrovia. Mario told us with pride that he had delivered a number of expensive cell phones to President Taylor's house earlier in the day. Mario spoke of Taylor in a stage whisper, "He is a wicked man. I know this in my heart. I know all the things he has done. I know who he is. But if you are not a smart man; you will love him when you meet him. I am not a smart man, and I love to talk to him. He is very intelligent, very charming. You know he can be very evil." Taylor impressed Mario: "If he tells a soldier to go to jail, the soldier just takes off his shirt and walks to jail. There doesn't have to be a guard and no one has to point a gun; this is how strong his command is. The boys around him will follow his orders no matter what. They would die for him, no problem."

Mario, being a good businessman, spread largesse when he visited Taylor's heavily guarded house, "I give his men some tips, some small money. Taylor wants his men to like the people he meets with." For a full year, the government had given Mario the exclusive rights to distribute cell phones in Liberia, something that would not have occurred without "arrangements" being made. "Business was incredible. I could not bring in phones fast enough." As we picked at the food on the table, Mario turned reflective, "Even though I like him, nothing will change until Charles Taylor is gone, that is the reality." I could tell Mario worried that he had said too much, and he was distant for the duration of the meal.

The next day we went to the U.S. embassy. Given that Liberians often flocked to the embassy seeking refuge during bouts of violence, the double layers of razor wire along the exterior wall were not surprising. The American diplomatic team in Liberia was in disarray. The ambassador was within weeks of finishing his tenure, and disputes between the State Department and the White House staff had gridlocked U.S. policy. The embassy was short-staffed, and the war on terrorism had left Liberia a forgotten sideshow. Although many Liberians spoke instinctively about the "special relationship" between Liberia and the United States, it meant very little in Washington.

The political counselor was also wrapping up his tour. The State Department had not identified his replacement because, as he bluntly put it, "nobody wants to come here." The counselor's take on events was bleak. "The opposition, excuse my language, has no balls. They are afraid even to come back here." He viewed Taylor as irredeemable and noted, "I have worked in some pretty bad places, and this is as bad as I have ever seen. There is just a total blight of young, promising people. You know those people who you meet and right away you know they are smart and capable? I do not see them here. Would Taylor's replacement be any better than he is? This place is as close to hopeless as I have ever seen."

The political counselor had just returned from the port city of Buchanan and he described the scene, "There are huge bucket cranes that used to load iron ore on to ships that are rusted and falling down. The train tracks that brought in the ore are choked with weeds. Little kids play on top of old piles of iron ore. The other part of the port is still busy, that is where they handle timber shipments, and it is all run by militia boys. But other than that, there is no economic activity, nothing. This is an area firmly controlled by the government, and where there has been no rebel activity. Think about what it is like in the rest of the country. The whole economy is collapsing."

The political counselor was adamant that no peacekeeping force would deploy until there was a ceasefire. Neither the rebels nor the government were likely to accept a ceasefire unless they saw it as being to their tactical advantage. He thought the LURD rebels were making steady advances, and would eventually attack the capital, which was everyone's worst case scenario. But a LURD attack on Monrovia would be far from the end of the war. "Maybe the LURD wins. Maybe Taylor wins; he is not afraid of a long fight." None of the scenarios were good.

On some days, the meetings ran together in a blur of names, faces, and small run-down offices. Even then some moments stood clear: the civil society activist who insisted he never received a Mercedes as a bribe from Taylor; the lawyer who feared that he and his family would be jailed because he was trying to get imprisoned journalist Hassan Bility released; and the local BBC reporter who told us that we should not accept coffee in meetings with government officials because they had been known to poison visitors. A Venezuelan relief worker commented on his drive through the countryside, "I know the militia boys looted the hospital because they were all at the checkpoint playing with crutches and one was sitting in a wheelchair. They are just boys, fourteen, maybe fifteen, years old, drunk, stoned, with guns that seem as big as they are. It is funny in a way, but it can be dangerous."

On a Saturday, we drove well out of town to visit the Firestone rubber plantation and meet Carlos for our promised round of golf. The sign at the entrance proclaimed, "The World's Largest Rubber Plantation." The plantation was like another world. The streets were clean, its buildings were well maintained and the plantation had its own hydroelectric plant, grocery store, and health clinic. It even had several tennis courts and a fitness club. Acre after acre of rubber trees were aligned in tidy rows and affixed with small red buckets to collect the latex bled from them. The plantation had a colonial feel, and Firestone only made money because the cost of labor was so low. It was a jarring enclave of orderliness in a place where everything else had broken down. Carlos led the golfing expedition in a ratty sleeveless T-shirt and Ray Bans, with a cigarette dangling from the corner of his mouth.

On Sunday, I explored the town. Not far from our hotel was a hill that overlooked the entire city. A large Free Masons Lodge, once an architectural gem, was deserted. A chipped and faded statue of one of Liberia's former presidents looked out forlornly on the capital below, as did a smaller statue depicting a slave with broken chains. The Free Masons Lodge looked like the set for a gothic horror film. Over the years, local teens, Nigerian peacekeepers, and militia men had scribbled graffiti on the walls.

Behind the lodge was a raised platform with several rusted Italian artillery pieces guarding against long-forgotten foes. Nearby, weeds threatened to overgrow a monument to Liberia's founding. On the monument's side was carved a scene of freed slaves freshly arrived in Africa wearing suits and shaking hands with tribesmen. The message was remarkably arrogant: the Americo-Liberians had arrived back in Africa to set everything right. A short distance from the monument was a former luxury hotel; its fifteen stories empty and ruined. This was the highest point in Monrovia, with a commanding view in every direction. The hotel's windows were broken or boarded up. A loose scree of garbage led down to the sagging fences of a clay tennis court. A few squatters hung wash by a swimming pool that had a bent shopping cart and a pile of dead leaves sitting in its deep end. Ten years before, reporters had stood on the same veranda and watched fighting rage between militia factions on Monrovia's bridges.

Because it was Sunday, Monrovia's Broad Street was quiet. Almost everyone was in church. Although most of Liberia still practiced indigenous religions, Christianity had always had a strong foothold in Monrovia. The city was host to an incredible number of churches and denominations. In one of the churches, everyone was dressed in their Sunday best, with the women wearing towering and colorful hats. The minister shouted and broke into song as he exhorted his congregation. Children looked fidgety and impatient under the vigilant watch of their mothers. A small girl peeked at me over the back of her pew. It was refreshing to see a slice of normal life.

Comfort and I visited the UN headquarters on the outskirts of town and toured several nearby camps for the displaced and refugees. There was an unusual amount of activity on the roads, and there was a heavy armed presence on the streets. A number of intersections were blocked off and people were intently listening to their radios. The taxi driver explained that President Taylor was making a surprise visit to the troops on the front lines near the city of Tubmanburg. Government-controlled radio covered the news with the enthusiasm of hometown sportscasters and declaring, "Rest easy people of Tubmanburg, you will soon be free."

The first camp we visited was populated with refugees from Sierra Leone who had fled the earlier war in their country. The camp was relatively small, maybe 2,000 people, and it had been in place for several years. There was a school and a health clinic, and the refugees were living in small huts rather than hastily assembled lean-tos constructed with plastic sheeting. It was more a village than a camp. Little kids played in the rows between the huts. Many of the refugees had started returning to Sierra Leone, not because they felt confident about the situation in their home country, but mainly because they feared Liberia's fighting would soon engulf them.

We spent more time speaking with the internally displaced than the refugees, because we were focused on the situation within Liberia. It was a classic example of how the internally displaced were often given inferior treatment compared to refugees. The UN had delivered assistance to the refugees from Sierra Leone for years, but as Liberia's civil war intensified, more and more Liberians fled their homes with almost nothing. Many of the internally displaced reasoned that if they went to the refugee camps, the UN would have no choice but to take care of them. The UN was not able to, but the displaced did get some assistance from private relief groups.

The Liberian government exploited the displaced camps to its own advantage. The government regularly inflated estimates of those in the camps so that it could skim off food and other supplies to funnel to the war effort. The government also forcibly recruited young boys from the camps to serve in its militias. Relief groups understood exactly what the government was doing, but also knew that withholding assistance would only hurt the sick and the hungry even more. This was humanitarian relief in the real world, and like every other conflict in recent memory, aid workers were presented a devil's bargain.

The displaced camps were much newer than the refugee camps. People were crowded under plastic sheeting and squatting in abandoned buildings. One of the displaced camps offered painful insight into the way Liberians still viewed their relationship with America. Many of the displaced Liberians had gathered at the large complex that formerly housed the Voice of America radio complex at the height of the cold war. Even though the compound had been deserted for years, the Liberians believed that if they gathered at the former American facility, U.S. marines might eventually evacuate them.

An aid worker explained that most of the displaced camps had been set up remarkably close to the road because many of the displaced had already relocated several times with the shifting tides of the front lines. They were ready to move again on a moment's notice. Torrential rains only added to the distress.

As we returned to Monrovia, security on the streets was already scaled back. President Taylor had returned to his residence. We headed to the Foreign Ministry to chat with the Deputy Foreign Minister, Tambakai Jangaba. Jangaba has been in the news after a heated exchange with the U.S. ambassador at a fourth of July picnic at the U.S. embassy. The ambassador had assailed Liberia as a failed state, and Jangaba insisted that "foreign powers" were to blame for the country's suffering.

During our meeting with Jangaba, several young Liberian men sat in, giving the impression that they were keeping an eye on the Deputy Foreign Minister. Jangaba looked uncomfortable, fearing that he would be seen as complicit just by speaking with us. In an awkward exchange, he offered to provide us with written answers to any questions we might have. He eventually and grudgingly agreed to a more informal conversation. We were treated to a heavy dose of propaganda, and the guys on the couch all smirked. Not even they took the party line seriously. We listened patiently.

That evening Comfort got a call from the Ministry of Information, run by Reginald Goodridge. A ministry official demanded that we immediately register as journalists or be deported. He said that we needed to go to the Ministry to file the proper papers, even though it was well after working hours. Given that we planned to travel well out of Monrovia the next day, we recognized that we needed to resolve the situation. We took a taxi to the Ministry of Information, a sprawling mint-green building adjacent to the Executive Mansion. Despite the building's size, only a handful of people actually worked there. An assistant to Goodridge told us that we would each have to pay a $100 fee to register as journalists. The shakedown annoyed me, and I argued that we were not journalists and that we did not have to register as journalists before.

I made little headway. The ministry official was melancholy in the extreme and told us, not once but twice, "I should just commit suicide." He explained that local journalists had to pay a $25 registration fee and international journalists had to pay a $50 registration. We asked why we had to pay twice the amount of international journalists. "Your organization makes policy, and policy matters. Your group recommended sanctions, and the UN put in place sanctions. So you pay $100." We insisted that he was overstating our influence. We asked to either see the regulations in writing or speak with Minister Goodridge. He claimed that Goodridge had left for the evening, although his jeep *Pajero* was still parked in front of the building and his secretary was sitting at her desk. We argued for a long time, and the man took it personally that I did not want to pay a bribe. He eventually grew so irritated with my repeated requests to see a copy of the regulations that he told us to leave.

Just as we got back to the lobby of the Mamba Point, we could hear the hotel's Lebanese owner talking on his cell phone. The conversation was about us. The owner called us into a back room. He had just spoken with Minister Goodridge. If we did not pay the registration fee, the authorities would come to the hotel and deport us. The owner was sympathetic, but did not want to be involved in the matter. He had a business to run.

We called Goodridge, who carefully detailed why "anyone doing research or writing in Liberia" needed to register as a journalist. It was not about the money, he demurred, it was about following the "proper process." We had little choice but to pay the money and register, particularly because we would be traveling to Gbarnga in the morning and passing through a lengthy series of militia checkpoints.

I asked Goodridge if he would be willing to meet with us and give us his perspective on the political situation. He said he would consider it. We dutifully took a taxi back over to the deserted ministry and paid $100 each for a piece of paper declaring us journalists. Goodridge's assistant smirked as we handed over the money, laughing at our insolence in challenging the power of a government that could do as it pleased.

GBARNGA

We were up early the next day, ready to drive to Gbarnga, a city in north-central Liberia. LURD rebels had briefly occupied Gbarnga before the government retook it. Over breakfast at the hotel, an international aid worker, Jeff, told us that the local government controlled radio station—KISS FM— had mentioned us on air that morning. According to the report, officials were complaining that we were misrepresenting ourselves as journalists,

somewhat ironic given that the government had forced us to register as journalists the night before. A local group loyal to the government had objected
to our activities, and a government official had said our status was under
review. We assumed the story was a fallout from the previous evening's
discussions at the Information Ministry. However, the idea of being out in
the countryside on the same day the government radio was denouncing us
gave me a knot in the bottom of my stomach.

Paul, the human rights activist, showed up early with a driver, David,
for our trip. Paul's attire and choice of vehicle spoke volumes about his
street smarts. The car, a small sedan, was plain white, making it resemble
a UN or donor vehicle without actually misrepresenting it as such. Paul,
who usually wore khakis and a dress shirt, sported a black baseball cap, a
black T-shirt and long black denim shorts with sunglasses perched on his
head. His wardrobe was perfectly geared for dealing with the militia boys
manning checkpoints. Sorting out who was who in this war was incredibly
difficult, and Paul knew that if he projected authority and looked like a
militia guy many people would be afraid to question him. As we stopped at
checkpoints on the way out of Monrovia, Paul was brusque with the soldiers
who stopped us and it seemed to speed our passage.

A light drizzle was falling and we were both uneasy from the night before.
Going through checkpoints was never a good experience. Clusters of bored
and heavily armed young men guarded the homemade barricades, which in
some cases were nothing more than a rope stretched between two barrels. In
other places, militias had constructed small guardhouses and sandbag fortifications. Men with guns peered into the car, looking to see if anything was of
interest. A different faction of government forces manned each checkpoint:
the Anti-Terrorist Unit, the Armed Forces of Liberia, the Special Operations Division, and some militia boys in no uniform at all. Under Taylor,
the security forces had become incredibly Balkanized. He played one group
off against another as a means to ensure that no force was positioned to
challenge his rule. There were so many militias that the minister of defense
was largely irrelevant. Operating a checkpoint was also a commodity, since
it gave soldiers a means to extort bribes. There were always young boys
hanging around at the posts because they were attracted to the guns and
the authority. Throughout Liberia's conflict, very bad things had always
happened at checkpoints.

The elite Special Operations Division soldiers, known locally as the SOD,
were swathed in black. Many Liberians darkly murmured that the acronym
actually stood for "Sons of Devils." After passing through one of their
checkpoints, Paul turned in his seat, "If you saw the Sons of Devils in
action, you would never want to set foot in Liberia again. You would never
come to Liberia again in your life. I tell you the truth." I had no reason to
doubt him. Paul was also concerned about Roosevelt's safety as Comfort
and I had discussed earlier, "He will have to leave Liberia soon. He is vocal;

too vocal. If he does not leave, he will be killed." Roosevelt had gone into hiding since we had met with him.

The road to Gbarnga was almost deserted. There was activity in the small towns that we passed through, but virtually no traffic between towns. The lush green and rain-streaked landscape stretched out like forgotten territory. The only thing that periodically broke the sameness of the terrain was the large displaced camps. In the displaced camps, thousands of families were sprawled across slick, muddy hillsides stripped clean of vegetation.

We arrived in Gbarnga after more than ten checkpoints and several hours. Our first stop was the local police office, where we informed the commander of our presence and our intention to speak with a number of officials during the day. The commander, a rough looking guy, assured us that the security situation was well under control and that the government had decisively routed the LURD guerillas. When asked about the problems facing locals, he stolidly maintained, "There are no problems." The commander assigned a uniformed policeman to accompany us.

Our escort was easily the most dapper policeman I had seen in Liberia. As we walked toward our vehicle several bystanders called out, "Respect the Police." The officer broke out in a wide smile and waved. This curious scene was repeated everywhere we went, and the officer was treated like a celebrity. Eventually, he explained that in addition to his police duties, he was a pop singer. His biggest hit had come with his song, "Respect the Police." He sang the chorus, and it lightened the mood as we made our way around the heavily militarized town.

We tried to meet with the city's superintendent, a distant relative of Taylor's. He demanded to see our authorization. We showed him the letters of accreditation as journalists we had gotten from Minister Goodridge the night before. The superintendent quickly turned angry, not with us, but with Minister Goodridge. "This is a trap set by the Minister of Information. I report to the Minister of Interior. I have many insights that I could share with you, but only if I am instructed to do so directly by the Minister of Interior. The Minister of Interior understands this. I cannot help you. Talk to whoever you want here in town, but I cannot help you." Liberia was an incredibly paranoid place.

We spoke mostly with representatives of the different security forces deployed in the town, including the SOD, the Anti-Terrorist Unit, and the Armed Forces of Liberia. The government fighters we spoke with in Gbarnga were notably happier than those in Monrovia. The reason was simple: they had been allowed to loot Gbarnga after the LURD was repulsed. They were the only fighters we spoke with that had no complaints about back pay.

One of our more surreal discussions was with a local militia faction composed largely of child soldiers. We sat with them in an abandoned building that looked like it might once have been a small schoolhouse. Several boys stood on the front stoop cradling guns. They were no more than fourteen or fifteen years old. The commander of the group was seventeen. He was engaging and happy to chat with us. The boys leaned their automatic weapons in the corner during our discussion. The commander must have been shot in the jaw at some point. His speech was labored, and he had a profound scar across much of his face. His job was to fight, nothing else, and he was unvarnished and honest. He freely discussed who supplied the rebels with weapons and the organization of Taylor's field forces. For the teenage boys, having a gun was the only way to make a living, to gain prestige, and even to stay alive.

After the militia boys, we talked to James, a local human rights lawyer, in his modest home. James explained that government forces had conducted most of the looting in Gbarnga. He also told us a large number of suspected LURD collaborators had been disappeared by the security forces. James feared that he might need to again flee to neighboring Ivory Coast if the situation deteriorated further. James spent much of his time lobbying local military officers to release people that they had rounded up, and from observing his casual interactions with several soldiers that we came across, he maintained a good relationship with the military in the process. There was an AK-47 propped up in the corner of his office. Being a human rights advocate in Gbarnga was not for the faint of heart.

We spent several hours in Gbarnga. It would take us several hours to drive back to Monrovia, and we did not want to be on the road in the dark. Militia men were often drunk and disorderly after the sun went down. We stopped at Liberia's largest displaced camp, Totota, during our return. Most of the people in the camp had already moved several times because of the fighting. Rich mud caked on our shoes as we walked through the camp and talked with the displaced. Thin trails of smoke from anemic cook fires daubed the rainy sky. The displaced were exasperated: with the power-hungry rebels, the ravenous government, the donors that had lost interest in Liberia, and the terrible violence that had conspired to leave them on a soggy bare hillside trying to stay alive. A group of officials associated with the official Liberian government aid agency quickly attached themselves to our conversation, and they went out of the way to assure us that no government security forces interfered in the camp's operations. Others quietly told us this was not true and that the militias continued to forcibly conscript boys from the camp.

Paul was iridescently angry when we climbed back in the car. He was outraged at what had happened to his country and to Liberians. He blamed the people's misery on President Taylor, and was incredibly frustrated that people who advocated peace could do so little against the people with guns. There was little to say. As we neared the outskirts of town upon our return, we passed President Taylor's residence. A small fleet of new black sport utility vehicles filled the driveway.

The next day we learned that Minister Reginald Goodridge had consented to meet with us. We returned to the Information Ministry. The session started badly. Reggie swept into the room with a small entourage, including a camera crew and a lawyer. I thought we were going to be deported. Reggie said that he wanted to film our meeting, "just for our records. We will be happy to provide you with a copy." We knew he could use the tape for disinformation, but there was little to do about it. We also thought it possible that Reggie was taping the session to demonstrate to Charles Taylor that he was still loyal.

Reggie, like Cyril Allen, had a way with words. While not berating us, Reggie did his best to be ingratiating. "I went to school with the U.S. ambassador at Syracuse University. We were all so happy when he was appointed ambassador that it was like a carnival when he arrived. But your country is bent on destroying us, and the ambassador has been a deep disappointment."

He launched into a long attack on the previous Crisis Group report on Liberia and what he alleged were factual inaccuracies. "We are not the worst country in West Africa, not by any means. Do you feel safe here? Have you been harassed?" Reggie took issue that we had reported that the country's former vice president, Enoch Dogolea, was seen with security officials shortly before he turned up dead, apparently poisoned. Reggie pushed a stack of photos toward me with the relish of a prosecutor making his case before a jury. It took me a second to focus on the pictures as Reggie continued his harangue.

"The vice president had lifelong liver problems. Did you talk to his wife? Did you talk to his bodyguard?" I was appalled when I realized he had handed me autopsy photos showing the former vice president on a dingy gurney with his chest and stomach cut open. I suppressed a grim little smile, almost overwhelmed by the sad absurdity of it all.

"Do you think this is funny?"

I noted that I was not a trained medical professional, and that even a doctor would be able to tell little from such photos. Eventually, Reggie's long monologue drew to a conclusion and, with the camera still running, I posed a series of exceedingly polite questions. Reggie responded at length about the special relationship between the United States and Liberia, "You may not know it, but we are cousins. Comfort and I are sisters, but you and I are cousins." He cited the large numbers of officials in the government that attended U.S. universities. Reggie also spoke a great deal about President Taylor as "a great leader of regional reconciliation efforts and peace in Sierra Leone."

I gently inquired if, as part of his commitment to reconciliation, President Taylor would be willing to go before the Special Court convened in Sierra Leone to investigate war crimes during the conflict. Perhaps, Taylor could help explain Liberia's regional role during such an appearance. Reggie responded angrily, "Will you take him to the tribunal? Is that your plan? Will you indict him? Is that your plan? You two are agents. You are trying to subvert our country. Make no mistake about it, no matter who you say you are—you are foreign agents."

Like a storm that passed quickly, Reggie soon regained his composure. He was pleased with his performance for the camera. The meeting concluded not long after. I asked for a copy of the videotape for our files. Reggie said he would be happy to pass it on. We also made a pitch for a meeting with President Taylor. This too touched a nerve, and Reggie confrontationally asked, "Why? What do you want to tell President Taylor?"

"We don't want to tell him anything. You have said that our last report contained inaccuracies. Who better to explain the situation in Liberia than President Taylor himself?" Goodridge rolled his eyes, but said he would look into the matter. Our expectations for a meeting with Taylor were almost zero. Remarkably, several hours later, we got a call from Reggie's assistant, Kennedy, "The meeting you requested with the president has been arranged, come to the Information Ministry at two in the afternoon."

CHARLES TAYLOR

In rushing around before going to the ministry, we had little time to reflect on the man we were meeting. Charles Taylor was infamous for his brutality, and local legend had it that he threatened to burn down his high school after losing a student council election. He ran his army as a virtual personality cult, and he had killed too many people to count. Taylor was more criminal overlord than president, and he was not a man used to answering questions.

After returning to the Information Ministry, Kennedy escorted us for the short walk to the Executive Mansion. Built in the 1960s, the Executive Mansion had lots of curved concrete in a style that had aged poorly. A broad reflecting pool and fountain in front of the building were stagnant with moss and weeds. We passed through a cursory security inspection and then taken into a holding room where several Liberian dignitaries were also waiting to meet with Taylor. I assumed our discussion would amount to little more than a courtesy call.

After a short time, the president's press secretary came for us. Instead of heading upstairs to the president's office, we were escorted out to the large back lawn of the Executive Mansion. Walking down the broad concrete steps that looked out across the sea, I tried to remain nonchalant. It was not easy. Young muscular men toting automatic weapons and dressed in t-shirts patrolled the grounds. A workman pushed a lawnmower in a far corner of the lawn. I did a double take upon spying several ostriches, remarkably large birds when viewed up close, grazing on the patchy grass between the bodyguards.

They took us to a large gazebo where President Taylor was holding court. We were taken aback when we realized that the president had assembled much of his senior cabinet for the meeting: Vice President Moses Blah,

National Security Adviser Lewis Brown, Foreign Minister Monie Capatin, Information Minister Reginald Goodridge, the chief of staff and several others. We shook hands with Taylor. He sat in a large wicker chair with his cabinet flanking him on either side. Several reporters clicked photographs before Taylor dismissed them with a wave of his hand.

Taylor was dressed in a cream-colored sports jacket. His gold watch and ring were conspicuously large. Sitting on the small coffee table in front of Taylor was the videotape of our earlier discussion with Reggie. Taylor yelled at an assistant who in turn yelled at the man mowing the lawn. The lawnmower was turned off.

As we sat down, Taylor admonished us to take out our notepads: "So you do not make any mistakes about what I say." The Liberian president continually referred to Comfort, who had been born in Nigeria, as his "African sister." Taylor gave us a long scolding lecture. His assembled ministers provided periodic punctuation by nodding their heads in agreement or solemnly intoning, "Yes, Mr. President."

Taylor seized on the issue of the war crimes tribunal in Sierra Leone, which I had referred to in our earlier meeting with the Information Minister. President Taylor had directly supported the militia faction that had committed the worst abuses in Sierra Leone, and there were growing calls for Taylor to be hauled before the court. Taylor's vehemence toward the tribunal convinced me that he was deeply nervous about a potential indictment.

Taylor also went on at length about the LURD rebels. With September 11 still a fresh memory, he mimicked the language often used in Washington, "The LURD are terrorists. We want them to come out of the bushes, lay down their arms, and participate in the democratic process." The Liberian President called the rebels "Islamic fundamentalists," although only a portion of the group's followers were Muslim, and almost no one outside of Liberia had suggested that they were part of a terrorist network. Taylor also denied allegations that he had been involved in money laundering, through diamond sales, for al-Qaeda.

Turning history on its head, the Liberian President tried to tie the RUF rebels in Sierra Leone—the militia group he directly supported—into an Islamic conspiracy. "The way the RUF has been cutting off people's arms, maybe this is a *sharia* practice. I do not know." Taylor insisted that his own forces had been very well behaved, "We were so careful. War is not child's play." Taylor did not touch upon the large numbers of child soldiers in his ranks.

Taylor passionately argued that the world was treating Liberia unfairly. He insisted that because of the LURD attacks he had no choice but to circumvent the arms embargo, "This is a clear and present danger; any country would do what we are doing. Our actions are in keeping with the United Nations charter." Taylor blamed the United States and Britain for backing the LURD, and he felt the two nations were hell bent on his removal.

When we asked what he wanted from Washington, his answer was simple: "We need to talk. Senior U.S. government officials have not contacted or engaged us. They cannot talk at us. We are not children to be lectured to. Washington should engage with us." I noticed the foreign minister was craning in his seat trying to read my notes as I wrote them.

Taylor was incisive in critiquing his Liberian political opponents. He noted that one prominent opposition leader, Ellen Johnson Sirleaf, had worked with him as he was founding his rebel movement. Taylor claimed he had met with Sirleaf in a Holiday Inn in Paris where the two made plans to overthrow Samuel Doe. He also criticized her for living abroad. "Ellen has done nothing for her village. She has done nothing for her people. We can go to her village and you will see. She does not even take care of her own house. How can a person who does not take care of her house or her village lead this country? Her own people do not respect her. I am the democratically elected leader of this country, and I will win the next election as well."

Taylor glossed over the general suppression of political dissent in his country. He blamed the vicious murder of his former rival Samuel Dokie on disgruntled members of his own tribe—despite the fact the Vice President was last seen in the custody of security forces before the burned corpses of Dokie and his wife appeared by the side of a road outside of Monrovia. Similarly, the beating of an opposition leader in prison was dismissed as "an unfortunate incident." President Taylor offered to let us visit the detained journalist, Hassan Bility, "You want to go see him?"

After taking us to task, Taylor's tone became more personable. He insisted that we not impose our worldview on Africa. "You see my brother, political feuds border on hatred in Liberia. You cannot expect first world standards. Things are just different; everyone wants power. It is not like the politics you know. Comfort, my African sister must understand this. I live well and have no regrets. I am a good Christian. I lived and studied in Boston. All these men sitting around you have advanced degrees, most of them from good universities in the United States. But a politician from America could not survive in Africa no more than I could survive in Alaska."

I politely interjected, "President Taylor, I am convinced that if you moved to Alaska, you would be governor within eight months." President Taylor laughed, and a number of the cabinet members grinned at the thought.

Glancing around the gazebo, I could not help but remember Cyril Allen's comments about going to the Executive Mansion, killing President Taylor and eating his heart fresh from his chest. Looking at the men gathered around Taylor, I knew they all lived in constant fear of falling out of favor, of being betrayed, or becoming victims of the same violence they used so capriciously. They were afraid of Taylor and they were afraid of each other. As the ostriches and armed thugs wandered across the lawn, I realized that Allen was not simply warning me, he was also terrified. Allen, like those in the cabinet, knew that if someone killed Taylor and triumphantly held the president's bloody heart in their hands, his world of patronage, privilege, and expensive Thai mistresses would collapse like a house of cards. No matter how frightening he might be, Charles Taylor was just a man, and he was vulnerable.

Our meeting with Taylor stretched the better part of two hours. The Liberian president concluded by commenting, "If your next report contains these same inaccuracies, we will think it was not done in good faith." He delivered his threat with a sharp smile. We fielded a few press questions as we walked away from the gazebo. I said only that we welcomed the chance to discuss the current situation with the president.

As the reporters left, I turned to the press attaché, Kennedy, and asked a question that had been on my mind since we arrived, "What is the story with the ostriches?"

"The president likes animals," Kennedy replied, "There are three ostriches. There used to be four ostriches. One ostrich swallowed a cell phone, and when it rang, the bird went berserk. The bird was so badly injured that he died. The president was very upset." Kennedy found the entire ostrich incident routine, and his face remained expressionless.

After the meeting with Taylor, both Comfort and I were drained. Paul, who picked us up, looked like he was in the company of two people who had just met Satan himself. Comfort had not slept for several nights, and the stress of dealing with Monrovia was starting to take its toll. That evening, we were told that we had been criticized on the evening news, with a local "civil society" group again complaining that we were harming Liberia. We did not get much in the way of specifics, but we were scheduled to leave the country the next day, and the timing seemed good. We were both ready to go.

THE MAN IN THE RED HAT

Our bags were packed early, and we were both excited with the prospect of our departure. However, we were also greeted with more critical media coverage. An article in the local *Inquirer* newspaper reported that a group, the Patriotic Consciousness Association of Liberia (PACA), wanted to bring charges against Comfort and I for "criminal coercion and impersonating officials." We learned that PACA billed itself as a veterans' group, but was little more than another government militia. In a three-day span, our work had been attacked in the newspaper and on both radio and television. We agreed that Comfort should purchase additional credit for her cell phone in case we encountered difficulties. We planned to catch a UN flight to Sierra Leone. Roosevelt materialized out of hiding to bid us farewell.

Comfort's phone rang. It was Reginald Goodridge, the Minister of Information. Reggie informed us that Charles Taylor wanted us to drive out and see Ellen Johnson Sirleaf's house and village. The president wanted us to witness first-hand how she did not take care of her house or village. Reggie said the president's "personal car" would be at our disposal. We pointed out that we were supposed to catch our flight. The Information Minister was insistent, but we assured Reggie that the next time we came to Monrovia we would make Ellen's village our first stop.

We dropped Roosevelt off and, after a quick farewell, he melted into the crowd. Paul and David drove us to the airport. We arrived early, and David parked the car what seemed to be a long way from the largely empty terminal. He wanted to keep out of the view of security. Comfort and I sat at a small kiosk outside the terminal taking in the local scene. A few money changers milled about flashing wads of local currency. Their girlfriends chatted with each other. An older man sold warm soda and cigarettes across a small wooden counter. Two women with pails of kabobs trolled half-heartedly for customers. A couple kids chased each other across the parking lot and on to a dirt road that lay beyond.

It was a sleepy scene. The man running the kiosk fiddled with his radio trying to find music. Static and commercials faded in and out as he spun the dial. While I was only listening with half an ear, I heard with perfect clarity my name being announced on the radio. The man quickly spun by the station, and the news item was finished by the time we convinced the vendor to turn the dial back. I hoped the mention was only in reference to the meeting with Taylor the day before, but I was ill at ease.

Eventually we were ushered into the airport's waiting lounge. We were the only two people scheduled to be on the flight from Monrovia. Since we were taking a UN flight, a Liberian working for the UN High Commissioner for Refugees took our passports and some cash for our exit fee. He was gone a long time. When he returned, he indicated that the flight was on its way. However, we then overheard the local UN officer telling his boss, a Frenchman whom Comfort had met before, "There is some problem." The two men disappeared.

A short time later, the Liberian UN official escorted us into the airport immigration office. There were about fifteen immigration officers packed into the small office, along with two policemen and a beefy guy wearing a shabby sports jacket, a red baseball cap, and a scowl. There was a steady buzz of conversation in the room. Everyone was too excited for it to be good news.

The head immigration officer sat behind his desk. He was arguing with the man in the red baseball cap. It sounded like they had been over the same ground several times, "Their papers are all in order. They have paid their exit tax and development fee. There is no problem with their visas. As far as we are concerned, they are free to go. It is not our job to arrest them." This agitated the man in the Red Hat—who looked like a militia guy. I sat down on a small wooden chair in the crowded office. Red Hat pulled a folded piece of paper out of his pocket and thrust it at me. "This is a writ. You are under arrest. You must come with me."

I could feel the color rising in my face as I read the writ. A Justice of the Peace in Monrovia had issued the arrest order, and it was a complaint from "W. Knowlden, Vice Chairman of PACA"—the same militia group that we had read about in that morning's paper. The warrant was sloppily typed and its grammar was poor. It might have been funny under different circumstances. Much of the writ described comments that we were alleged to have made to Mr. Knowlden—a man that neither one of us has ever met. We were quoted as saying: "Your government is full of murderers, murderers, murderers, rogues, rogues, rogues." It continued, "If you tell anyone that we are posing as journalists we will ruin you W. Knowlden, just as we are ruining your country. There is nothing you can do." According to the document, we were "wicked" and to be charged with criminal coercion and impersonating officials. In essence, the court had charged us with espionage. The charges were a shoddy fabrication, but it was still an arrest warrant and we were still in Liberia.

It was apparent that Red Hat was with PACA. I asked his name and affiliation. Red Hat responded with an angry shrug, and refused to answer. I handed him back the writ, "I do not know who you are. I do not know where you work. You cannot serve me with an arrest warrant. Anybody could type this up." Red Hat was momentarily perplexed by the logic, and a few of the policemen laughed at his expense. If he was unwilling to establish his identity, he probably could not serve us the warrant. Red Hat handed the writ to a policeman standing next to him, and the policeman handed me the writ. I then asked the policeman for his identification, which caused him to get both flustered and annoyed as he stood in middle of the overcrowded room searching for his papers.

The French flight operations manager walked into the room. He loudly announced to the head immigration officer that the UN plane would not be touching down in Monrovia because of "this embarrassment by your government." While his comments were supportive, it was not reassuring that we no longer had a way out of the country. Upon prodding by Red Hat, the police officer demanded, "You must come back with us to town." We were informed that we had a court date several days later on Monday.

As we stepped out of the immigration office, the Frenchman tried to be encouraging, "I used to live in the Congo. I ran a hotel there. I would get arrested every other week; all the time. They used to arrest me if the hotel was full and they could not book a room. Don't worry. It will be taken care of." As we headed out of the terminal, a scrum of people surrounded us: immigration officers, police, the UN officials, a few militia guys with Red Hat, airport security, and curious bystanders. Almost everyone was male and under thirty. Comfort called our headquarters in Brussels on her cell phone and informed them of the situation. I scribbled some emergency numbers on a business card and gave them to the Frenchman. One of Red Hat's associates objected to Comfort using her cell phone, but he quickly became distracted by a new squabble.

Red Hat and the policeman wanted us to get into a taxi with a large hand-drawn placard in its window declaring, "PACA." We objected. We insisted that we needed to let our own driver know what was happening. I started to walk in that direction and this triggered a great deal of shouting and gesticulating, "You must ride in this car."

"I only want to tell our driver so he knows where we are going." I argued that they should allow us to ride in our own car and follow the taxi. Red Hat and the cop strenuously objected. We proposed that we could instead ride in the UN vehicle and argued that we were not trying to escape. "But you are under arrest," wheedled the policeman, upset that we were not being more compliant. Comfort continued to make calls as I negotiated.

A young man dressed in civilian clothes appeared, and he was apparently the head of airport security. He and Red Hat quickly become embroiled in a heated confrontation. Listening in, I walked back closer to the terminal and further away from the taxi. The head of security was adamant that the airport had a strict policy regarding arrests and that we could not be detained without direct orders from the Minister of Justice. For a moment, it looked like the argument would come to blows, and I was glad that only some of the men were armed. Red Hat was only restrained by the fact that his group was badly outnumbered by the airport security officials.

The airport security chief was unfailingly polite to us despite the rising tensions. He explained his position, taking great care to say that he was making no judgment as to the merits of the case against us, but resolutely maintaining that procedures needed to be followed. "Do you want a soft drink? You can wait in my office." I thanked him for the offer, but added that we were more concerned with leaving the country. Comfort had managed to get through to Brussels, and the Frenchman had informed the local European Union office of our detention. We made a flurry of phone calls, and Comfort stood to the side talking as two Liberian security officials tried to eavesdrop.

Red Hat and the head of airport security engaged in dueling cell phone conversations. Red Hat called the justice of the peace who issued the arrest warrant as well as a low-ranking official at the Ministry of Justice. The head of security telephoned the airport manager. In mid-conversation, Red Hat handed his cell phone to the head of security, leaving him to explain to the person on the other end of the line that we could only be arrested upon direct order by the Minister of Justice. I could hear an angry response on the other end of the phone, pushing the security chief, who had been quite patient, to angrily interject, "Please do not accuse me of lacking patriotism. I fought a war to bring this government in power." Red Hat leaned in and sneered, "*We fought* a war to bring this government to power."

Comfort had gotten hold of both senior staff members in Brussels and the British High Commission. We also learned that there was a commercial flight headed to Sierra Leone at five-thirty that evening. I felt like we would be in a much stronger negotiating position if we had a plane that we could board—otherwise we would have to head back into town. We tried to reach Reggie Goodridge, hoping to remind him that President Taylor had assured us that we would be able to do our work without harassment. The head of airport security said that we should go wait in the airport lounge and again suggested that we have a soft drink. We were happy to head into the lounge because it got us further away from the militia guys and closer to an airplane. Comfort, doing her best to preserve her battery time and calling minutes, only took incoming calls. The clock moved steadily toward five-thirty.

We had our money counted and were ready to purchase commercial tickets if we would be allowed to leave. Unfortunately, while the lounge was more comfortable, it also cut us off from listening in on the talks between the security staff and the militia guys. Comfort finally got hold of Reggie, "You are still here? I thought you had left." Reggie initially maintained that his hands were tied because "PACA is a private group." This caused the usually soft-spoken Comfort to snort with derision. One of our vice presidents in New York called to complain to the Liberian ambassador in Washington who professed with some resignation, "I am not surprised, there is always some shit coming out of Liberia."

It was now after five. We were told to leave the terminal to speak with the security chief. Trudging back out to the parking lot was discouraging. Reggie called Comfort and told her that we were "not under arrest," but should return to the Mamba Point Hotel and remain as "guests of the government of Liberia" until the situation was resolved. It would essentially be house arrest, but Mamba Point sounded nicer than jail. Red Hat and his crew again tried to get us into the taxi, and again I objected. "No. No. No. We are not under arrest. The Minister of Information was just very clear, we are not under arrest." I insisted that we could arrange our own transportation. At that moment I saw an AID vehicle dropping off someone. I asked the understandably confused driver to radio his supervisor to see if he could give us a ride into town. This would also have made it possible for the driver to take us directly to the U.S. embassy. We were no longer sure if Paul and David were at the airport and figured that they should be left out of things for their safety. The PACA thugs were nervous that we would hop in the AID car and speed off. The arguments continued.

The airport manager arrived on the scene. He was around fifty, and had a reassuring sense of gravity. He was irritated with the entire fiasco. He sent us back into the lounge. The political counselor from the U.S. embassy called, and I explained our situation. He laughed when I told him the Liberian bureaucracy was "having some problems." He indicated that the AID car would wait for us if needed. It was now past five-thirty. The plane to Sierra Leone had been loaded with cargo and its passengers were impatiently waiting to board. Although it appeared less likely we would be sent to jail, our chances to escape Monrovia were slipping away. We got a call from Paul. Apparently he and David had been punched several times and harassed, but not arrested.

We then got a call from a different embassy that assured us that our situation was under control. The embassy informed Comfort that there would be "technical difficulties" with the commercial plane to Sierra Leone until we could board. The embassy also indicated that they had a person at the airport, although this individual would not make their identity known to us. This was welcome news—in a cloak and dagger sort of way.

Around six, the airport manager reappeared. He apologized for the confusion and said he was awaiting word from the Minister of Justice. His cell phone rang a short time later. After a brief conversation, the manager hung up and informed us of the Minister of Justice's decision. The Justice Minister had explained that the justice of the peace was a lower court and was not of sufficient level to bring espionage charges against us. The minister had dismissed the charges. We were free to leave.

In a rush, we paid cash for tickets on the commercial flight, thanked the airport manager, and made a few phone calls to let people know that we were headed for the plane. The plane lifted off as the sun set. We both felt a huge burst of anxious energy and relief. After touching down in Sierra Leone, we had a well-deserved drink—at the Mamba Point Hotel in Freetown of course.

The next day, I said goodbye to the team, and thanked Comfort. I was scheduled to fly to Ghana and then on to London. My ticket indicated that it would be about four hours before I arrived in Ghana. Exhausted, I fell asleep as soon as I got on the plane. I did not wake up until the wheels of the plane screeched on the tarmac.

Rubbing the sleep from my eyes, I glanced out the window. I looked once. I looked twice. I was horrified. The large sign above the airport terminal read, "JJ Roberts International Airfield." I was back at the Monrovia airport. My ticket to Ghana had not indicated there was a stopover in Liberia. Competing emotions filled my head. On one level, it was absurdly funny; on the other level, I could be totally screwed. It was Saturday, I had no cell phone, and nobody knew I was in Liberia. There would not be a lot of goodwill from the Liberians if I reappeared the day after they tried to arrest me.

I took a deep breath, unsure of my choices. The pilot came on the intercom and announced that we were free to remain on the plane during the layover. I did, spending the next forty minutes slumped low in my seat, keeping an eye on the terminal. The second departure from Liberia was no less sweet than the first.

A Brief Reflection

BETTER AND WORSE

Kathmandu, Nepal 2006. We sat across the table from a remarkably senior group of Maoist military commanders. All were men, and they were predominately in their thirties. They were not imposing. Most of them were slight, and only a few scars here and there spoke to the toll of combat. Yet, appearance was illusion; the People's Liberation Army officers were some of the most feared in Nepal. Armed with often basic weapons, they had managed to tie the 90,000-strong Nepalese army in knots during a brutal decade long hit-and-run campaign. In the rugged mountains and jungles of Nepal, few could match their ingenuity, ferocity, and guile.

Months before, it would have been unthinkable for these men to gather openly in Kathmandu. Much had changed in a short time. Massive street protests led by a shaky alliance between mainstream democratic parties and the Maoists had ended Nepal's absolute monarchy. The Maoists and the political parties were trying to negotiate a permanent ceasefire and rewrite the constitution, but the process was messy and uneven.

I had left the International Crisis Group and joined a small United Nations team assisting the ceasefire talks between the Maoist rebels and the new coalition government. Both the Maoists and the army were encouragingly fatigued of the battlefield, and we were trying to get the peace process across the finish line. It was not easy work, and the years of violence had fed intense distrust. All sides wanted the UN to monitor a peace agreement, but they had difficulty sorting through the details involved in getting everyone to lay down their arms.

The Maoist commanders had practical questions: *Will I be able to carry a gun during the ceasefire? Will the army be able to use its helicopters? What will the UN do if the army attacks us?* Both the Maoists and the government were eager to have the UN tell them the "best" way to go about making peace. It felt awkward to tell them that peace could only come from them, not us.

I glanced down the table at our negotiating team. We were led by a veteran British human rights expert, Ian Martin. Our military adviser was a Norwegian one-star general. Our elections adviser hailed from Romania. I was the senior political adviser. In our own way, we were disaster gypsies one and all. These were good people, and I was lucky to work with them.

Although there were no shortages of daily catastrophes in the international system, and the UN did lots of ill-advised things, I was still profoundly impressed by the dedication and compassion of those with whom I served. At the end of the day, most wanted nothing more complex than to leave the places they worked better than they found them. It would be easy to fall into the trap of writing solely about all-too-human failings and succumb to cynicism, but it still felt like we were on the side of the angels.

My first week back in Kathmandu had been a reunion, filled with warm greetings and familiar faces. I had worked with about half of the team before, including Suman, our Nepali political officer, who I had recruited to join the International Crisis Group three years earlier when he was a journalist. Other members of our team had worked together in East Timor. Several of the military experts had served together in peacekeeping missions in Lebanon. It never took six degrees of separation to find connections in the disaster industry.

During a brief intermission in the negotiations, the Norwegian general, Jan Erik, announced in his lilting Norwegian-inflected English (or "Norglish" as he liked to call it) that he was stepping outside for five minutes "to do something my wife will not let me do at home." His comment provoked a ripple of laughter among the internationals—even though we knew full well that he simply was eager for a cigarette. A sense of humor helped preserve the sanity.

It would have been easy to look around the world and think that everything was going to hell in a handbasket. The situation in Iraq at the moment was nothing short of ghastly, with scores being killed every day in fantastically brutal sectarian violence. The agony of Darfur in Sudan continued to be largely ignored by the world—in no small part because Iraq was already in flames. Lebanon had just suffered incredible destruction after warfare between Israel and Hezbollah. Afghanistan was turning out to be as hard and chaotic as all the people in Kabul had told me it would be without more troops on the ground.

What was frustrating about Iraq in particular was that almost every important lesson the world had learned since the early 1990s about dealing with conflict had been ignored in the wake of the U.S.-led invasion. For example, the entire Iraqi army had been dismissed virtually overnight with no thought given to finding the soldiers new jobs or reintegrating them into society. It was no surprise that angry, disaffected, and unemployed Iraqi soldiers flocked to a growing insurgency. Important reconstruction jobs were given to political cronies from Washington rather than specialists. The entire dismal situation was a painful reminder of what happened when you stopped listening to experts on the ground. Hubris was no substitute for the slow, trudging work of cooperating with allies to develop practical solutions.

Yet, as hard as it might be to believe from the daily newspapers, much has actually changed for the better in the world since the early 1990s. The number of conflicts around the world has steadily dropped. The numbers of people being killed by deadly conflict continues to decline, and often quite dramatically so. It is not by accident. Amid all the false starts and frequent disasters, the world has gotten much better at responding with both humanitarian relief and effective political interventions. Peacekeeping missions often make a real difference and, importantly, there is a much better understanding of the conditions that need to be met for peacekeeping to be effective.

There is also growing recognition that governments cannot abuse their own citizens with impunity. The architects of some of the conflicts in which I worked—men like former Yugoslav President Slobodan Milosevic and my old friend Liberian President Charles Taylor—had been hauled off to The Hague to appear before war crimes tribunals. There are more and more experts available to help prevent countries from veering into bloodshed. There are organizations that specialize in rebuilding societies that do fall victim to war. There has never been more or better early warning information available to politicians and diplomats around the globe. No matter how uneven, and often reluctant, the world has gotten better at dealing with the hard business of conflict.

As the Maoist guerillas huddled among themselves and fielded calls on their cell phones, I reflected on the long road that had led me from my first service as a novice relief worker in Rwanda to working as a negotiator with the United Nations in Nepal. I was fortunate. I had seen horrific things, but I still remained hopeful. I honestly believed there was no war that could not be solved by the right people and a lot of hard work. No hatred was so deep that the urge for peace was not ultimately more compelling.

As our meeting concluded, there were handshakes and plans for further discussions. Stepping out into the crowded Kathmandu streets, the Maoist commanders were flocked by their security detail. The security men all had small backpacks and bags; they did not want to be seen carrying their weapons in public. Incongruously, the Maoist commanders all hailed taxis to take them off into the evening.

I did not know if Nepal's war was over or not. I could think of countless reasons the talks might stumble out of greed, stubbornness, misunderstanding, or even just habit. However, the negotiations had a measure of momentum and, in villages across the Himalayas, families were returning to their homes, planting crops, and getting on with their lives. For the moment, that was enough.

INDEX

Also by John Norris

Collision Course: NATO, Russia, and Kosovo

"... No one has told this important story in more detail or uncovered so many points at which things went disastrously wrong."
Times Literary Supplement (London)

"The definitive book on one of the most important American military actions since the end of the Cold War."
Former Ambassador to the United Nations, Richard Holbrooke

"... No one has pulled the war's tale together quite as Norris has—teaching even those who had central roles, such as the Finnish president, Martti Ahtisaari, things they did not know."
Foreign Affairs

"The story is a dramatic one, and Norris tells it well, drawing the reader into the web of relationships within and between the countries involved."
Political Science Quarterly

"An important and exciting story told with verve and a lot of detail by the author."
International Affairs

About the Author

JOHN NORRIS is the senior political adviser with the United Nations Mission in Nepal. He also served as the Washington Chief of Staff for the International Crisis Group while conducting a wide range of fieldwork in Asia, Africa, and the Balkans. Earlier in his career, he was the Director of Communications for the U.S. Deputy Secretary of State, and served both as a relief worker and head speechwriter at the U.S. Agency for International Development. In addition, John has worked on Capitol Hill and has a graduate degree in public administration.